Architect of Air Power

AMERICAN WARRIORS

Throughout the nation's history, numerous men and women of all ranks and branches of the U.S. military have served their country with honor and distinction. During times of war and peace, there are individuals whose exemplary achievements embody the highest standards of the U.S. armed forces. The aim of the American Warriors series is to examine the unique historical contributions of these individuals, whose legacies serve as enduring examples for soldiers and citizens alike. The series will promote a deeper and more comprehensive understanding of the U.S. armed forces.

SERIES EDITOR: Roger Cirillo

An AUSA Book

ARCHITECT

OF

AIR POWER

General Laurence S. Kuter
and the
Birth of the US Air Force

BRIAN D. LASLIE

UNIVERSITY PRESS OF KENTUCKY

Scholarly publisher for the Commonwealth,
serving Bellarmine University, Berea College, Centre College of Kentucky,
Eastern Kentucky University, The Filson Historical Society, Georgetown
College, Kentucky Historical Society, Kentucky State University, Morehead
State University, Murray State University, Northern Kentucky University,
Transylvania University, University of Kentucky, University of Louisville, and
Western Kentucky University.
All rights reserved.

Editorial and Sales Offices: The University Press of Kentucky
663 South Limestone Street, Lexington, Kentucky 40508-4008
www.kentuckypress.com

Library of Congress Cataloging-in-Publication Data

Names: Laslie, Brian D., author.
Title: Architect of air power : General Laurence S. Kuter and the birth of
    the US Air Force / Brian D. Laslie.
Other titles: General Laurence S. Kuter and the birth of the US Air Force
Description: Lexington, Kentucky : University Press of Kentucky, [2017] |
    Includes bibliographical references and index.
Identifiers: LCCN 2017019447| ISBN 9780813169989 (hardcover : alk. paper)
    ISBN 9780813174044 (pdf) | ISBN 9780813174051 (epub)
Subjects: LCSH: Kuter, Laurence Sherman, 1905-1979 | United States. Army Air
    Forces—Officers—Biography. | Generals—United States—Biography. |
    United States. Air Force—Officers—Biography. | World War,
    1939-1945—Aerial operations. | United States. Air Force—History—20th
    century. | Air power—United States.
Classification: LCC UG626.2.K87 L37 2017 | DDC 358.40092 [B] —dc23 LC
record available at https://lccn.loc.gov/2017019447

This book is printed on acid-free paper meeting
the requirements of the American National Standard
for Permanence in Paper for Printed Library Materials.

Manufactured in the United States of America.

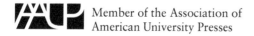 Member of the Association of
American University Presses

This book is dedicated to
Donald J. Mrozek, scholar, mentor, and Renaissance man

I am responsible for what I think was the greatest contribution to Air Force history in the [creation of] the Oral History Program. I organized the meeting of Frank Lahm and Benny Foulois with Tooey Spaatz as monitor at Maxwell [Air Force Base] in the interrogation room where they appeared to be alone with two bottles of whiskey. Tooey poured drinks for both Lahm and Foulois and took a big one himself and said, "Who really was the first military aviator?"

—General Laurence S. Kuter, USAF (ret.), 1974

Contents

Photographs follow page 117

Preface

The idea of wanting to write a biography is challenging. The medium is a victim of its own success, and I have been told that scholars shy away from it. Each year another popular-history biography is published and eagerly purchased and read by masses of people. In the academic community, the biography has become something *not* to do. Maybe this is because, in writing a biography, historians must tread the perilous course of being objective while at the same time proclaiming why the subject needs individual attention in the first place. Too much of the former, and the subject can come across as uninspiring. Too much of the latter, and the historian becomes a cheerleader and hagiographer instead of a biographer. There is also the danger of going native and losing one's objectivity. Lloyd Ambrosius tells us in *Writing Biography: Historians and Their Craft* that a biography presents "the dual challenge of telling history and telling lives."[1] So it was with great trepidation that this historian approached the task of telling the story of a little-known founding father—to use a gendered term by way of explanation—of air power. However, my fears are assuaged when I look at the many magnificent and growing number of biographies on air force leaders, including George Kenney, Carl Spaatz, Pete Quesada, and Claire Chennault, to name just a few. There is also excellent autobiographical literature from Hap Arnold, Jimmy Doolittle, and others. Still, there are many others whose biographies have yet to be written: Nathan Twining, Earl Partridge, Haywood Hansell, and Lauris Norstad come immediately to mind. Larry Kuter falls into this latter category. Yet the story of Laurence Sherman Kuter is a history, a biography, and, in a sense, the autobiographical story of the US Air Force. Kuter's career dovetailed with the rise of an adolescent air power and ended with a fully grown and mature air force capable of global monitoring and response.

Introduction

On 30 September 1974, General Laurence S. Kuter, US Air Force retired, sat on a small chair in his apartment in Naples, Florida. He wore an open-collar button-down short-sleeved shirt and pants with a pattern of crossed golf clubs. His skin was a deep bronzed color thanks to the days in retirement spent on the golf courses of the southwestern Florida coastal city. At nearly seventy years of age, he still looked every part an air force general. With the general in his apartment sat two air force historians who were there to conduct an oral history interview to preserve the historical value of the general's life from his earliest days through World War II and his experiences in the newly formed US Air Force of the 1940s, 1950s, and 1960s. It was part of a program that Brigadier General Kuter himself authorized in the early days of American involvement in World War II when he directed that the Air Staff Historical Section gather history "while it is hot" and that "personnel be selected and an agency set up for a clear historian's job without axe to grind or defense to prepare." That directive, signed in July 1942, and the documents, interviews, mission reports, and other items collected during the war became the nucleus of the official archives of the US Air Force, now held at the Air Force Historical Research Agency. This was made possible because Kuter directed that that material be collected, preserved, and archived. Kuter himself might have been unaware at the time that so much of his own story would be captured by this program and that years later his personal remembrance of events would itself be archived away as an official report.[1]

Only the most ardent of air power historians know the name of General Laurence S. Kuter despite the fact that he welded a B-17 wing into a cohesive fighting force, was the deputy commander of Allied tactical air forces in North Africa, and later served as commander of the Military Air Transport Service, the Air University, and the Far East Air Forces (later Pacific Air Forces), and finally as a commander in chief of the North American Air Defense Command (NORAD). He was a rated command pilot, combat observer, technical observer, and aircraft observer. In his career he logged more than eight thousand flying hours, including

1

thirty-two hundred hours as a command pilot, an unheard of number by today's air force standards. He flew in early biplane trainers and ended his flying time in F-106s and 747s. During World War II, he flew the B-24, the B-25, and the B-29. By 1952, his career had taken him around the world seven times visiting air force installations. At the beginning of World War II, he helped write the strategic plan for the air war, and, during the war, he served in every major theater of war in addition to tours in Washington, DC. He was everywhere, and, although he stayed in some places only a few weeks, he made enormous contributions to the development and changing of air power concepts, doctrines, and tactics everywhere he went.

Perhaps one of the main reasons there has been no major biography of Kuter is that, as the author James Parton unfairly accused him, he "never proved himself in combat." Parton was partially wrong in this assessment. Parton served as an aide to Ira Eaker in the European theater, and the thoughts that Eaker held on Kuter early in the war (discussed later) obviously colored Parton's perceptions. More importantly, Kuter is also overshadowed by other soldiers, sailors, airmen, and marines of his generation. As the historian Daniel Mortensen noted: "Neither [Sir Arthur] Coningham nor Kuter gained, at least in American eyes, the grand celebrity status granted to their colleagues in Africa—Eisenhower, Tedder, Montgomery, Patton, and Doolittle, to name the most obvious. However, working behind the scenes, refining doctrinal bulkheads, and putting words in the mouths of their service chiefs, Coningham and Kuter benefited American and British air organizations. Their efforts helped establish doctrine that supported more efficient, effective, and expert air force control over tactical air resources, an arrangement that eventuated in a less abusive treatment of air units working with surface forces."[2]

There are two reasons for this. The first was that Kuter was junior to these more well-known luminaries. As a brigadier and a major general, Kuter did not stack up to the three- and four-star-generals above him, even in his own service. The second was that he was never in one location long enough to make much of a name for himself. It seemed that he was always influential in the building of a command but transferred shortly after things got going.

Kuter spent barely six weeks as commander of the First Bombardment Wing in England under Major General Ira Eaker before Lieutenant General Carl "Tooey" Spaatz requested that he be sent to North Africa. In North Africa, he served as Air Marshal Sir Arthur Coningham's deputy of the North African Tactical Air Forces; a position he held for only a few months before finding himself ordered back to Washington to serve as Henry H. "Hap" Arnold's director of plans for the army air force. From that point forward, he operated in the background. Despite being influential in the organization and equipping of the air force during the Second World War, he mainly operated behind the scenes. However, his fingerprints are on every aspect of air force operations during the war. He spent time in every theater, and, perhaps more importantly, he left an enormous paper trail for the historian to follow in each of these theaters. The search for his actions during the war is not entirely different from the air force itself: global.

Opinions of Kuter remained mixed. Mortensen called Kuter "the epitome of a headquarters type with very limited operational experience," even though he served in the European, Mediterranean, and Pacific theaters during the war. But the historian Phillip Meilinger called him "one of the more accomplished air planners and staff officers in Air Force history." Meilinger listed Kuter among "some truly great airmen" whom "biographers have virtually ignored." Perhaps the reason Kuter does not already have a full biography is that he falls into somewhat of a gray zone. During the Second World War, he was not a three- or four-star general leading a corps, an army, or a major command, and he was not a more junior officer serving as a company or squadron commander. He was one among hundreds of one- and two-star generals/flag officers whose rich contributions to the war effort have been overlooked, preference going up and down the chain of command to the strategic and tactical leaders of the war. Despite the paucity of material written on him, he was universally praised for his contributions to the air force. After his death on 30 November 1979, the *Air Force Magazine* called him a "strategist, tactician, planner, educator, military statesman, and commander of strategic, tactical, airlift, and air defense forces." The *New York Times* called him the "Architect of Air Power."[3]

His colleague and lifelong close friend Haywood "Possum" Hansell said after Kuter's death: "Larry contributed to the development of and advancement of American Air Power at every step up the ladder." His contributions to the US Air Force and air power in general were "too numerous to name." One thing is clear: whether the attention is on his time as a combat officer or his time as an Air Staff planner, virtually nothing has been written on Kuter outside the odd chapter here and there. This must change.[4]

Perhaps there exists a lack of focus on Kuter because he is remembered much more for his mind, doctrinal development, and organizational skills than he is for his flying ability. In the air force, whose great icons did things in the *air*, his important actions took place on the ground and, to a great extent, behind the scenes. He was more in the mold of George Marshall than that of Tooey Spaatz or Curtis LeMay.

Laurence Kuter is an important and unsung hero of the earliest days of the air force who helped mold it into a cohesive and organized fighting force. A biography of him is long overdue, and it fills a gaping hole in the historiographic record. Even his associate authors of Air War Plans Division–Plan 1 (AWPD-1)—Haywood Hansell, Ken Walker, and Hal George—have been studied by historians, and each has had an individual biography or extensive studies written about him. Hansell wrote two books after the war and has a biography. Walker, who would die in the Southwest Pacific, would receive the Medal of Honor and a biography decades later. Only George and Kuter, both deserving, do not have book-length treatments. In particular, Kuter, a man who spent time not only in Washington, but also in every theater of war, needs individual attention. He did publish two books in his own right: *Airman at Yalta* and *The Great Gamble* (on the development of the 747). He was working on an autobiography when he died in 1979.[5]

This work is the first, but will certainly not be the last, to attempt to correct this missing piece of air force history. It is, first and foremost, a biography of Larry Kuter, but it is also a biography of the origins of the US Army Air Corps, the US Army Air Forces, and the independent US Air Force. What follows here is as much about what was occurring around Kuter as it is about the man himself. For Kuter's life is also the story of the prewar army, the story of the Air Corps Tactical School, the story of the organizing, training, equipping, and creating of a hitherto nonexistent air force to engage in global conflict before and during the Second World War. It is also the story of the early years of the Cold War, the Berlin Airlift, the Korean conflict, and the development of NORAD. It is also the story of the birth of an air force, its independent organizational struggles, and its growth into a service capable of monitoring the globe every minute of every day. Kuter was involved in each of these stories. He is a central player in them. This is a social, cultural, political, and military history.

Throughout this book, I have endeavored to allow Larry and Ethel Kuter to speak for themselves as much as possible. It was my hope that their own words would be more powerful than any description I could ever give. Their collected writings and memoirs are already enough to fill shelves in multiple archives across the United States. This is the story Larry Kuter never had the opportunity to finish himself.

1

Beginnings, West Point, and Early Assignments

It was the same story told in a different location. Young man of humble origins rises to important position and influences history by altering events. The same could be said—and has been many times—of many of his contemporaries. As if men and women who performed great deeds must somehow be ushered into life through something other than the way we all come into this world. Laurence Kuter's story started no differently than the stories of other men of his generation. At least Kuter recognized this when speaking on his own birth, noting that it was "an event totally ignored by the press."[1]

Laurence Sherman Kuter was born on 28 May 1905 in Rockford, Illinois, eighty-five miles west of Chicago. He was the grandson of Simon Kuter and the son of Maynard Washburn Kuter, men of German stock who were so ardently American that no German was permitted to be spoken in their house; nor would "S. A." Kuter, as his grandfather was known, join any German American society. It was his grandfather who insisted that the last name was pronounced to rhyme with *pewter*, although the common mispronunciation was, and still is, with the short *o* sound as in *Cooter*. At West Point, when he was asked for his name and he replied with "Kuter," the upperclassman in front of him yelled back: "Cuter? Cuter than what?" Laurence's response was: "Cuter than hell sir!" Years later, when Kuter was asked whether there was any anti-German feeling toward his family after the First World War because of his last name he quipped: "Kuter doesn't sound German enough. . . . If it was Eisenhower . . . or Stratemeyer, even Spaatz . . . [then] there might have been some resentment."[2]

It is a familiar story to historians of the time: a small community, a devoutly Methodist family, and a young boy running a paper route making twenty dollars a week to support a struggling family. Kuter was a quiet young man, not distinguishable from the rest of his classmates and coming of age in the aftermath of the First World War, and his life story was not unlike the stories of his later colleagues. He had his first taste of military life at the age of eight when he joined the Loyal Temperance League, an offshoot of the Women's Christian Temperance Union. He and his fellow members were "talked to a while" and then "given red fezzes and red sashes and wooden replicas of rifles." It was a rather uninspiring start to a lifetime spent in uniform.[3]

Kuter was likable enough to become class president in high school. He seemed to have no recollections of favorite subjects or classes outside English, and that preference can be attributed to the fact that a pretty girl, Ethel Lyddon, who had captured his attention, also enjoyed the subject. Thankfully, Ethel was a diligent diarist from the early age of thirteen and recorded much of her and Larry's high school experiences together. It is her words, not his, that give us the best picture of the young Laurence Kuter. He first appeared in her diary in January 1922, and his name slowly eclipsed every other subject in her diary. She described him as "an old peach" and "a fine fellow." She later admitted to herself: "I don't get crazy over him, just like him, good and steady." Laurence did, however, remember that it was his high school English teacher who sat him next to Ethel and that since their lockers were next to each other they walked to class together. As he later remembered: "We have walked together ever since."[4]

By their senior year (1922–1923), they were considered a steady item. They spent time with each other's families, she taught him to dance, and they went to movies and plays together. For high schoolers of the time living in Rockford, it was truly an age of innocence. Their favorite song was "All the World Is Waiting for the Sunrise." During the second semester of their senior year, Laurence's name was rarely absent from any entry in her diary. He was "perfect," and she "adored him." She would feel the same way about him nearly six decades later.[5]

Although Kuter did not have a favorite subject, he enjoyed the ROTC in high school, and Captain Harold H. Fisher pushed him to look into West Point for college. Kuter was initially uninterested and wanted to go to the University of Cincinnati, but Fisher was so ardent that he secured not only Kuter, but also two other boys' appointments to the military academy on the Hudson. He actively contacted every congressman in northern Illinois to obtain the needed appointments. He was initially successful in getting acceptances for Kuter's two classmates but not Laurence. He did secure Kuter an alternate's slot through the office of Congressman Charles E. Fuller of the Twelfth District of Illinois, but this would work out only if one of the two primary candidates failed to meet either the academic or the physical standards. Kuter apparently went forward with the physical and academic entrance exams for West Point despite being only an alternate, but this would prove beneficial shortly. He also accepted the alternate appointment via handwritten letter signed by both himself and his father in December 1922. The alternate slot was not good enough for Fisher, who struck out to find Kuter a primary appointment.[6]

Kuter continued with his plans to enter the University of Cincinnati in the fall of 1923 when he received a long-distance phone call that June, just days before his high school graduation. Fisher was on the other end of the line and standing in the office of Senator William B. McKinley. All McKinley's appointees had failed either their entrance or their physical exam. If he was willing to accept on the spot and be prepared to leave for West Point within a week, Kuter could have the appointment. Kuter looked around to his parents and, after a brief discussion during which he was told that the choice was his, returned to the line and said: "Yes, sir." And with that he spoke his last words to the "man who made a crusade of getting his young men into the service academies and who taught us leadership, loyalty, team-play, pride and discipline, not by books or lessons but by personal example day-in, day-out and by the quiet subtle influence of a great teacher." Fisher hung up the phone and Senator McKinley appointed Laurence Kuter to West Point. The confirmation letter was dated 16 June 1923 and approved by the US Military Academy on 20 June, a mere twelve days before Laurence Kuter was to report to begin his training.[7]

In later years, Fisher was also able to secure other young men from Rockford appointments to the Naval Academy. Kuter felt that his former ROTC instructor was responsible for his opportunity to attend the US Military Academy and corresponded regularly through letters. However, in an apparent case of class consciousness, a recognition of the type of officer that West Point was respected for producing, Fisher wrote Kuter an odd note in his third year: "You are an established West Pointer; you are going to graduate. As a West Pointer, you will be in a class by yourself, and you won't want to deal with people like me. So we'll agree that this has been a good relationship. I'm pleased to have gotten you in there, and we will say goodbye." Kuter never heard from him again, and he would later say: "I was very fond of him, and he just wrote himself off." Years later, Kuter wrote that Fisher's behavior was an odd form of "intense reverse snobbery, an enormous inferiority complex, or a gross underestimation of the quality of his own education and training."[8]

Laurence and Ethel attended every graduation and senior year event they could together that June 1923, including dances, picnics, and the graduation ceremony itself. For graduation, she bought him a Scheaffer fountain pen, and he bought her a monogrammed silver compact. The high school held commencement on 21 June. Laurence gave the commencement address. Nine days later, he boarded a train for the US Military Academy. His parents and Ethel saw him off at the train station. After saying good-bye to his folks, he turned to Ethel: "I'll be seeing you in a few years." They both knew that he would not have leave until after his sophomore year.[9]

West Point

Kuter, along with two of his high school classmates, stepped off the train on the morning of 2 July 1923. He was greeted by the senior cadets known to every cadet ever to attend a military college. Holding his one suitcase, he was told, "Drop it!" then immediately, "Pick it up!" and then again, "Drop it!" Life at West Point had begun. The business of "beast barracks" left no time to get homesick. Like thousands before and after him, Kuter learned that simply accepting the punishment of indoctrination was considerably better than attempting to fight the system as "any resentment of the hazing led immediately to an intensified treatment" from the upper-class cadre. Beast barracks ended in September, and Kuter, along with the rest of the class of 1927, set about the daily life of the plebe, which now included academics in addition to the military life.[10]

The West Point of Laurence Kuter's tenure was one where Chaucer was still taught and class position mattered more than anything else in determining where a graduate would be placed in the active duty US Army. Those at the top of each class became engineers, those at the bottom went into the infantry, and those in the middle joined the signal corps, the cavalry, or the field artillery. Despite the American experience in the First World War, the Civil War remained the benchmark of all military tactics and Gettysburg the most important battle referenced during map and field exercises. At West Point, Kuter was on the boxing team, but, as he put it, he was "too heavy to avoid the heavyweight category and too gangly and not grown up enough to fight in it." He was therefore a "good punching bag." The hazing of freshman was an accepted form of indoctrination, but this did not bother Kuter because it kept his mind off of his girlfriend back in Illinois. Beast barracks did not trouble him either. Despite being awake and under pressure for more than sixteen hours each day, he said of the experience that it was a "fine thing." His pleasant attitude lasted through the first four months, which coincided with the moment that the curriculum passed everything he had learned in high school.[11]

The first months at West Point did not hinder Kuter's communication with his girlfriend. Starting on the train ride to West Point, and continuing unabated nearly every other day for the next four years, Kuter meticulously wrote Ethel every chance he had, even during the earliest and toughest weeks of beast barracks. Ethel wrote to Laurence even more often. She hand-delivered the first of these letters to him at the train station as he departed for New York. The early letters detailed Laurence's daily routine, his formations, mess times, and interactions with classmates and upper classmen. Kuter penned twenty-five letters during beast barracks and kept up an ever-increasing stream of letters thereafter. In total, he wrote 510 letters to Ethel during his time as a cadet, the last one dated 11 June 1927, the "last letter from West Point." She returned the favor writing a total of 517 letters to him. One letter, written that first summer, has her pondering: "In twenty years from now . . . [will we] still have them . . . will [they] be priceless treasures or scraps of paper or ashes?" In September 1923, she went off to gain her education as well and entered Northwestern University in Evanston, Illinois. In September of her sophomore year, she transferred to the University of Illinois at Urbana-Champaign.[12]

Kuter had no trouble keeping up with his new life as a cadet, but he did note to Ethel: "Don't think that you ever worked—unless you have been a plebe at West Point." He tolerated, if he did not enjoy, the military aspects of that first year. Known for his seriousness and lack of emotion—something Ethel commented on in her high school diary—he had no problem maintaining an "undertaker's countenance" at mealtimes as he sat on the front six inches of his chair. His early letters demonstrate that the military life was not the only new experience he was having. A young man who had as yet had limited opportunities to travel, he met young men his age from all over the United States: midwesterners, southerners, and northerners were all thrown together for the first time. Kuter recalled the difficulty he had understanding his Marylander roommate when he said: "Ahm goin to write mah sweetie or this whole —— ahmy can go to ——."[13]

Cadets at military academies and colleges throughout the United States recognize that there are two primary draws on your time as a cadet. These are military matters and academic matters. Kuter excelled at the military aspect, but it did not take long until he found himself academically stranded, primarily because he had not spent any time studying. The college curriculum rapidly sped by everything he learned in high school, and he found himself falling behind. The correspondence to Ethel indicates that he had other things on his mind—something that many cadets in his position have felt since the creation of these unique institutions—including cadet knowledge, uniform preparation, and, of course, writing to Ethel. Things did not improve much for him over the course of the first semester. Although he survived the Christmas cuts—when the academically delinquent were sent home—he found himself at the bottom of his class. As classes formed up in sections by their academic standing, he lined up in the rear of each class—alone. He rectified this situation by doing the one thing he had not been doing up to that point—studying. It paid off in the long term. He graduated forty-fourth in his class, well within the top 25 percent.[14]

Kuter's years at West Point were demanding. His time not in class was spent learning the life of an army officer. Each cadet was expected to learn about each army branch and to make his preferences known prior to graduation. Kuter's letters to Ethel indicate that at one point he considered leaving the army after his initial commitment, but by the spring of his junior year he had committed to staying in. He wrote to Ethel: "You see yourself as a potential theater leader, I see myself as a future general, probably neither of us will reach those aims." It was also at West Point that Laurence became Larry. His classmates at the academy called him Larry, and he decided that he preferred this to his formal name. He later asked Ethel to call him Larry, at least in front of others.[15]

Since grades and class ranking mattered in the assignment of an army branch, a cadet might not get his first or even his second or third choices, especially the lower he was in the class. Summers were not free time for the cadets; visits to military bases and maneuvers were the norm during the 1920s, and each cadet became acquainted with their future possible occupations: corps of engineers, infantry, cavalry, field artillery, and signal corps (to which the nascent air arm belonged). This was the reason he did not see Ethel or his family until the summer between his sophomore and junior years. It was the next summer that Kuter had his first brief exposure to the US Army Air Corps.

During the summer before his senior year, Kuter visited Mitchel Field and broke the bonds of the earth for the first time, taking two rides with an air corps flyer. His first flight was in a DH-4 and the second in the ubiquitous JN-4 Jenny. The pilot took him on quite a ride, under the Brooklyn Bridge and around the Manhattan skyscrapers. Despite this, the ride did not represent the birth of a lifelong love of aviation and did not kindle in Kuter a desire for a future in flight. There were two possible reasons that he did not take an immediate interest in the air arm. The first was discussion among cadets that the "flying club life. . . . and flowing scarves of parachute silk"—that is, members of the air arm—did not want uptight, overly disciplined West Pointers interfering with their business. The second and undoubtedly more important reason was an incident that occurred on his last day at Mitchel Field when the first aircraft down the runway crashed on takeoff, killing the pilot and Kuter's classmate, Cadet Bill Point. The realities and immediate dangers of work in the air corps were readily apparent to the cadets standing on the field that day as they watched the black smoke boil into the sky. Kuter stated that he had no real "consciousness of air power" and chose field artillery as his occupational specialty.[16]

Kuter's senior year got off to a rocky start, but through no fault of his own. His letters speak often of the *hazing* that occurred at West Point, but the word did not have the same connotation as the pejorative it has become in the twenty-first century. *Hazing* was simply the accepted word for the military rigors of the fourth-class system at West Point that every freshman endured his first year. This included the strained exaggerated posture of attention known as *bracing,* the silent mealtimes sitting on the forward portion of the chair, and the great amount of often ridiculous knowledge that freshmen had to memorize. However, during beast barracks of his senior year, a freshmen quit the school and found a sympathetic ear in a newspaper that quoted him as referring to "vicious hazing." Four of Kuter's classmates were implicated, and the fourth-class system was immediately suspended. This meant, among other things, no double time in the barracks, no bracing, no freshman knowledge, and no front six inches—"straight back . . . shoulders back and down, chin back, ears high"—at the mess table. Upperclassmen were allowed to address freshmen with formal commands only while marching. Nothing else was permitted. No one was more upset than the freshmen themselves, who wanted the "traditional West Point" experience. To that end, the freshman class staged something of a rebellion, and it began at Cadet Larry Kuter's mess table.[17]

At dinner the day after the new orders went into effect, Kuter remembered, the freshmen at his table rebelled: "[They] opened the bottom buttons on their uniform blouses, and boisterously started to eat. Having finished they lounged on the table, tilted their chairs back and crossed their legs. One put his head down on crossed arms on the table and appeared to nap." Larry Kuter was in a real fix, for there was no formal military order that he was allowed to give to the freshman. The behavior quickly spread to the other tables. At breakfast the following morning, the behavior and unruliness of the freshmen continued, but now the commandant of cadets was in the mess hall observing. Immediately after breakfast, the commandant reinstated beast barracks. To ensure the press that the initial claims of hazing had been dealt with, the commandant issued orders that no upperclassmen could any longer strike a plebe and that no paddling of plebes would be tolerated either. Kuter noted that the new rules sat fine with the cadets since that type of behavior was not tolerated at West Point anyway. The freshmen of the class of 1930 received what they wanted, a traditional West Point experience.[18]

As their senior year drew to a close, Larry and his fellow cadets began to pay more attention to class standing and the quotas for each branch of service as well the available postings for each branch. The corps of engineers and the cavalry typically filled the fastest, but there were other considerations to take into account. As this was the height of the interwar period, most cadets did not take the possibility of fighting into account. Rather, uniforms, choice locations, and officer housing were the topics most often discussed. Corps of engineers officers typically resided in larger cities and near oceans or rivers. Cavalry officers were known for their high boots and swagger sticks but had a much higher chance of being sent to undesirable locations. Those who chose coastal artillery were certain to be near water but also at older, established bases where the housing was more likely to be nicer than that at interior posts. There was also one more consideration that several of the cadets were now taking quite seriously. As Kuter remembered: "High among the criteria that influenced cadets' choice of branches was the likelihood of the assignment to attractive geographic locations of stations, particularly if the cadet was planning on a wedding after graduation." And Kuter was certainly in that small group planning on being wed shortly after graduation. In February, he wrote to Ethel: "Mid [his best friend at West Point] and I have found another post that would not be so hard to take: The Presidio of Monterey, California . . . Monterey on the coast, in the heart of California's best section. Not bad, wot?"[19]

Kuter chose field artillery prior to graduation and was commissioned a second lieutenant in the branch in June 1927, the same year Ethel graduated from the University of Illinois. They would rendezvous back in their hometown after graduation for the wedding and then depart for Larry's first duty station: the Presidio. If location and accommodations for his new bride had been on his mind, Kuter could not have landed a better spot, although by his own admission this might have had more to do with help from a classmate's mother than any other factor. His friend, "Mid" Condon, a transfer from the naval academy, was also planning on wedding shortly after graduation. His mother, "Mother Fan," apparently intervened to ensure that, if the pair chose field artillery, she would make sure that they would be stationed together. Help from mothers of important persons was nothing new, and no less a persona than Douglas MacArthur was also implicated in having his mother's help in landing a plush first assignment.[20]

"June Week" found Kuter preparing for graduation and departure from West Point. His family arrived from Illinois, and he and the rest of the class of 1927 endured the never-ending succession of parades marking the end of another year at the military academy. Ethel did not travel to Larry's graduation, and his last letter to her from West Point expressed his discontent that the superintendent of the school assigned him to escort the daughter of the secretary of war around for graduation. Kuter ensured her that there was nothing he wanted less than such an assignment and nothing he wanted more than to travel home to see her. Larry graduated from West Point on 14 June, and Ethel graduated from the University of Illinois the next day with a degree in dramatics, an education, and a passion that she would exercise throughout Larry's career. They both headed back to Rockford to plan the wedding.[21]

On 8 September, Laurence married his longtime sweetheart, Ethel Lyddon, in the home of her parents at 1518 Chestnut Street in what the *Rockford Register Gazette* called "one of the prettiest weddings of the season." It was the tradition of the time for a wedding to take place in the bride's home. Promptly at noon, the harpist played the West Point Alma Mater, which also happened to be to the tune of Ethel's sorority—Pi Phi—sweetheart song. Next came the Wedding March as Ethel descended the stairs. The two married in the company of around forty guests. They visited friends and family in Milwaukee and Rockford before beginning their honeymoon trip across the country on 11 September bound for San Francisco and the Presidio. They departed on an afternoon train from Rockford and traveled through Laramie and Salt Lake City, making stops along the way of the six-day trip.[22]

First Assignment

The Presidio was a known quantity to the new lieutenants headed in that direction in the late 1920s and had everything a newly minted second lieutenant in the US Army could hope for in a first assignment: a storied history, a beautiful location near a major city, and leading regiments in both artillery and cavalry. It was a highly desired assignment and one that Larry Kuter and his new bride always remembered fondly.

Kuter was assigned to Battery D, 2nd Battalion, 76th Field Artillery, 11th Cavalry. He arrived at the Presidio from San Francisco, where he had dropped off his new wife of nine days with a former classmate who was currently residing in Berkeley. He was met at the train station by two fellow officers and taken to dinner. This reception eventually stood in sharp contrast to his later arrivals at other bases. He told Ethel that he would telegraph once he was settled and housing arrangements had been made, which did not take him long. He telegraphed Ethel that night: "Wonderful place—wonderful people—wonderful girl—be on tomorrow's train." The next morning, he officially reported in and was assigned as the executive officer of a field battery unit. Since he was the only other officer in the unit, his additional duties included battery mess officer, battery supply officer, battery school officer, and battery stable officer. That afternoon, as was customary for the protocol-heavy US Army, Lieutenant and Mrs. Kuter were met at their residence by a caisson pulled by six draft horses and attended by three officers and driven over to the Officer's Club for an official welcome reception with all the officers and wives present on post.[23]

After the reception, Kuter and his new bride returned to their quarters to find the door locked—another tradition of the time—and themselves without a key. After surveying all doors and windows, Kuter was forced to hoist his wife up on his shoulders and through a kitchen window, where she was dumped into the sink. Kuter recalled forty years later: "That is not the traditional way to welcome the bride into a house, but that's the way that one happened." Ethel remembered that, rather than being carried over the threshold, she was "pushed in over the kitchen sink."[24]

The Presidio of the interwar years stood at the crossroads of old and new. Artillery pieces were still pulled by teams of horses, and the horses still required the attention of a stable sergeant. On 2 December, Kuter received a certification for "proficiency in the care of animals." Coincidentally, he later served on the committee that reorganized the War

Department and officially ended the role of the cavalry in the US Army. Daily work at the Presidio began with a stable call at 7:00 A.M., followed by two hours of horse-drawn field artillery exercises. Kuter enjoyed these maneuvers even though the surrounding forests and beaches—which, according to him, were far superior to the "monastic conditions of life at West Point"—made focusing on work difficult at times. Maneuvers were followed by sighting practice with French seventy-five-millimeter field artillery pieces or shooting on the pistol range. Field work ended at noon, and the remainder of the afternoon was taken up with "practically mandatory" polo games.[25]

The assignment at the Presidio also exposed Larry and Ethel to another new experience: alcohol. While they both had surely been around intoxicating drinks before, neither of them ever mentioned partaking until their first assignment. This was also the time of Prohibition, so the alcohol they did consume was mostly homemade. The fault seemed to rest on the shoulders of Kuter's company commander, Captain Richardson, who, as Ethel noted, "introduced Larry to his bootlegger." She continued: "We succumbed." It was simply "the thing to do." Larry remembered that evenings included "bath tub gin and home brewed beer in staggering quantities." While many of the officers distilled whiskey, Larry put his German ancestry to use and became a local brew master of some renown.[26]

It was an ideal existence for a newly commissioned officer and his new bride in the interwar US Army. Ethel put her drama degree to good use by joining a local entertainment troupe called the Presidio Players. Her acting time was limited, however; within six months of arriving, she was pregnant. The Kuters' daughter, Roxanne, arrived at 10:20 A.M. on the morning of Monday, 5 November 1928. The battalion issued orders announcing her arrival and presented her with a silver spoon.[27]

During battery firing exercises, Lieutenant Kuter had his first exposure to army aviation. A DH airplane flew from San Francisco and landed on the Presidio's polo grounds. The aircraft's crew would gather their orders, fly more or less in the "general vicinity" of the target, and make "nonchalant observations" about the artillery fire. Kuter recognized that the utility of the observers would improve greatly if they would simply fly over the target. He then made an important decision, one that would change his life. He applied for flight training. His friend Mid Condon also applied, but he did not pass the flight physical. Their paths "went in different directions thereafter." After the flight physical, Kuter received orders in May to report to Brooks Field, Texas, on or about 25 June 1929 to attend the Primary Flying School of the US Army Air Corps. His service in the field artillery had lasted less than two years.[28]

Flight Training

Kuter's path to flight training in the late 1920s was not unlike that of many other air power pioneers who joined the army air corps either directly out of West Point or shortly thereafter through a transfer, and their reasoning has become somewhat of a cliché in the histories of such men. Each felt that air power offered something different and unique to the understanding of warfare as it was practiced in the interwar years. Too young to have served in World War I, the airplane presented to them a means to an end, be it observation of artillery or flying artillery capable of crippling an industrialized society through well-placed and precision attacks. Most were not yet disciples of Giulio Douhet or Billy Mitchell, but the religious fervor would manifest itself shortly. Still, Kuter did not want to learn to fly out of a desire to change careers or from any sense of the greater contributions that air power could offer to warfare or, more narrowly, to his career. (This conversion would come later and bring with it religious devotion.) He did it simply to improve himself as an artillery officer, saying later: "My entry into a career of aviation was motivated only by my intention to be a better field artilleryman." What began as a way to affect their current assignments would turn into a new style of warfare capable of affecting the outcome of the war—or so Kuter and others like him eventually came to believe. His origins in field artillery are important from the perspective that Kuter knew what it was like to be the soldier on the ground looking up at an airplane, and this perspective demonstrated itself later, especially in North Africa.[29]

The Kuter family departed the Presidio on the morning of 18 May, heading east toward family in Illinois; neither set of parents had yet met six-month-old Roxanne. They traveled in their newly purchased, but used, Willys-Knight automobile. The trip to Rockford was nothing short of miserable. Four days into the trip, Larry's military bedroll fell off the car with no one noticing. It contained Larry's raincoat, Sam Browne uniform belt, all of Roxanne's clothes, some of Ethel's clothes, flatware, and linens. Luckily, an army major driving in the other direction came across it, and it was eventually returned to them. The same day, they had their first flat tire. By 25 May, the car was in desperate need of attention, which required Ethel's family to wire them fifty dollars for repairs, which included a second flat tire. On Larry's twenty-fourth birthday, May 28, they departed Kansas City only to have the fan belt break early the next morning. The Kuters limped into Rockford on the afternoon of May 29 after an eleven-day journey. After three weeks visiting family and friends and showing off Roxanne, they departed on 21 June for Texas.[30]

Kuter arrived at Brooks Field on a "burning hot" 25 June, accompanied by his wife, his wife's fifteen-year-old sister Ruth Ann Lyddon, his six-month-old baby, and a grand total of $22.00 cash in his pocket. According to the historian Rebecca Cameron, Brooks Field, outside San Antonio, was "hardly palatial," and Kuter and his family were appalled at the differences from the Presidio. Kuter later said: "The attitude of complete indifference to student officer housing or other welfare requirements . . . was in sharp contrast to the situation at Monterey." He spent a lengthy amount of time wandering around the field until he came across "one squatting Sgt. who seemed mildly interested in the arrival of student officers." After in-processing and handing over his orders, he was unceremoniously told that officer housing was not available at that time and that the school "did not wish to be bothered by incoming students" until the start of training on 1 July. He temporarily moved his family into a tourist cabin until other housing arrangements could be made. In the sweltering heat, Roxanne immediately broke out in hives. Larry was forced to take her to the hospital at Fort Sam Houston, where the doctor prescribed an oscillating fan to keep her cool, which Kuter purchased on the return trip to Brooks Field for $18.00, leaving the family a grand total of $4.00.[31]

The army air corps that Kuter experienced on his arrival was not the air force of later decades. This was years before the air force would gather the reputation of being better housed, better fed, and better taken care of generally than were the members of the other services. Kuter surely questioned whether his motivations were correct in this venture, especially considering the lifestyle to which he and his family had become accustomed at the Presidio. He did wonder whether he was still in the same service as the one he had left behind in California. The only piece of good news he received was that flying students were to be paid the same as full-time aviators, which meant a 50 percent increase in his pay. If his living conditions were worse off, at least his wallet was about to grow fatter.[32]

At Brooks Field, Kuter entered into a flying class of roughly sixty to seventy students composed of recent college graduates and regular army types like himself, including about a dozen of Kuter's classmates from West Point. On his first day of training, the local commandant read the standard post rules and then turned the class over to the director of flying training, Captain Claire Chennault. Chennault launched into a discussion about his students' possibilities for success in the flying arm, which were, to his mind, dim. More than 50 percent of the class was expected to "wash out." The only way to avoid being sent packing was to meet with the "wash out board," which Chennault chaired. On being removed from flying training, the washout was to pack his bags, pay his bills, and leave base immediately.[33]

As did all such classes, this one began with ground school, which included readings and tests. During one of these tests, Kuter noticed some of his classmates blatantly cheating with barely concealed textbooks under their desks. When he informed the instructor, he was curtly informed that he "was no longer at West Point." He was shocked that cheating was indirectly tolerated, a dismissible offense at the academy. In his opinion, this was another strike against the army air corps.[34]

The West Point in Kuter never left him. He did not tolerate lying, cheating, or stealing, and he would not allow it around him. He was already a stickler for doing things the correct way, and this episode certainly helped reinforce the honor code for him. If the early aviators—men like Curtis LeMay and Jimmy Doolittle—were cowboys, then Kuter represented the first-generation lawman who came to town to impose order.

Having successfully made his way through ground operations, Kuter and his class moved on to flying training. Things did not go well for Kuter. Besides being verbally berated by his instructor in the front seat of the PT-1 aircraft, he began to suffer migraine headaches, owing in no small part to the Texas heat, the tightly fitting helmet, and the blinding sun. He kept these headaches secret from his instructors and classmates, choosing instead to buy an expensive pair of shaded goggles to deal with the glare of the sun and have Ethel hand-knit a better-fitting helmet (there was no standard headgear at this time). However, his nerves were also getting to him. Along with the sweating and dehydration that came from the unending heat, he was losing weight. He dropped thirty pounds and weighed less than he did his freshman year at the academy.[35]

The washout rate was indeed high, with many of those affected being Kuter's West Point classmates. Perhaps there was truth to the legend that the flying arm truly did not want West Point men in its ranks as well as to Kuter's previous encounters with flying instructors. Only three of Kuter's thirteen West Point brethren remained after a few weeks. Most were sent for a final check ride with Captain Chennault and told they lacked "inherent flying ability." They returned to their previous assignments and disappeared from Brooks Field. By the end of the course, Kuter alone remained of the members of the West Point class of 1927—and, by his own admission, just barely.

As the end of primary flight training approached, Kuter was sent for a check ride with Chennault, the precursor to being washed out. The two took off to practice "figure eight patterns," and, after several mechanical turns, Chennault took control of the aircraft and returned to base. Kuter knew he was finished. As they stood beside the aircraft, Chennault asked Kuter why he flew the way he did, so rigidly. Knowing he was finished anyway, Kuter let loose with the truth that he had been trained to fly that way and that he knew he could do better. Chennault intoned rudely that apparently Kuter thought himself better than his instructors and ordered the lieutenant back into the air for another go. This time, rather than do as he had been instructed, Kuter applied gentle pressure to the rudder and lazily made the figure eights. On landing, Chennault told Kuter that, starting the next day, he would have a new instructor and never mentioned the incident again. Kuter survived being washed out. And he survived Captain Claire Chennault.[36]

Kuter was at this point transitioned over to Kelly Field for advanced flight training. His headaches subsided, and his weight returned to a respectable 172; he had survived. The advanced course was designed to familiarize officers with a number of aircraft types: PW-9s and P-12s for pursuit, A-3s for attack, and MB-1s for bombardment. This was long before the days of being selected for an airframe of one's choice. Kuter chose bombardment. He also decided that he would never return to field artillery. He was seriously considering a future in the air arm and began to explore the applications of air power. Those who chose bombers were paired up with another officer to switch the right- and left-seat assignments of the "big" bombers. Kuter was paired Second Lieutenant Delmar T. "Del" Spivey, and the two developed a close working relationship. Many years later, when Kuter commanded the Air University, Major General Spivey lived next door to him as the commandant of the Air War College.[37]

Kuter and Spivey sailed painlessly through this portion of the curriculum, and both were adept at the required night and formation flying. They breezed through their "cross-country" test, which saw them flying from San Antonio to Austin, Fort Worth, Midland, El Paso, and back to San Antonio, having never left the state of Texas. The graduation was a muted affair, although the guest speaker was one of the first American military aviators, Brigadier General Frank Lahm. Ethel pinned Larry's wings on his chest in full view of his parents. That afternoon, as was air corps policy at the time, Kuter made three separate flights in an A-3, one each carrying his wife, mother, and father on a thirty-minute familiarization flight. Afterward, Larry and Ethel loaded their possessions onto a train and headed north. Lieutenant Larry Kuter was an army air corps pilot, and he was headed to Virginia's Langley Field.

Langley Field

Still a second lieutenant, Larry Kuter was now assigned to the Second Bombardment Wing, Langley Field, Virginia. Langley is one of the oldest military flying installations in the United States. Named for a former head of the Smithsonian, Samuel Pierpont Langley, the base has been in active use since its creation in 1917. In the spring of 1916, the army, the navy, and the National Advisory Committee for Aeronautics jointly decided to construct a facility. The army agreed to search for such a site, appointing a board of officers to search for a location. The board, its members sometimes posing as hunters or fishermen, investigated fifteen locations before deciding on a site just north of Hampton. The location met all the requirements: flat land bordering on a large body of water, east of the Mississippi, and not more than two hours travel time, by train, from Washington, DC. A citizens' committee of what was then Elizabeth City (now Hampton) acquired options on the land and in November offered it to the army for $290,000. On 30 December 1916, the government purchased the parcel, which totaled about 1,650 acres. Construction on the fledgling field began in the same month that the first contingent of soldiers arrived, April 1917. Without any available facilities, the soldiers billeted at "Fortress Monroe" until moving into a cottage on the Sherwood Plantation. In mid-June, they were organized into the field's first unit, the 5th Aviation School Corps. On 7 August 1917, the Aeronautical Experimental School, as it was initially called, became the first unit at Langley Field. In the early 1920s, Langley became the proving grounds for new air power concepts. Brigadier General William "Billy" Mitchell claimed that air power could destroy any surface ship with torpedoes and bombs. In 1921, the 1st Provisional Air Brigade was formed to put to rest the heated controversy raised by Mitchell's claims. In July, a series of successful "attacks" were made against some captured German ships, including the huge battleship *Ostfriesland*. In July 1922, the 2d Bombardment Group arrived at Langley and remained there until

October 1942. For several years, the 2d represented the air corps's only bombardment group. Besides its military mission, it flew airmail missions during the mail crisis of 1934. In 1937, it became the first to receive the new B-17 *Flying Fortress*.[38]

When Kuter and his family arrived on 10 July 1930, they were assigned to a brick duplex within walking distance of the flight line, offices, and maintenance hangars and a leisurely stroll to the officer's club as well. It was no Presidio, but it was a vast improvement over the conditions at Brooks Field. Kuter also met Haywood Hansell that summer. Shortly after arriving, the Kuters threw a housewarming party. Kuter's recent appreciation for alcohol also landed him in hot water that same night.[39]

At the party, Kuter distributed the brew that made him a famous brew master at the Presidio. At some point during the evening, he and his intoxicated guests heard a series of loud explosions. The beer in the basement was literally bursting at the seams. The party guests, drunk and in possession of illegal alcohol, took to the streets of Langley. It was probably the mass exodus that attracted base security. Only one party attender stuck by Larry when the authorities arrived: Haywood Hansell. Luckily for both Hansell and Kuter, the officer of the guard was also a home brewer. He admonished Kuter and Hansell and then offered "excellent technical advice on preparation and storage of home brew and went his way." Nearly five decades later, Hansell remembered that the incident was "without merit except for an important side-result: it cemented a friendship that lasted through forty-nine years and two wars."[40]

Kuter's entrance to Langley was also his introduction to the very forward-looking air corps. While the field was dotted with LB-3 and LB-5 bombers, talk was already circulating about what was going to come next from Boeing and Douglas. The Air Corps Tactical School (ACTS) was still at Langley—although looking to move to Alabama's Maxwell Field shortly—and this also added to the overall intellectual atmosphere of what air power might contribute to the future of warfare, although the ACTS intellectuals had little time for the line pilots. Kuter was assigned as the operations officer of the 49th Bombardment Squadron, part of the 2nd Bombardment Group, under Captain Eugene Eubanks.[41]

Langley Field was the heart of the prewar air corps. Not only was it the home of ACTS, which moved to Maxwell Air Force Base in 1931, but it would also become, in 1935, the home of the newly created and quasi-independent (from the US Army) General Headquarters Air Force. One month after his assignment to the 49th, Kuter was officially transferred out of field artillery and over to the air corps. During his Langley Field assignment, he participated in the annual army air corps bombing competition. Just off the end of the runway and after following the Back River out, but before the pilot entered the Chesapeake Bay, was Plum Tree Island. The pilots at Langley drew out shapes of battle cruisers to practice bombing and strafing runs. The ACTS students and instructors and those assigned to the 2nd Bombardment Group were already using the airplane against possible future targets.[42]

It was at this time that Kuter became reacquainted and finally friends with Claire Chennault and flew with the acrobatic "Flying Trapeze." His initial poor performance on his lazy eights seems to have been forgotten. He was never a full-time pilot with the unit and flew as a replacement only on occasion because, as he put it, "I could just barely stay with the Flying Trapeze." This did not strictly refer to the flying maneuvers: "The hardest drinkers were the most vigorous fighters. You can't be much more vigorous than Claire Chennault, and Claire was a good hard drinker too." This group might be considered a precursor to the modern air force Thunderbirds or navy Blue Angels as it was the first recognized aerial acrobatic team in the military service. Kuter flew alternate wing position with Chennault when one of the other members—Haywood Hansell, Red Williams, or William McDonald—was absent.[43]

Kuter also worked on the development of the experimental B-9 Boeing twin-engine bombers, which pioneered high-altitude bombing techniques and tactics in the US Air Force. The bomber was notoriously dangerous and deadly owing primarily to its flimsiness. The aircraft had a monocoque fuselage, meaning that the structural support for the aircraft was its skin, much like the shell provides structural support for the egg. Kuter noted: "[If you] jammed down the rudder and looked back at the fuselage, you could see the monocoque twist. Well, you didn't twist egg shells very successfully." Of the nine planes in his squadron, six were eventually damaged beyond repair. Kuter's only aircraft accident came at this time. Since Langley had been located near water for amphibious aircraft training, the base had an older Sikorsky amphibian. Because he was the only pilot checked out as an instructor in this aircraft, Kuter flew it often, but, if pilots did not push the nose down on landing, the plane would skip like a rock over the water. Over time, this skipping damaged the supporting struts. While landing the aircraft in the Back River, a wing strut separated, and the propeller cut into the aircraft directly in front of Kuter, destroying the instrument panel, and spraying Kuter with parts. The investigation determined that the accident was 50 percent mechani-

cal failure and 50 percent pilot failure. Kuter always resented having half the blame placed on him.[44]

Kuter spent his time at Langley in the 49th flying new and untested aircraft. These tests were often conducted at night, four miles in the air. This was still the age where pilots continued to determine what an aircraft could do and what utility air power offered. The unit flew the new B-9 before the program was terminated, participating in a demonstration mission that perhaps conclusively proved—in a rather comedic manner—the effects of bomber aircraft on morale. At the Aberdeen Proving Ground, a large "target" was laid out in white panels, well within sight of the observers in the grandstands. As the planes approached the target on the day of the demonstration, winds cut across them, causing the pilots to "turn" into the wind to remain on the correct approach path. Unfortunately, the day's narrator failed to inform the audience that, although it appeared as if the Keystone bombers were coming directly for the grandstands, they were not. The army generals and congressmen present later reported that the air corps had directly threatened their safety. Nothing could be further from the truth, and Captain Eubank had to spend many hours explaining to the viewers that his pilots were not actually attempting to kill them.[45]

The interwar period was not viewed as such by the members of the air corps. It was, if anything, a quiet time for America's armed forces. The early 1930s were a slow time in general in America. The market had crashed in 1929, Franklin Roosevelt was not yet president (Herbert Hoover still held that office), and Hitler had not come to power in Germany. If bombardment was the future of warfare, it was certainly not evident yet to Lieutenant Larry Kuter. Beyond practice bombing runs, Kuter moved from squadron operations officer up to the wing staff—working for the wing's commander, Colonel Dargue—where he now ran operations for the whole wing. One such glorious assignment in the summer of 1931 was leading cadets from West Point around and taking them on familiarization flights. The first cadet Kuter flew with was J. P. McConnell, unbeknownst to either of them a future chief of staff of the US Air Force. Kuter, himself a West Point man, remembered his first flight while still a cadet well and was doing his best to counter the stigmatization of the air corps that he felt existed in the military academy. These flights were to be more realistic, "not for thrills," and demonstrate to the cadets what life in the air corps was really like. Kuter wanted more academy graduates to apply for direct commission into the air corps, which is exactly what McConnell did on graduation. This professionalization is significant. It demonstrated that Kuter wanted the air corps to be taken seriously, viewed as a professional arm of the military and enticing to newly commissioned officers as a viable career path. Slowly, but surely, he was making an impact on the air corps.[46]

Flying the Mail

In early 1934, America's postmaster general, James Farley, could not come to terms with the rates paid to commercial airlines to deliver the mail. President Roosevelt canceled all commercial air contracts and ordered the army air corps to fly the mail. The chief of the air corps, General Benjamin Foulois, called his subordinates Hap Arnold, Horace Hickam, and B. Q. Jones to his office, where they divided the United States into three zones: Eastern, Central, and Western. This was the beginnings of the army air corps mail operation. It soon turned into a complete fiasco and a black eye for the air corps. There existed no facilities specifically designed to support air corps pilots flying large quantities of mail across the country. The pilots had less than two weeks to prepare for the operation, and most of these men were reserve officers with limited flying experience and no experience at all flying the airmail routes. Arnold later said of what became known as the "Airmail Scandal" that, while air corps pilots had the will to do the mission, "the price of our doing it was to equal the sacrifice of a wartime combat operation."[47]

From February to June 1934, Kuter served as operations officer of the Eastern Zone. The wing commander, Colonel Dargue, called Kuter in and told him to pack a "side arm" and "civilian clothes," take a P-6 Hawk up to Washington, DC, report to Lieutenant Colonel B. Q. Jones, and "be prepared to stay." Jones was already in over his head and needed an officer with an organizational mind to help get things in order. Kuter fit the bill. He arrived at the War Department munitions building only to be told that Jones was moving the entire operation to Newark Airport, in essence to run the operation from anywhere but Washington. Kuter was informed that he was the "rear echelon" and to man the phones until Jones called for him. He was also told that, when he departed for Newark, he was to fly the new "Air Corps Airplane Number One," a Curtis Condor transport plane, to the new headquarters. When he pointed out that he had never even set foot inside the aircraft before, much less logged any flying time in it, Jones told him: "You're the only bomber pilot I've got. You should have no trouble flying the No. 1 big ship." Dumfounded,

Kuter stood by as Jones and the rest of the staff departed. He was left to wait for the phone call to join the rest of escaping mail operation staff.[48]

When the phone call did come, Kuter reported to Bolling Field, across the Potomac, to find the Condor preflighted and ready for take-off. He signed for the aircraft, climbed aboard, and threw his meager belongings down. He noticed that every seat was laden with boxes of sta-tionary marked with the letterhead of the army air corps. In his rush to escape Washington, Jones had failed to take any with him. Kuter climbed into the cockpit and sat in the left-hand seat beside his unknown copilot. These were certainly not ideal circumstances in which to have to learn to fly a new aircraft. Kuter familiarized himself as quickly as possible with the controls and taxied the aircraft to the end of the runway. He needed to get airborne quickly to beat an approaching front that was rolling in. He virtually ignored the man in the right-hand seat, who did not seem too inclined to be of much use anyway. He pushed the throttles forward and sped down the runway, wondering whether there was enough power to get the aircraft into flight. Pulling back on the controls, he just cleared the trees at the end of the runway and banked north. He told his copilot to pull up the wheels. The bewildered man looked over at him and said, "What wheels?" Amazed, Kuter asked whether he was the crew chief, to which his passenger replied, "I don't know anything about airplanes. I'm a clerk-typist." The only reason the man had chosen to sit in the front seat was that the others were stacked so high with stationary.[49]

Kuter was now flying an unfamiliar aircraft with no copilot, racing an approaching storm, and headed for a "foggy, smokey [sic], strange airport among oil refineries in the Jersey Swamps." Finding Newark proved to be no easy task. Kuter made several false approaches to what turned out to be filling stations along the Jersey Turnpike. He was finally able to land the Condor and taxi to a small hangar marked EZAACMO: Eastern Zone army air corps mail operation. He had barely turned off the aircraft's engines when a winter storm set in, stopping any further operations.[50]

Having now discovered that his move to Newark was ill advised, Jones looked to get the mail operation up and running. Of pressing con-cern was finding lodging for his officers and enlisted personnel, none of whom could afford the local hotels. He eventually convinced a Coney Island hotel to house his men, but the accommodations were far from adequate. Beyond housing, He also decided that Newark did not main-tain suitable facilities for running the mail and, again, moved his head-quarters, this time to Floyd Bennett Field in Brooklyn. This led to all the assigned aircraft having to be moved during the winter gale. Kuter, also again, found himself flying an unfamiliar aircraft—a P-26—to Brooklyn.[51]

The army air corps quickly learned the difficulties involved in carrying the mail. Across the country, air corps pilots crashed their aircraft, and several pilots died. America's World War I flying ace, Eddie Rickenbacker, called it "legalized murder." One pilot, lucky enough to "land" his aircraft in a winter storm, reported to Arnold that his aircraft was a "bit damaged." When Arnold questioned just what a "bit damaged" entailed, he was told: "Well, it has no landing gear . . . the lower wing is off . . . the tail surface is broken, and the engine flew out of the fuselage."[52]

Kuter, running the operation in the Eastern Zone, also had to contend with a difficult boss who found himself in a wrangle with the New York mayor, Fiorella LaGuardia. Both wanted to be in charge of the airfield. The fact that LaGuardia was a World War I aviator did not help matters. Jones followed through on his promise to, yet again, move his headquarters "far enough away so that the Mayor couldn't get his Goddamned hands on it." Jones again left Kuter as rear echelon and moved the headquarters a third time, this time to Mitchel Field. As Kuter closed up the limited operations at Floyd Bennett, the mayor and an entourage pulled up outside the hangar. LaGuardia demanded to see Jones, and Kuter was forced to inform him that Jones had absconded that afternoon and that, in all honesty, he had no idea of his current whereabouts. LaGuardia and his staff left in a huff, knowing that Jones had escaped the confrontation the mayor wanted. Kuter was left alone to await the phone call from Jones to bring what remained of the EZAACMO staff and aircraft to Mitchel Field.[53]

The growing list of aircraft accidents in the few months of the air corps operation in the Eastern Zone alone became an atrocious casualty list: "Major Kirby—P-12—caught fire in air, ship destroyed, pilot sustained fractured skull and burns; Lt. Jackson—P-12—collided with ground target, ship destroyed, pilot killed." A zone supply officer attempting to make a comprehensive list of damaged aircraft conceded that accidents occurred so regularly that his list was only "somewhat as follows."[54]

Kuter's own personal recollections of the Airmail Scandal attempted to vindicate the air corps, pointing out what it had accomplished in the face of such overwhelming odds, including poor knowledge of mail procedures, instrument flying, radio beam flying for night operations, and meteorology. The army air corps was better able to deliver the mail than the civilian airlines were, but Kuter ignored the costs. That winter cost the lives of dozens of airmen flying a mission that they were not properly trained to accomplish. Even with Kuter's organizational panache and record on-time rates, the deaths far outweighed the accomplishments. Kuter later remarked that he was also shocked that the major papers made front-page stories of these incidents while also ignoring the accomplishments of the air corps. This was his first experience, but not his last, with the impact that public relations has on military operations.[55]

Kuter was the last officer relieved from this duty, having been held over to write the final report and history. At this time, he already had an intuition that the events he was participating in would be historically significant, and he took great pains to write an exhaustive 439-page report covering details minute by minute. He also had an impact on the collection of history during the Second World War, but even at this early stage in his career he was providing an invaluable paper trail for future historians and was already on his way to being the father of air force history.

Kuter's final version of the "Eastern Zone Army Air Corps Mail Operations Report" was more honest than his later remembrances and stated that this was a job for which the air corps was "not trained, equipped, or organized" to conduct. His focus on proper training for the aircrews was an important note on his part and something that he emphasized time and again in his own commands. Again, his insistence on a professional air arm was a significant step in paving the way for a more autonomous branch. Interestingly, the cover of the final report depicted a moss-covered gravestone giving the birth and death dates of the air mail operation and the epitaph "Requiescat in Pace, rest in peace."[56]

Kuter returned to Langley Field on 12 June to find his next orders and move awaiting him. His days at Langley were over. He had been selected to attend ACTS, Maxwell Field, Alabama. In a career of less than ten years since his graduation from the US Military Academy in June 1927, he had already transferred from the field artillery to the air corps. He earned his pilot's wings and left his ground life behind. He earned a specialty rating in bombardment aircraft and now had experience at the squadron, group, and wing levels and had proved himself a capable organizer. His mettle, and that of the army air corps, had been tested during the airmail crisis.

That he was selected to attend ACTS was no accident. He had a reputation as a sharp and capable officer with potential for doing great things in the future. Attending ACTS would not only test his ability to think critically; it was also a stepping-stone along the road from tactical operations to operational and strategic thinking. Kuter's concepts for future theories, doctrines, and operations could flourish at Maxwell Field, as he would be surrounded by the best and brightest officers, not unlike himself, that the US Army Air Corps had to offer. He was also entering the school at what would prove to be a pivotal moment for the future air arm. A unique collection of air power thinkers was already there, and Kuter's class and his instructors proved to be the right men, in the right place, at the right time to meet the storm clouds of future conflict then gathering on the horizon.

2

The Air Corps Tactical School

The air domain, not just the military application commonly called *air power,* experienced exponential growth in the interwar years. The many ways in which air forces had contributed to military operations during World War I were studied, expanded, expounded, and developed into new, forward-looking—and sometimes fanciful—theories in the 1920s and 1930s. Air power as an important, if not decisive, force found a home inside the Air Corps Tactical School, more commonly referred to by the acronym ACTS, which Kuter attended in 1935 and where he stayed on for four years afterward as an instructor.

The historian Phillip Meilinger stated that the true changes began at ACTS in the 1930s. He notes: "There began arriving on the ACTS faculty [around that time] a number of original and creative minds who deliberately and effectively altered the debate on airpower." These air power luminaries included Harold George, Haywood Hansell, Hoyt Vandenberg, George Kenney, Claire Chennault, and Larry Kuter. Not every student was as intellectually curious or willing to engage in debates about air power theory; Curtis LeMay would later say that he learned "not much" during his time as a student. So much of history seems to be timing, the fickle hand of fate placing individuals at certain places and at certain times that will forever affect their futures. Those students and instructors at ACTS in the years immediately preceding World War II were one such group. They studied, instructed, debated, refined, and then put into practice an entirely new way of waging war that would have consequences that none of them could have imagined. Even the most ardent of advocates for bombardment aviation could not comprehend the global impact that their decisions would have.[1]

The intellectual underpinnings for the development of American air power after the First World War took place at ACTS, located at Langley Field from 1920 to 1931 and thereafter at Maxwell Field in Alabama. Early student classes—those held at Langley Field in the early 1920s—

had many officers with flying service in the First World War interspersed with more junior officers. The historian Alan Stephens has called ACTS "a vibrant, innovative environment, in which the evolving and often competing schools of air power doctrine . . . were argued with a passion." ACTS graduates became a veritable who's who of senior leaders in the army air force during World War II. Beyond the list of instructors already mentioned, ACTS graduates included Joseph McNarney, Elwood "Pete" Quesada, Ira Eaker, and Carl Spaatz. If the school was a vibrant and innovative environment, it was not always one in which differing opinions were accepted. Stephens is right in his assertion that schools of thought were argued at ACTS, but although a wide range of views was discussed seriously, one school of thought was primus inter pares: bombardment. At the 1920s ACTS, pursuit stood equal to bombardment, but, as the debates for an independent air corps grew and Billy Mitchell sacrificed himself on the altar of public relations, the mind-set at ACTS began to change. By the time Kuter and Hansell arrived, the "basic premise of the school was complete"; bombardment was the clear choice for prosecuting warfare in the future. So deeply ingrained and accepted was the idea of bombardment that tactical aviators, such as Pete Quesada and Claire Chennault, found themselves maligned, sidelined, and left out.[2]

ACTS became a preferred alternative for US Army flyers instead of the Command and General Staff School (CGSS) at Fort Leavenworth, Kansas. Kuter never attended CGSS. His name was on the eligible list for three years, but, since he was instructing at Maxwell, it was continually "scratched off." CGSS was in his opinion "widely considered in the Air Corps a waste of time in maneuvering companies and battalions on the Gettysburg maps." However, it was acknowledged as "an important leg up on the promotion ladder in the army," and ACTS graduates still hoped to attend if for no other reason than to keep their careers on track. However, flyers who attended the course, including Hoyt Vandenberg, considered it a "wasted year." In the long run, not attending did not hinder Kuter's promotion opportunities.[3]

The main concepts that emerged from ACTS during the 1920s and 1930s argued that air power should be viewed as an inherently offensive weapon; even a defensive use of air power, as in a patrol over one's own airfield, becomes offensive once aircraft are engaged, as opposed to the use of ground forces, which could operate in a purely defensive manner. The second tenet, first quoted by British prime minister Stanley Baldwin in 1932 before Parliament, became a mantra: "The bomber will always get through." Even though, as the historian Alan Stephens noted, "competing schools of air power doctrine . . . were argued," one quickly surpassed the other. The importance of the development of bombardment aviation cannot be overstated. Pursuit aviation was justified only as a means to provide some support for bombers, and it was subsumed into bombardment theory.[4]

Kuter's intellectual pursuits had until this point been limited to being a tactician and to understanding the job of piloting an aircraft. Being assigned to being a student changed all this. As he later recalled: "Until I left Langley, I was solely concerned with the physical aspects of air tactics—flying, bombing, shooting, gunnery, everything related to the physical equipment. There was no intellectual activity of any sort among my group or, I think, at Langley Field. . . . We had our first introduction of any sort to air strategy [at ACTS]. We never heard the name of Douhet until I was a student at the Air Corps Tactical School." This at least proves that by the mid-1930s Douhet's ideas were, if not accepted, indeed being discussed.[5]

In the summer of 1934, a twenty-seven-year-old Laurence Kuter, along with his wife and daughter, arrived at Maxwell Field. Kuter would later remember: "[That academic year] had a greater effect on my career than any single event since entering West Point." Following closely on the experience of the airmail fiasco, he was entering ACTS at the nadir of the interwar air corps. Kuter also noted he was leaving, at least for the time being, the active flying life behind and moving into the world of theory, strategy, and planning. Finally, this also proved to be a time for the Kuter family to settle down and truly make a home and connections. They would be posted to Maxwell Field longer than anywhere else in Larry's career, a total of five years.[6]

Kuter arrived at ACTS in the incoming class of 1934–1935. He graduated at the top of his class on 4 June 1935, a testament to a growing appreciation of the theoretical approaches to and the future applications of air power. The ACTS school that Kuter entered that summer was divided into four sections: the Department of Air Tactics and Strategy, the Department of Ground Tactics, the Department of Command, and Staff and Logistics. Kuter attended lectures, developed staff estimates, prepared combat orders, and gave lectures about his former branch. Ironically, and despite the dislike of moving pieces around the maps at CGSS, the maps used for exercises at Maxwell were still of Gettysburg because they were the only maps readily available for such a purpose. The Battle of Gettysburg finally had an air campaign.[7]

Even though there was the Department of Ground Tactics, more than half the year was devoted to the study put forward in the Department of Air Tactics and Strategy. In this department were the truest of Billy Mitchell disciples, including Hal George. By 1934, the air tactics and strategy section included readings on and by Clausewitz, Billy Mitchell, and Douhet. George's lectures ended with the conclusion that air power overcame traditional land and sea concepts of warfare and provided effects "independent of armies or navies." The independent air strategies executed during the Second World War had already found fertile ground at Maxwell Field, and Kuter noted that these ideas "grew with vigor." Interestingly, at this time no member of the faculty spoke for air corps independence, and, despite being in the "cradle of the Confederacy," secession from the ground arm was not presented as an official position, but it was certainly discussed by staff and students alike.[8]

The air tactics and strategy section was further subdivided into specialized compartments: observation aviation, which included aerial photography and reconnaissance; attack aviation, including direct support to ground commanders; pursuit aviation, headed by Claire Chennault; and, finally, bombardment aviation. The bombardment aviation section had more direct contact hours than any of the other three aviation sections and, by default, more hours than any other section in the entire curriculum.[9]

Inside the bombardment section, the concepts of attacking a country's major industries was already deeply entrenched as the best method of destroying an enemy's ability to resist and its will to fight. The "industrial web theory" dictated that all industrialized nations were internally linked through their major industries and that attacks against these industries would, if conducted correctly, eventually lead to the collapse of a nation's means of resistance—and, by extension, eliminate the need for ground operations against. Since it was then, and remains today, unfashionable to describe by name the countries with which one is most likely to go to war, they were called by either a different name or a color, or, as was the case at ACTS, the Northeast United States served as the primary target. The bombardment section therefore looked to determine how many well-placed bombs it would take to turn off the electric grid, destroy oil and gas refineries, and destroy military production facilities. From this number of bombs, the number of aircraft needed and the size of the attacking air force could be extrapolated. Bombardment proponents were therefore reverse engineering the solutions to their problems. That is, they were doing exactly what Sherlock Holmes once warned against: "It is a capital mistake to theorize before one has data. Insensibly one begins to twist facts to suit theories, instead of theories to suit facts." Kuter became very caught up in this methodological practice.[10]

Classes began for Kuter on 5 September 1934. He and the other fifty-eight students walked to class that fall morning. Student families lived in a semicircle of duplex houses immediately behind ACTS headquarters, which contained the instructors' offices and the lecture halls. Instructors lived in larger homes, but they were still within walking distance. Notables in Kuter's class that year included his friend from Langley Haywood Hansell, Hoyt S. Vandenberg, and Muir S. "Santy" Fairchild, both destined to greatness but simple company-grade officers in 1934.[11]

Still, these men were members of the air section within the US Army, and vestiges of the "old army" remained. ACTS commandant Colonel John Curry required his officers to participate in twice weekly equitation lessons. This was no problem for an old horseman like Larry Kuter, but not all the officers appreciated this, including Fairchild, who felt he was sure to break a leg and be taken off flying status. Curry also encouraged the wives to participate in a riding club or as part of weekend horse shows, something Ethel enjoyed immensely. Roxanne was also given her first riding lessons while the family was at Maxwell Field.[12]

Kuter's year at ACTS ended with examinations and exercises. His classmates, including Vandenberg, received orders to attend CGSS, and, while, as we have seen, many air corps members considered it waste of time, Kuter knew that it provided a step in the direction toward command and promotion, and he was disappointed not to be following his classmates to Fort Leavenworth. Instead, he was one of the few chosen each year to remain at Maxwell Field as an instructor and faculty member, this in addition to the fact that he was the second youngest and most junior-ranking member of his class shows that members of the ACTS faculty saw potential in him. If there was a silver lining to not attending CGSS, his closest friend as a student, Haywood Hansel, also remained at Maxwell as an instructor. The Hansells had been at Langley with the Kuters, and an important relationship and friendship continued to grow between the two officers. Kuter was assigned to the bombardment aviation section, and, after a year on the faculty, he became the chief of bombardment for the class of 1936–1937. Staying at Maxwell had other benefits. The Kuter family moved from the duplex across the street from the ACTS building and into the permanent party officer's housing quarters: no. 267, built in the "French Provincial" style with "Italianate influences." These homes continue to house senior leaders and other instructors assigned to Maxwell Air Force Base.[13]

Historians have been guilty of overlooking the home life of their biographical subjects, and, while this work focuses on the officer Laurence Kuter, it is important to remember that every day after classes ended, whether as a student or as an instructor, Larry Kuter walked home to be a husband and father. Ethel, as would be a continuing practice, stayed involved in the local community and enjoyed her time at Maxwell and in the local area. Besides seeing to the raising of Roxanne and serving as a leader of first her Brownie troop and then her Girl Scout troop, she acted in numerous plays and served on the board of the Little Theater in Montgomery. She also taught drama at Huntingdon College and had a fifteen-minute-a-week "daily women's radio program" on a local station. The Kuters attempted to expand the family, but without success. Ethel had a miscarriage in February 1935. She remained in the hospital for much of February and was confined to her bed for much of March.[14]

It was during his years on the faculty that, as has been mentioned, Kuter developed a deep and lasting friendship with Haywood Hansell. The two were close enough that they coordinated Halloween costumes that October for the staff party, posing as "young and old mountain man," and Ethel placed a photograph of them in the family album. It was this friendship that helped drive a wedge between the two men and Claire Chennault. Kuter and Hansell both had a long history with Chennault despite their differences in age. Both had flown with him, Hansell more extensively as part of Chennault's Flying Trapeze. It was Chennault who aided Kuter in passing his final flights at pilot training, and it was now ironic that Kuter helped drive Chennault out of the air force.

There were two aspects of what was going on at ACTS that historians have focused on. The first was the conflict between the proponents of pursuit (fighter) aircraft and the future "bomber mafia." The second, once the first had been more or less resolved by the instructors, was the doctrine that issued forth from Maxwell Field: high-altitude precision daylight bombing. The historian Conrad Crane stated: "Precision-bombing doctrine, attacking factories instead of women and children, offered a way for the Air Corps to be decisive in war without appearing immoral." These two schools of thought—pursuit versus bombardment aviation—were discussed inside the classroom and argued about by the faculty members outside the classroom.[15]

Claire Chennault was the leader of the pursuit crowd in the early days of ACTS. A 1931 ACTS graduate and member of the faculty until his departure in late 1936, he argued vehemently in favor of pursuit aviation. Kuter undoubtedly had him as one of his instructors during the 1934–1935 school year. Chennault's biographer, the historian Martha Byrd, said that he "championed pursuit with a vehemence" as he attempted to "save bombardment from itself." On the other side from Chennault were Kenneth Walker, Harold George, and, after their graduation, Kuter and Hansell. The doctrinal debates went on for the better part of the 1930s. As students realized that bombardment was the dominant arm, both inside and outside the classroom, they joined the bomber mafia in growing numbers, leaving Chennault more and more marginalized. Chennault's attempts to win over students to the importance of pursuit aviation began to wane. Kuter noted that "Chennault was not articulate" and that those opposed to him were "a very articulate group." Chennault found himself alienated, not just from the students, but also from his fellow instructors. Kuter said that the bomber proponents, of which he was now the chief, "just overpowered Claire . . . just whipped him." This was a personal affront to Chennault, especially coming from Kuter, a man whom he considered a friend and whom he had personally saved from return to the regular army on his last check ride at Brooks Field. Kuter would not even be at ACTS had it not been for Chennault. Chennault's health also took a turn for the worse owing in no small part to his penchant for chain-smoking.[16]

In 1936, an offer came in that allowed Chennault to leave Maxwell Field and the US Army Air Corps entirely. It turned out that, contrary to what was being taught at ACTS, pursuit aviation was important, and China was very interested in pursuing this style of aerial combat against the Japanese. Chinese officials contacted the American government looking for any fighter pilots who might be willing to trade in their American wings for a chance to lead and fly with the Chinese. Chennault put the offer in the back of his mind, but it took less than a year for the marginalization he felt at the hands of the bomber mafia to send him into a final downward spiral. He became depressed and prepared for retirement in 1937 at his twentieth year. Byrd said that "his spirit seemed to break," but the offer from China offered a final escape from his depression and frustration, the US Army Air Corps, and the wrong theories pursed by his fellow instructors. He separated from the air corps, boarded a plane, and flew away from his troubles, but it was far from the last time he and Kuter would cross paths.[17]

When asked years later whether it had been an intentional move to place bombardment in front of pursuit aviation, Kuter answered: "We did everything we possibly could to establish that dogma." By the mid-1930s, the dominance of strategic bombardment theory gripped the minds of all who attended ACTS. It was a domination that would follow throughout the coming war, and its adherents would not be strongly questioned until the post-Vietnam era. As Kuter put it: "We just closed our minds to it; we couldn't be stopped; the bomber was invincible."[18]

At this time, as the storm clouds brewed in Europe, Kuter and the other bombardment proponents moved from the theoretical to the practical and began attempting to establish what a strategic bombardment campaign might look like. Kuter spent his time on two important subjects: bombing accuracy and the industrial web theory. The web theory, as Phillip Meilinger noted, involved identifying "industrial bottlenecks," "those factories or networks integral to the effective operation of the entire system and whose destruction would have disproportionally negative effects throughout the economic structure." Haywood Hansell, speaking to the Air War College in 1951, said: "[The theory] reasoned that other great nations were not unlike our own, and that analysis of American industry would lead to sound conclusions about German industry, or Japanese industry, or any other great power's industry."[19]

The school was beginning to develop the role of strategic bombing in future warfare. Prior to this, planning had been directed to defensive and supporting roles. ACTS instructors began to grapple with how a wartime air corps might be organized. The ten-thousand-plane air force envisioned in Captain Kuter's lectures taxed imaginations at that time, but the ACTS instructors and students put their lessons to a practical purpose: developing what a wartime air force needed to look like. As the historian Michael Sherry phrased it: "Officers like Kuter . . . were trying to link the aerial weapon to national policy, that is to justify its potential not only for winning wars but for sustaining peacetime policies." Kuter's thoughts broadened from the tactical to the strategic level of war, a place in which the air corps and later the air force always preferred to operate in its theories.[20]

Despite being asked to stay on as an instructor in the bombardment section, Kuter recognized that he was a junior officer teaching students older than he himself was. In an attempt to fix this, he grew a pencil-thin mustache to make himself look older. (He kept the mustache for the rest of his life.) He traveled extensively to prepare his lessons and during the summer of 1935 probably met Hap Arnold for the first time on a trip to Wright-Patterson. His first year of teaching gives more insight into what his year as a student was like. Ethel recorded the lessons Larry offered, which included "Appraising the Situation," "Probabilities I and II," and "Formations," three of the fourteen First Lieutenant Larry Kuter taught in his first year.[21]

His assignment to the bombardment section was certainly fortuitous and benefited Kuter's career. Even though war in Europe was not on the horizon, it was in the not too distant future, and Kuter was poised to get his thoughts and opinions heard. His penchant for recognizing the historical significance of his work gives an insight into what it was like for the students at ACTS, and, because he was nothing if not meticulous, he typed his notes, not in outline form, but exactly as he wished to deliver his lectures. Kuter was also something of an air power pack rat. He apparently refused to rid himself of any paper, article, or typed manuscript that he might conceivably one day need again. His personal papers also include other instructors' course notes and reports written in the aftermath of the First World War, many from years prior to his arrival in Montgomery. Thanks to these notes, modern researchers can almost attend one of his classes. Again, Kuter seemed to have had a premonition that the work he was accomplishing was historically significant.[22]

After being assigned to the faculty, Kuter had sixty days of academic leave to prepare his lesson plans. Although assigned to the bombardment section, he taught other courses, including "American Air Power: School Theories vs. World Facts," and a lesson titled "Naval Operations (Air Force Section)." Throughout his lectures on bombardment, he hammered home what he believed to be a few universal truths over and over again. The accuracy of aerial bombing depended entirely on two factors: training and equipment. The latter included accurate bombsights and bombs with uniform ballistic characteristics. In each course he taught, he made these same two points time and again.[23]

On 4 January 1937, Kuter walked into the classroom to begin his bombardment course lecture. Interestingly, he began with a note for each student to read the course mimeograph, what any student who has ever sat in a college class would know as being instructed to read the syllabus. He set his typed notes down next to copies of Training Regulation 440-15 and the ACTS "Bombardment," which dated from 1 November 1935 and was "about the size of the Pittsburg telephone directory and not much more interesting." He began by telling the students that they had reached the "ebb point in morale of the students at the Air Corps Tactical School": "This Deepest, Darkest, bluest, Monday on our schedule has gained its bitter reputation during the past years." But all that was about to change because as he noted: "We enter the field of bombardment aviation." Kuter went on to state that, as an instructor, he was not infallible: "If all students in this school accepted as gospel every statement enunciated on this platform, a great portion of this school's advantages would be lost. By no means are you expected to accept as gospel everything we give you." His introduction to bombardment continued:

> We do not exist to destroy surface objectives on land, nor do we exist specifically to destroy objectives on water. We are not organized to destroy only undefended objectives but to destroy objectives regardless of the presence, absence or intensity of hostile defense. We are not trained to only destroy objectives from high altitudes nor are we restricted in our training to operations in daylight only, but our equipment is such as not to restrict our operations to any particular condition of time or visibility. Likewise our function is not restricted to destroy near or distant objectives, or large or small objectives, either massive or fragile objectives, or large or small objectives. The scope of our task is unrestricted. We exist to destroy material objectives wherever they may be, whenever ordered, and however may be most effective.

In the end, he offered a reminder: "Never use a bomb heavier than necessary to accomplish the desired results."[24]

Another of the classes Kuter taught was "American Air Power School Theories vs. World War Facts," which he taught between 1936 and 1937. Prior to his taking this particular lecture on, he traveled to Chicago for research. The school commandant recommended that he extend his travel to meet with a local army instructor. Kuter wrote: "This I did not bother to do." He was already pressed for time and did not feel that he should use his limited research time to meet with an unknown national guard member. He later wrote: "This obscure N.G. Instructor was then Colonel George C. Marshall."[25]

Kuter began his "Theories vs. World War Facts" course with more hyperbolic discussion of air power: "Students of air power of all nations are proving that large ground armies, even corps, cannot exist in the face of hostile air power." At least he recognized his fellow instructors' penchant for the oratory inflation of air power theory: "Perhaps we in the Air Corps have been carried away by the oratory of instructors in Air Corps Tactics and Employment and the enthusiasm of the staff of the GHQ Air Force." He was not finished: "Let us assume that modern theorists have been deluding zealots who have led us, far from the paths of fact, into a garden of fanciful air power, where all pilots are colonels with free beer and six months flying pay in advance." He then turned to a more realistic appraisal of his methodological approach and cautioned his students: "Let us be especially critical of the employment air power." In this lesson, Kuter also noted: "Opinions are being formed by the horrors of the First World War." However: "Proper training could have led to different results, that with a properly trained bombardment unit, rail lines would have been destroyed and air power successful." He used the 1st Bombardment Group as his example for bombardment in the First World War. His main line of thought was phrased thusly: "Why was the 1st Day Bombardment Group so poorly employed in the Meuse-Argonne?" Ironically, in a few short years, Kuter would have the opportunity to pose the same question to himself when he commanded the very same unit, now the 1st Bombardment Wing in the early days of the combined bomber offensive. Kuter's lessons contain a bent of the futurist. Even while providing historical examples, they do demonstrate, not what air power did, but what it could have done. Another way of looking at it is that it is never that there is not something that bombardment cannot do but that bombardment could have done something more if employed correctly.[26]

Kuter also taught "Naval Operations (Special Course)—Air Force Section," saying during the course of his lectures: "The details upon which the air and naval authorities disagree concern the degree of the effectiveness of bombs and the degree of effectiveness of antiaircraft fire." The air power advocates thought little of antiaircraft artillery, a desire on their part to believe in the very best of air power and the very worst of ground forces firing back at them. Kuter went on to state: "The factual results of navy tests are not available for our examination. Whatever these conclusions may be, if air attack is practical and is effective with relatively small and relatively very inexpensive elements of an air force, there must follow a considerable readjustment of our former ideas concerning sea power." Whether or not one looks for proof of Kuter's predications to the results of Pearl Harbor or later sea battles where American antiaircraft artillery and pursuit aircraft wholesale destroyed Japanese air power, conducting a concerted attack is to a certain degree irrelevant. What bears closer attention is Kuter's desire, and that of the rest of the growing bomber mafia, to see the very best in air power.[27]

The indictments against the bombardment instructors are many, but at least Kuter recognized that his advocacy of air power was viewed by others as zealotry: "We realize that we, in the Air Force section, may be extravagant air enthusiasts. It has been more than once inferred that the exponent of the effectiveness of air power has the ability to magnify his own powers and minimize the opponent's powers approaching dangerously near the brink of mania. We have made an honest effort to temper our zeal."[28]

Nor did Kuter honestly believe, at least in his days as an instructor, that what would come to be known as high-altitude precision daylight bombing was proscribed. In fact, he instructed his students that violating doctrine was not a sin against the air corps but that, if they chose to violate doctrine, they should recognize what they are doing: "Battles have been won too often by the judicious violation of doctrine. . . . Disagree with doctrine in the conference room—be familiar enough with it to violate in the conference room—but know it well enough to know what it is and why you are violating it."[29]

On 14 June 1937, after his first year as an instructor, Kuter was promoted to captain, placing him on a par with his fellow instructors. This was long before the day when captain was a virtual guarantee after four years of service, and it was the beginning of his tenth year on active duty. His diary noted that ACTS was more than once suspected of "intolerable deviations from the military party line" by senior officers, and the War Department General Staff had the curriculum investigated by no less a persona than Brigadier General Leslie McNair, himself the CGSS commandant. Even four years before America entered the war, there was already a growing disconnect between the ground and the air arms.[30]

Although Maxwell Air Force Base is still sometimes jokingly referred to as a "sleepy hollow" for its laid-back atmosphere and its remoteness from Washington, DC, there was certainly no belief that what was said at ACTS would stay at ACTS, as Kuter found out. In one of his lectures during the 1938 school year—most likely the naval operations course—he detailed how a squadron of B-17s could easily defeat battleships attempting to escape a harbor. News of the lecture reached Washington—in all likelihood directly from the one navy officer on the ACTS staff—and the commandant of ACTS, Brigadier General H. C. Pratt, was forced to publically reprimand Kuter in front of the entire student body. Whether anyone really wanted to hurt Kuter's career is conjecture. The answer is that they probably did not, that they just wanted ACTS to go on record as disavowing the course material. However, shortly thereafter, Kuter received his officer evaluation report, which rated him perfect in all areas. He later remarked: "Jesus couldn't have had a better one." It was this episode and the investigation by McNair that inadvertently helped his career. Although he was just a captain in the army air corps, he was being noticed by the right people. His name was being openly discussed in Washington as an officer who spoke his mind.[31]

Beyond his duties as an instructor, Kuter also published articles in magazines and newspapers. These pieces included such titles as "The Bombardier Meets Pursuit and Antiaircraft Artillery Simultaneously," "The Bombardier Disperses Antiaircraft Guns," and "The Bombardier Evaluates Antiaircraft Artillery." One of these, for *The Coast Artillery Journal,* which discussed bombardment operations and antiaircraft artillery, was found by the public relations branch of the War Department General Staff to be "exaggerating" a purported dispute between the air and the antiaircraft artillery arms of the US Army where none existed. Ironically, in his letter forwarding Kuter's articles to the journal, Pratt noted: "There is, of course, a healthy rivalry between the Air Corps and the Antiaircraft artillery, but here at the school we endeavor to use that rivalry for the benefit of both."[32]

The content of the articles demonstrates the relative ignorance that air corps officers displayed of antiaircraft fire, which would, indeed, prove effective in the Second World War. If air power advocates were looking forward to what bombardment *could* do, they ignored advances in what surface-to-air fire *would* do later. To counter the idea that antiaircraft artillery could effectively shoot down a bomber, Kuter used the "big sky, little airplane" theory: "Shells from all guns miss small targets quite frequently. A maneuvering airplane at long range or high altitude is the most difficult target ever assigned to any piece of artillery." This ignores that massive bomber streams would not be maneuvering on approach to a target and that they would not have the opportunity to maneuver against incoming fighter aircraft either, preferring to stay closely boxed in for protection. Kuter would go on to state that antiaircraft artillery would indeed sometimes find targets: "Antiaircraft shells will not always miss bombers. Antiaircraft shells will not always hit bombers." He believed that the best option for the flyer in combat was to ignore incoming fire. A student of his flying a bomber mission over Germany during the Second World War thought to himself as shells exploded around him: "I sure wish Kuter was here to ignore this!" Kuter also acknowledged that the relative merits of both antiaircraft artillery and aerial bombing would be determined only during an actual conflict.[33]

On 30 December 1938, the new ACTS commandant, Colonel Millard "Mif" Harmon, forwarded portions of Kuter's lectures on the power and effects of demolition bombs to the recently installed chief of the air corps, Major General Henry Arnold. As Arnold read through the course notes, he would not be able to help but notice across the top of the paper "Instructor: Captain L. S. Kuter." Kuter's work was now being circulated at the highest levels of the air corps. This lecture, part of the bombardment aviation section, focused on the destructiveness of bombs when used against ships but allowed for their use against "any other type of objective." The course notes point to the sinking of the battleships and dreadnaughts off the Virginia Capes in 1921. Years after Mitchell's court-martial, the army air corps was using these tests as proof of the airplane's effectiveness: "Our point in this is that demolition bombs, properly placed, have the power and effect to destroy the usefulness of any naval vessel." Kuter's lecture also indicated an early belief in what would later be understood as "effects-based operations."[34]

It was not necessary to sink a vessel; all that was required was removing it from combat. The effect of doing so was equally as good as sinking it. To this end, Kuter referenced Mitchell: "Where he used the word 'sink' we substitute the phrase 'effect a material reduction in the combat effectiveness or navigation efficiency, or both.'" The problem with this line of thinking is that it allows for a vessel to be repaired and returned to combat action. It would be impossible to argue on the evening of 8 December 1941 that the eight American battleships at Pearl Harbor did not have a "material reduction in the combat effectiveness" and that only two of those battleships were complete losses.[35]

Oddly, the lecture also distanced itself from the importance of accuracy, which was to become a cornerstone of the high-altitude precision daylight bombing practices of World War II. In it, Kuter said: "Let me emphasize that the point in bombing accuracy is not included in this lecture. Do not infer that this degree of accuracy can be expected every trial, every other trial or once in ten times. Today we are concerned with the effect of bombs." While this is certainly true, it went against later dogma stating how important accuracy was to bombing operations and how much time Kuter himself would spend on improving accuracy. As would come to be proved, every bomb that was not placed accurately on a target caused wanton destruction and damage. The effects of bombardment could not be removed from the accuracy of bombardment.[36]

1939

After more than four years at Maxwell Field, Kuter found his time at ACTS coming to end. His years spent as student and instructor transitioned him from air power practitioner to an operational and strategic thinker. While his perceptions about the validity and possibilities of air power, particularly bombardment, were not unusual in the air corps, he was among the most ardent of bombardment proponents. In retrospect, there existed many ideas about air power, ardently held, that proved to be incorrect. The most obvious of these were those marginalizing both pursuit and attack aviation. More debatable opinions included the general invulnerability of bombing aircraft carrying out a concerted assault even in the face of a determined enemy. Despite all this hindsight, at the time Kuter was an established air power thinker and strategist who already had a reputation for attention to detail and organization. He was both a bomber pilot and an advocate. Despite the fiasco that the airmail crisis became, Kuter proved his determination and skill in the face of adversity during its course. By all accounts, he was articulate and respected in his community. Still in his early thirties, he was a known commodity inside the army air corps and was recognized as a rising star. The investigation into his incendiary remarks about the navy also brought him to the attention of officers outside the air corps. At the time, none of this was obvious to Kuter himself.

The ideas Kuter learned as a student and later helped develop at the school were to play an important role in the coming war and in official policy regarding US war aims. However, of more immediate concern to him than the growing tensions in Europe was his next assignment. He eventually ended up assigned to the Operations and Training Division, War Department General Staff, Washington, DC. He was ordered to report for duty on 1 July 1939, but it was not smooth sailing from one location to another. For a time, he thought his career would see him waste away in obscurity.

A new program under General George C. Marshall, who had recently become the chief of the War Department General Staff, called for the experimental assignment to the staff of aviators, young and junior officers and officers who had not attended CGSS. Captain Kuter's assignment represented all three phases of this experiment, but, as far as Kuter knew, at this time he was going to instruct at ACTS for another year.

Colonel Harmon traveled to Washington that summer to determine which of his section chiefs he was going to be able to retain at Maxwell for the coming school year. He was informed orally and in writing that his bombardment chief, Larry Kuter, would remain in residence at Maxwell despite having been on the ACTS staff for four years. With the knowledge that he was to remain at Maxwell, Harmon dispatched Kuter to the West Coast for a tour of the bombardment groups at March Field. However, as soon as Kuter stepped out of the aircraft in California, he was instructed to report to the base operations building, where he was handed a telegram stating: "Orders revoked . . . proceed to Washington DC and report on July first to Chief of Staff for Duty." He was thunderstruck. This was not what he had expected at all. Worse, he was not going to CGSS. He was now assigned to the Office of the Chief of Staff. Interestingly enough, the officer who probably plucked Kuter from obscurity was Brigadier General Leslie McNair, who was now the War Department assistant chief of staff. The General Staff wanted aviators, and Captain Laurence Kuter was going to Washington.[37]

Ethel discovered this new assignment before Larry did. While Larry was in the air headed west, Ethel went to the ACTS headquarters to pick up his mail. A large group of men circled around his office, which immediately scared Ethel, knowing that Larry was currently flying. She always worried when he was flying, and considering the amount of accidents common during this time, especially during the airmail fiasco, she can hardly be blamed, but this was, from a certain point of view, very good news. One of the officers handed Ethel the telegram they had been passing around. She read the note and, on seeing the orders to the General Staff, blurted out: "Oh Hell! He wanted to go to Leavenworth!"[38]

The assignment to the War Department in 1939 was not going to hold Larry Kuter's career back, nor was his not attending CGSS going to hinder his career progression in the long run. Quite the opposite proved to be true; he was headed to Washington at a very opportune time for young officers. Someone in the War Department recognized that he was an up-and-coming officer, and they were going to put his talents to good use. But, even with a war approaching, it could not be known how much influence Larry and other junior officers in the air corps, particularly the core group of instructors at ACTS, could have on the organization. Kuter's experience thus far, but most importantly his teaching tenure at ACTS, shaped his thinking on air corps organization, doctrine, and tactics. From the macro to the micro level, Kuter held a very clear understanding of how an air force should be organized, trained, and equipped.

3

The Coming War

Laurence Kuter was not initially thrilled about the Washington, DC assignment: "I believed that I was moving from the exciting development of the air power concept into the oblivion and inertia of an amorphous body of mind-bound elderly worshippers of the dogma of Napoleon and Hannibal [in other words, the regular army]." Having now spent more than a decade living on or near army posts, he was worried about this move to the "politically ambitious" city that was the nation's capital. Ethel located a suitable apartment at 3725 McComb Street NW very near the National Cathedral. At $85.00 a month, the rent was significantly higher than they were used to. But the location made Kuter's new office in the Munitions Building a short streetcar ride or a slightly longer but more enjoyable walk away.[1]

In 1949, a decade after arriving in Washington for his new assignment, Kuter noted in a speech: "One thing was apparent: whoever was running the Air Corps at that time, it wasn't the Chief of the Air Corps." He reported for duty on 1 July 1939 along with nine other new officers. He and his cohort were ushered into the office of the acting chief of staff, Brigadier General George C. Marshall. Marshall wanted Kuter and officers like him; he was looking for young officers—preferably those who had flying experience but no experience of the "War Department's stylized system of education." Kuter fit all Marshall's qualifications, and not attending the Command and General Staff School had not turned into a hindrance. Marshall made one thing abundantly clear: this was a wartime, not a peacetime, assignment and the officers were to treat it as such. The country was by no means on a war footing, but the War Department was going to start comporting itself as if it were. One of the immediate changes was the addition of an air section headed by General Frank Andrews to the G-3 (operations). Although this "raised some eyebrows," according to Kuter, it was not perceived as any great change. Besides, Marshall assigned only four officers to the air section, and how much impact could four company- and field-grade officers have on war preparations? It is worth noting the General Andrews was head of the air section of the General Staff and not the chief of the air corps, who, at that time, was General Hap Arnold. The air corps chief had not been briefed on what the General Staff planners were putting together, essentially operating in a vacuum. No one seemed to have a firm control over the US Army Air Corps.[2]

The problem of separate air corps staffs was not fixed until mid-1941 when Arnold combined the segmented offices into a single cohesive Air Staff under Brigadier General Carl Spaatz. This eliminated General Headquarters Air Force and streamlined all air corps activities under Spaatz, who reported to Arnold. One thing was clear to Kuter. He had approached this assignment with dread, believing it to be nothing more than a staff tour, the long-dreaded assignment of many officers. His meeting with George Marshall changed that. The morning he walked into Marshall's office changed his perceptions of his duties. He "had approached that old Victorian-style building at a time of a country-wide euphoria of 'America First,' 'Peace in our Time,' and isolationism." He left it in a "state of shock."[3]

It is important to note that Kuter was serving not on the Air Staff, under Arnold, but instead on the General Staff, under Andrews, as a deputy in the directorate of operations. He began his first Washington assignment working on Army Regulation (AR) 95-5, which allowed him to input an airman's perspective into official doctrine. Although the Air Corps Tactical School (ACTS) influenced like-minded air officers for years, there was still no official doctrine regarding what air power could or should accomplish. It was Kuter's belief that what occurred at Langley and later at Maxwell was self-contained. ACTS was important in developing and educating officers, but it did nothing in the way of official policy or doctrine until its graduates started arriving in Washington prior to the war. Change began small. AR 95-5 established a very small degree of recognition for air power.[4]

Kuter and the aviation community were also monitoring developments in Europe. The small group of air power enthusiasts inside the War Department took the events of the Spanish War and the operations of the German volunteers in the Condor Legion very seriously. The historian Michael Sherry stated: "Kuter made no exact analogy between what Hitler had accomplished with air power and what the United States might do. But his admiration for Hitler's achievement showed." This might be a bit unfair. Kuter certainly was no admirer of Hitler's, and he was not the only one to take note of air power developments around the world. It only made sense for air-minded officers to take note of what was going on in other countries' air arms, especially the European powers. Kuter was certainly not alone in showing appreciation for what any advancement in air power achieved around the world and wanted nothing more than to prove what American air power was capable of. He was shortly given the opportunity to do just that. There currently existed no overarching doctrinal statement or agreed-on formula regarding what the US Army Air Corps should look like. No one knew how many aircraft, aircrew, and support functions actually needed to exist for a war to be conducted.[5]

Air War Plans Division–Plan 1 (Munitions Requirements of the Army Air Force)

By 1941 and the creation of a dedicated Air Staff, Kuter found himself surrounded by familiar faces. Present in Washington now was Lieutenant Colonel Harold George, Lieutenant Colonel Muir S. Fairchild, and Major Haywood Hansell. Another, until this time known to Kuter only by reputation, was Major Kenneth Walker. With Hitler now in control of the European continent, planning for a general war in Europe was under way, but there existed nothing in the way of an air plan. A rough estimate of fifty-four groups had already been agreed on, but the makeup of this imaginary arsenal was not known. Marshall ordered Arnold to create an air annex to ongoing war plans.

It was in August 1941 that Kuter truly became a principal architect of the newly christened US Army Air Forces. General Arnold designated Lieutenant Colonel George to lead the Air War Plans Division of the army air force. George picked Kuter, now serving on the army air force A-3 for bombardment operations, to help write the annex. The air force operations staff included other ACTS classmates and graduates. including Kenneth Walker, Haywood Hansell and Hoyt S. Vandenberg. Kuter and the others around him now attached their names to history.[6]

Hansell noted that, after their "initial elation" over being tasked to write an air plan, the four men quickly realized they faced a daunting, if not completely overwhelming, task. War plans took years to put together, and four men were now being asked to create an entirely new plan in a few days. Being handed this unique opportunity, they "faced a very sobering problem." "From then on," Hansell recalled, "until we completed our task, we were at our desks from early morning until late at night."[7]

The air portion of the plan was centered on five "divisions." The first division was "to conduct air operations in defense of the Western Hemisphere." The second was to prosecute an air war against Germany as soon as possible. The third was to provide for strategic defense in the Pacific theater. The fourth was to provide air support for the eventual invasion of the European continent. Finally, after victory against Germany was secured, the fifth was to concentrate maximum firepower against Japan. These divisions were broken down into air tasks and then into target sets to include electric power, a transportation system, oil and petroleum systems, and by default the enemy air force that possessed the means to defend these sites.[8]

The planners wrote the Air War Plans Division–Plan 1 (AWPD-1), the first comprehensive air plan, in a scant nine days. All were former ACTS instructors, and the principal authors included Harold George, Kenneth Walker, Haywood Hansell, and Larry Kuter. In 1949, Kuter gave full credit for the creation of AWPD-1 to George, Walker, and Hansell. In later speeches, he did not include his name in this group, although, when referring to himself in the third person in his *Airman at Yalta*, Laurence Kuter was credited as an author of the document. That Kuter had no appreciable role in the writing of AWPD-1 was simply untrue and a case of Kuter focusing praise on someone other than himself. He is universally listed as one of the documents' principal architects.[9]

One of Kuter's traits was the ability to keep the spotlight off of himself. Hansell said that Kuter's principal contribution was spending those nine days calculating the actual number of forces needed for the plan to be successful using figures pulled from his ACTS bombardment notes. Kuter was not only one of the main authors of the AWPD-1; there is also no doubt that he had an equally important hand in the routing and briefing of the document through to its final approval.[10]

The four ACTS men—Kuter, George, Hansell, and Walker—believed that strategic bombing could win the war. They were the first of the bomber mafia, a moniker proudly held even in the modern incarnations of this group inside the air force. The document itself detailed the numbers of planes, men, equipment, bases, and other factors needed for the coming war. More than that, however, it gave the US Army Air Forces a mission. The historian Martha Byrd called AWPD-1 significant because "it defined a formal role for US air forces." As previously mentioned, AWPD-1 detailed five mission areas for the air force. Four were as follows: "conduct air operations in defense of the Western Hemisphere, strategic defense of the Pacific, wage an unlimited strategic air offensive against Germany," and, finally, "concentrate strategic air power against the mainland of Japan." The fifth—support of an invasion of Europe—would be conducted only if an "actual invasion was found to be necessary." Clearly, Kuter, George, Walker, and Hansell believed that the nascent air power of the US Army Air Force in the summer of 1941 could defeat Nazi Germany inside of three years since the air planners knew that a land invasion could take place as early as the spring of 1944. In fact, they believed that, by the time an invasion force could be readied, "strategic air power could have been built and employed over a sufficiently long period to undermine or destroy the German will and ability to continue to wage war." AWPD-1 explicitly stated that, if an air power offensive was successful, a land invasion would not be necessary.[11]

The plan was finished, but not finalized, on Tuesday, 12 August 1941. The same four officers who wrote the plan now set about briefing and selling it. It is a truism of the military staff officer that creating a project is only part of the work; it then has to be briefed and approved at every level to gain final approval and implementation. All four members of the planning team briefed the recipients, each taking turns in the two-hour presentation. Kuter later indicated that he did not believe the plan would be well received inside certain circles, particularly infantry officers: "The implication that strategic air alone might win the war violated long standing doctrine. It would be challenged by almost all members of the General Staff and would be anathema to many."[12]

The first recipient of the ensuing briefs was Brigadier General Harry L. Twaddle, later to command the 95th Division under George Patton, at the time the G-3 for the War Department Staff. Twaddle thus became the first full army officer to be presented with the plan that called for a strategic air war against Germany. While the army prepared for an invasion of the European continent, the US air arm would already be taking the fight to Germany. Twaddle was presented with the proposed numbers for the air force and the specific target sets. He approved the plan, and it went forward, next to Mr. Robert Lovett, the assistant secretary of war for air. Attendees at this meeting included Brigadier General Leonard T. Gerow and Brigadier General Carl Spaatz, both to assume increasingly greater leadership roles throughout the war. From there, AWPD-1 wound its way through the air corps, being presented to the chief of the air corps, Major General George Brett, and, finally, to the deputy chiefs of staff and the chief of staff of the US Army, General George Marshall, on 30 August 1941.[13]

The presentation to Marshall was the one that caused the most consternation among the four-man team. Hansell noted: "General Marshall was the one man in the War Department who could, with a gesture, dismiss the entire effort. If the plan did not have his endorsement as Chief of Staff, it stood no chance whatever of acceptance by the Joint Board, by the Secretary of War, or by the President." Along with Marshall, Hap Arnold also sat in on the briefing. Marshall not only approved the plan but also allowed it to bypass the Joint Board and be presented directly to the secretary of war. Hansell remembers Marshall giving the muted praise: "Gentlemen, I think the plan has merit." Kuter now believed Marshall to be an "unheralded aviation pioneer."[14]

With AWPD-1 now having received tacit approval from the military hierarchy, the plan needed to be distributed for implantation. Twenty-three numbered copies were made, Kuter having personal control of and responsibility for eighteen of those copies, which he kept locked in a safe. The others were distributed to senior administration officials. The secretary of war eventually approved the plan and asked to have the four architects present it to the president at a date to be determined. AWPD-1 was now a plan that could be implemented, and it had the backing of the military and the administration. Kuter remembered the acceptance as a major event: "A milestone had been established in the growth of American air power. The concept that had been laid out and developed at the Air Corps Tactical School and scoffed at in the twenties and thirties became the United States national military policy when the chips were down in 1941."[15]

AWPD-1 called for twenty-six thousand combat airplanes, another thirty-seven thousand training aircraft, and still another seventeen thousand aircraft to be delivered to the Royal Air Force (RAF). These were then broken down into specific units for a total of 207 groups. Obviously, these as-yet-unmade aircraft needed as-yet-untrained aircrews to fly them, 135,526 pilots, copilots, bombardiers, navigators, and gunmen. Aircraft also needed ground crews and logistics and supply troops, for a total of 2,164,916 men to be trained, fed, equipped, and transferred overseas to fight a war on an as-yet-undeclared enemy.[16]

On 4 December 1941, less than three days before the attack on Pearl Harbor, the *Washington Star* and the *Chicago Tribune* published a report under the headline "FDR's Secret War Plan Revealed." Published there in its entirety was the highly classified AWPD-1 in addition to plans for the ground and naval forces collectively known as the Victory Plan. Hansell said the report was a "verbatim" facsimile copy, which would allow the FBI to determine the specific copy it came from and therefore exactly who was supposed to be in control of it. He also noted that this represented a violation of trust placed in the United States by its ally Great Britain, who provided many of the classified details in the plan. Kuter knew that, even as he was reading the story sitting at his desk, many of the embassies to the United States, including Germany and Japan, would be sending copies of the report to their respective governments. Worse, he knew that he had responsibility for eighteen of the twenty-three numbered copies of the war plan. As he pondered whether this was treason, he looked over the top of the paper to see a pair of FBI agents approach his desk. He was forced to turn over every copy currently in his safe. The FBI then proceeded to trace each copy and every person who ever signed for a copy of the plan. Two days later, the FBI contacted Kuter and told him that his copies were "clean," as was everyone in his office. The leak had been traced to one of the five copies delivered to the White House. This was the type of story that typically could have dominated the headlines as the media struggled to locate the source of the leak. However, events in Hawaii on 7 December quickly relegated the story to obscurity.[17]

Kuter never established where the leak did come from, only that it was not from any of the copies he bore responsibility for. Thirty-five years later, he recalled the incident in a letter to a friend regarding the recently published *A Man Called Intrepid* (1976) by William Stevenson. The book detailed a highly fictionalized version of an English spy ring running rampant across Europe and in America. Kuter was none too pleased with many of the assertions made in the book, saying: "I cannot prove that he is wrong in stating that the AWPD-1 portion of the Victory Program was given to Burton K. Wheeler and that Wheeler passed it to the *Chicago Tribune* and *Washington Times-Herald*. I can't believe that Mr. Stevenson's research established the facts in this case. . . . He presented no evidence to support his allegations." The same was true of much of what else Stevenson discussed. It made good reading but bore little in the way of truth.[18]

Setting Up the Air Staff

In November 1941, after the approval and inclusion of AWPD-1 in American war plans, Major Kuter returned to the staff of the G-3 for air operations and shortly moved to be the assistant secretary directly under the army chief of staff, after the departure of his immediate supervisor, Colonel Omar N. Bradley. Bradley's departure highlighted a growing problem with the American military at the time, a dearth of qualified officers. While there was probably never any doubt that Kuter, still a major, could handle the assistant secretary job—his organizational skills were already a known quantity—the promotion showed that majors were now moving into billets normally filled by colonels. The US Army and the US Army Air Corps were desperately short of qualified senior officers. Kuter was sitting in his office on 7 December when reports of the attack against Pearl Harbor came over the radio. The other officers were told to get their uniforms on and return to the Munitions Building immediately; at the time, it was not unusual for officers to be at their desks in civilian clothes.[19]

The days immediately after Pearl Harbor were highlighted by chaos. During one meeting with Arnold, a secretary stepped in saying that there was an important phone call for Kuter from Colonel Gordon Saville in Lisbon, Portugal. Arnold waved Kuter out of the room, telling him it was likely indeed important. Saville told Kuter that he, Colonel Arthur Wilson, and General Joseph McNarney were at the Lisbon airport attempting to board the last Pan Am flight out of the country but were being told that there was no room on the aircraft for them, despite the fact that the personnel effects of Pan Am leadership, including golf clubs, were being loaded. Kuter knew that Marshall had personally recalled McNarney to Washington and told Saville that he was to tell whoever was in charge at Pan Am that the chief of staff, US Army, General George Marshall, directed that McNarney be on that plane when it departed.

Kuter thought nothing of it until Marshall called Kuter into his office and demanded to know why he had received a phone call that morning from the postmaster general demanding to know why Kuter ordered Pan Am to offload several hundred pounds of mail so that three of his "buddies" could be allowed to fly, all the while invoking his name. Kuter informed the chief of staff that it was McNarney he ordered on the aircraft and suggested that perhaps Pan Am should have used some common sense when it came to what was being loaded and offloaded, noting that perhaps the classified mail was a better travel investment for the company than someone's golf clubs. Marshall nodded and dismissed Kuter. As Kuter passed through the outer office, he heard the chief of staff shout to his secretary: "Get the Post Master General on the telephone."[20]

Kuter busied himself assisting Arnold and Marshall and whomever else he could. Still a major, he answered all kinds of inquiries, including: "How can the [army air force] succeed in softening up the enemy when the RAF . . . have been unable to do the same thing?" To answer this question, Kuter called on fellow field-grade officers to help him. They came to a very easy, controversial, and, luckily, classified decision to "avoid duplicating the errors of the RAF." This answer demonstrated the rift that already existed between the two air arms. Whereas the British attacked at night, the United States prepared to attack during the day. Kuter noted that the British method went against everything the army air corps, now the army air forces, trained and studied for at ACTS. He also noted that the Britons' method was clearly not working: "Their inability to hit the targets that have been located is due principally to their own failures in having initially expended their trained personnel, having trained before the war to a very low standard and with an inferior bombsight and in continuing to attack fixed precision targets knowing that their bombs may fall anywhere within six to ten square miles. . . . To a lesser extent, their inability to hit the targets that have been located is due to the effectiveness of the hostile antiaircraft searchlight and night fighter combination."[21] The United States had barely entered the war, and the US Army Air Forces had already found plenty to critique their comrades in the RAF about.

Kuter went on to be even more damning in this note, which clearly bespeaks his preconceived notions not only about aerial warfare but also about the entire army air force at the time, an organization that had not yet bloodied itself against the enemy:

> It is equally obvious that another reason for the failure of the RAF to exhibit the determined aggressiveness essential to successful bombardment—demonstrated by the Japs at Pearl Harbor—depends on adequate prior training. Attrition in airplanes in the Bomber Command of the RAF is over 50% per month and at the same time they are accomplishing no material results. The inevitable consequence of this vicious cycle which is initiated by entering combat without the training required to effect material accomplishment and at the same time having to withstand extraordinary attrition has resulted in the unpalatable fact that the bombardment combat crews of the *RAF are no longer trying.*[22]

This was a patently unfair critique of the RAF, but it echoed the sentiments of the army air force at the time and its belief that the war effort would see significant changes as soon as US aerial forces engaged the enemy. The RAF flew at night because its aircraft could not survive daylight bombing over Germany, and, as the war progressed, Bomber Command became adept at nighttime bombing, allowing for a "one-two punch" later in the war, with the Americans flying daylight missions. Kuter's criticisms were off target but represented the American view.

In January 1942, Kuter was finally, along with other members of his West Point class, promoted to lieutenant colonel, but this was only a stepping-stone. He remained a lieutenant colonel for a few days. It was in early 1942, while assigned to the General Staff, that he grabbed national attention for the first time by making a huge jump in rank. On 2 February, less than a month after being promoted to lieutenant colonel on 5 January, he was made a brigadier general, skipping the rank of bird colonel entirely. This made him, at thirty-six, the youngest general officer of his time and the youngest since William Sherman. By default, he was the first member of his West Point class to become a general officer. His archival holdings at the US Air Force Academy are filled with literally hundreds of congratulatory letters and Western Union telegrams; one from a former West Point classmate stated: "Congratulations on being the first in our class to wear stars." Kuter signed a thank-you letter responding to each and every letter or telegram.[23]

The press had a field day with the promotion list. Colonels jumped to general officer rank over other more senior officers, but it was Kuter's promotion that became notorious. His office was overwhelmed with reporters and photographers. One historian noted that the promotion "made good copy." Kuter was, in a sense, a dream come true for the press. He possessed a "coldly professional face that suggested efficiency and intelligence" and until a moment before was a major completely unexposed to the workings of the press. The jump in rank caused problems for him, some of which boiled down to simple bouts of jealously on the part of other officers who were none too pleased to see the very youthful Larry Kuter wearing a general's star. One such officer, Lieutenant Colonel Maxwell Taylor, passed him a note saying: "If you are not too busy with the press, General Marshall would like to see you."[24]

There was a method to the madness behind Kuter's and other junior officers' promotions. With the newly christened US Army Air Force rapidly expanding, Marshall had instructed Arnold to reach below the more senior men for a younger cadre of officers. Since so many of the more senior men were veterans of the First World War, he believed that more competent airmen could be found in the middle ranks of the field-grade officers. Larry Kuter certainly fit this description: "Kuter reminded people of an acetylene torch. Intelligence, dedication, ambition, and drive, mixed just right and burning hot enough to cut steel, yet never blazing out of control." Ironically, Arnold ignored Marshall's instructions to promote the midgrade officers, and, when Kuter's name did not come across his desk, Marshall added it to the promotion list himself.[25]

Despite the jump in rank, Kuter did not receive a new assignment. He stayed in the War Department. Brigadier General Laurence Kuter began setting up the Air Staff organization under Hap Arnold but continued to work in the secretariat office directly for Marshall. He gave thirty other officers the authority to sign General Arnold's name. Surprisingly, the resulting confusion and contradiction amazed him. It took him more than a year to drive down from thirty to only eight the number who could officially approve items for the air chief.

McNarney Plan and an Independent Air Arm

George Marshall quickly recognized that too many in the War Department in Washington, DC, were interfering with the field commanders' ability to do their job. He knew he needed to reorganize the offices under his direct control and to keep the work inside the War Department and the army in Washington focused on policy and, thus, allow field commanders not to be burdened by too much paperwork flowing out of the district. He placed McNarney in control of this shake-up along with Colonel William K. Harrison and Larry Kuter. The three officers met in the War Department's library, where they combed through historical records until they ran across a doctoral dissertation by Colonel Otto L. Nelson that revolved around Elihu Root's reorganization of the War Department. Luckily, Nelson was instructing at West Point, and he quickly found himself reassigned to the War Department and working directly for McNarney.[26]

The officers developed an organizational plan calling for five divisions inside the War Department but also reorganized the service into three operating agencies: army ground forces, army service forces, and army air forces. Although still a part of the regular US Army, army air force officers now had significantly more autonomy than ever before. They now had an entirely separate organizational structure from the regular ground army, reporting only to the chief of staff, George Marshall, himself considered to be very sympathetic to an entirely independent air force after war. The McNarney Plan also abolished all other air corps/air force organizations, including General Headquarters Air Force. The same thing happened to the army ground forces as well. This eliminated the abundant and often redundant offices and planning directorates under the previously numerous divisions. The overall purpose of the plan was to streamline the War Department. This ensured that Hap Arnold, who now became commanding general of the army air forces, had direct control over all aspects of the army air force as an organizational entity. General Leslie J. McNair now headed army ground forces, and he and Arnold reported directly to Marshall. General Brehon B. Somervell landed as the commander of army service forces.[27]

McNarney chaired a meeting of the new commanders, all of whom outranked him, and, although only a major general, opened the proceedings by stating: "Gentlemen, this is a briefing session to inform you how the War Department will be reorganized very soon. It is not a session in which to argue or debate the case." With Marshall's backing, there was little that the men in the room could do anyway, and War Department Circular no. 59 put the changes into effect on 2 March 1942. For better or worse, the US Army Air Forces had been liberated from the ground element. It was a separate organization planned by flyers and led by flyers. As one of the few officers working on the reorganization, Kuter played a major role in it, and this was another step toward the air arm's independence.

Kuter had now had a hand in both the development of the air force's war plan (AWPD-1) and the internal organization of the army air force. No other air force officer, including Hap Arnold, could say the same thing. Kuter later wrote: "With the Army Air Forces established separately and co-equal to the Army Ground Forces we had come as close as we could to establishing a separate air force."[28]

Once the reorganization went into effect on 2 March 1942, Kuter was reassigned as the deputy chief of staff, army air forces. In this position, he reported directly to General Millard Harmon, who reported directly to General Arnold. He oversaw the "A staff," including A-1 (Personnel), A-2 (Intelligence), A-3 (Operations), and A-4 (Logistics). His responsibilities centered around keeping the staff organizations functioning at a reasonable level of productivity and filtering items coming up the chain before they could reach Arnold's desk. Although a lengthy list, it bears showing exactly how the air force was now organized. Under Arnold, but administratively flowing through Harmon and Kuter, were four assistant chiefs of staff. These were Operations, the Directorate of Military Requirements under Brigadier General Muir S. Fairchild, the Directorate of Technical Services under Colonel R. G. Breene, and the

Directorate of Management Control under Colonel Bryan Gates. The new staff also included an air surgeon general, public relations people, and smaller special staffs.[29]

Also nested immediately under Arnold was the Air Force Advisory Council, composed of Lieutenant Colonels C. P. Cabell and Lauris Norstad. The advisory council ranged from two to five men throughout the war and acted as something of an action group for Arnold to bounce ideas off of. None of the other services had an office quite like it, and it even got the attention of General Marshall, who asked Kuter: "What is this 'council' I saw in the latest organizational chart of the Air Staff?" This forced Kuter to admit that it was a small office beholden directly to Arnold and no one else. Marshall was not pleased. The army air force staff had only just been approved, and now it seemed that Arnold was setting up some form of "super-staff." Kuter convinced Marshall that there was nothing to fear, that it was merely an organization that allowed Arnold to discuss ideas that might never go anywhere with an inner circle of trusted agents.[30]

It is apparent that Arnold relied heavily on Brigadier General Kuter. Arnold was not known for his desire to be involved in all policy decisions and preferred to have only the most pressing issues brought to his attention. This served the dual purpose of keeping him from being overwhelmed by the sheer quantity of policy and paperwork and of having his staff distill the important issues down to their most pressing and important components. Arnold was also known for assigning tasks to the first officer he crossed paths with inside the War Department. It became common practice for officers to save themselves from a possible undesirable task by diving inside the nearest office or men's restroom if they saw Arnold walking down the hall. Arnold would often assign tasks or projects to officers that were completely foreign to either their experience or what they were currently working on. As one staff officer remembered: "He would grab you by the shoulder and tell you to get it done." Arnold's decisions often seemed impulsive, but Kuter noted that his "batting average was awfully high."[31]

There was also the small problem that a member of his staff dropped dead while briefing Arnold. This added to the desire of many staff members to avoid contact with the general at all costs. Colonel Oliver S. Ferson, the director of war organizations and movements, had a massive heart attack inside Arnold's office, although Arnold obviously bore no responsibility for this. The incident still caused many both inside and outside the Air Staff to believe that Arnold was working his staff to death.

Arnold disliked the new Air Staff—not the organization or the staff itself, but its size. Kuter noted that Arnold "no longer had the small, tightly knit staff to which he had become accustomed, but an immense organization." Therefore, Arnold now acted as if the Air Staff was "not his own personal staff, not as an extension of his mind and will, but . . . an obstacle to be hurdled, to be dodged or evaded." To this end, Kuter served as something of an office manager and intercessor between Arnold, the Air Force Council, the Army Ground and Service Forces, the General Staff, the US Navy, the Joint Chiefs (Marshall and King), and the remainder of the War Department.[32]

Arnold's aversion to the larger staff made Kuter's job difficult. Kuter recognized that it was up to him to "assure that the suddenly autonomous [army air force] Headquarters managed our enormous expansion effectively, smoothly and very very quickly." The army air force was semi-independent, but Kuter had to make it function effectively for his boss and for the organization as a whole. He was no longer building the Air Staff; he now had to ensure that it worked, and to do so with a "fast acting, dynamic Chief who defied staff channels was no small task." It was the efforts of Harmon and Kuter that kept Arnold and the Air Staff functioning together.[33]

The Birth of the Air Force–Navy Rivalry

Despite the autonomy that the new War Department structure brought, many inside the army air forces still felt that they were under attack and not by the Germans or the Japanese but by the forces that sought to end the air force's independent momentum. Kuter remembered years later: "Another important function was to thwart wide-spread and high level authorities, outside the Air Forces, in their seemingly unending efforts to upset the strategy on which our growing Air Force was being built." It is interesting that, even while on a wartime footing, the air arm believed that it was under attack by external forces seeking to roll it permanently under the ground section despite the approval of Marshall and the Roosevelt administration. This culture of fear has long permeated the organization and seems to be a chronic disease the air force has never sought to cure, only to live with. However, in this case, the fear came with a certain degree of truth behind it.[34]

Although AWPD-1 had the approval of the president of the United States, there were still those who were not on board, namely large portions of the US Navy. These elements had Admiral Earnest J. King as their leader. In early 1942, King became "dual hatted" as the commander in chief of the US fleet and the chief of naval operations. These were not the same army ground elements that Kuter and army air force officers believed were out to destroy their independence, but they were out to siphon aircraft from the Europe-first mentality and divert them to the Pacific theater. Instead of the army ground forces, it was the navy that put up the biggest fight, and everyone "wearing Navy Blue" demanded massive augmentations to be directed toward the Pacific even though there were as yet almost no bombers in England.[35]

The disagreement over the number of aircraft being sent to the Pacific sowed the seeds of the air force–navy disunion. Although Arnold's and King's correspondence was never anything but civil, and although the two seemed to get along with each other and also with Marshall, the discordant aims of the two services at the beginning of the war were painfully clear. King wrote to Arnold in March 1942: "The plain fact of the matter is . . . that all of us—no matter what uniform we wear—must go to work to win the war." He added: "Therefore . . . I think it is high time that the trend toward a separate air force be given up—and that we face the *realities* of the situation with which we are confronted." As early as 1942, when the US military was training, equipping, and preparing for global conflict, the heads of the army air force and the navy were not singing from the same sheet of music.[36]

Although the navy was the principal proponent of moving more heavy bombers to the Pacific theater, the loudest voice came from General Douglas MacArthur. MacArthur was actually not a proponent of more bombers in the Pacific, unless of course they fell under his purview in the Southwest Pacific theater. He was fighting two wars. The first was with the Japanese. The second was between Nimitz in the Pacific theater and his allied forces back in Washington, DC.

In the fall of 1942, the army air force planners in DC dealt with the fact that, despite what was written down in AWPD-1, there were simply not enough aircraft in the nascent air force to fight a global conflict or to train at home, and Kuter was on the receiving end of these pleas for aircraft and pilots. Although it was clear that "Europe first" was the plan by which all branches of the military would fight, leaders in the Pacific theater—mainly any airmen working for MacArthur—were screaming for aircraft. Kuter received a memorandum regarding a recent inspection of Pacific air bases. In short, there existed "two recurring requests from the Pacific Area as a whole which we are incapable of meeting," those being a request for trained pilots and a request for aircraft types "superior to those which they now have." One of the things MacArthur wanted was an operational training unit (OTU) in the Pacific. As soon as pilots earned their wings, he wanted them ordered directly to the Pacific for further qualification.[37]

The memorandum to Kuter went on to state: "General MacArthur has twice requested additional personnel and additional combat airplanes so that he can set up an OTU system in Australia. We have been unable to grant this request since our continental OTU's are not functioning properly, due to shortages of personnel and equipment and, even if additional facilities were available to send to Australia, it would be better to increase our own OTU's than to duplicate them in Australia." In short, it was too bad that General MacArthur wanted more personnel and newer planes and a Pacific base to train them at because all of those things were in short supply everywhere and, even if they were not, it seemed that the Pacific was the last place they would be sent.[38]

General MacArthur was not the only general officer wanting aircraft. Even while the planners grappled with putting together an air force for the coming North African campaign, for which General Ernest Harmon was also requesting aircraft, General Delos Carleton Emmons was also requesting planes for the defense of the West Coast of the United States. All three were "continually hammering at us that the pursuit pilots we send them are not trained in pursuit, and the bombardment pilots we send them are not trained in bombardment." In a rare bit of military candor, the report admitted: "This [is] unfortunately true and is again a reflection of the shortage of training facilities in the United States."[39]

The problem of desiring newer pursuit planes was not an esoteric one. Current aircraft in the Pacific and soon North Africa were simply outclassed by their German and Japanese counterparts. Kuter was warned that "the recurring cry from these theaters is for pursuit airplanes superior in performance to the P-39 and P-40." Despite these pleas: "Neither the P-47 nor P-38 can be sent to these theaters in large quantities, as their primary assignment must be to Bolero where they operate against ME-109s and FW-190s. Already 100 P-38s have been diverted to General MacArthur as a result of his constant pleas." P-38s did arrive in North Africa later and were present there when Kuter arrived. Bolero was the ongoing buildup of the air force that would operate out of England.[40]

There was another reason for the aircraft shortages plaguing army air force units. Previously established agreements continued to send American-built aircraft to RAF units, particularly in North Africa. British production could not keep pace with the widening scope of the war, and the United States had the means necessary to churn out the aircraft the RAF so desperately needed. This remained a sore spot with American airmen—including Arnold—but it proved to be important as experienced RAF pilots proved more adept at encountering the enemy than were their unseasoned American counterparts early on in the war. Still, this never stopped American commanders from demanding more aircraft in their own theaters.[41]

General Harmon and General MacArthur also requested AT-6s for flight training. The request was denied because there was such an acute aircraft shortage that all the AT-6s in the continental United States were being used to train not only pursuit pilots but also twin-engine pilots. There were simply not enough planes to go around. Arnold did authorize six C-78s each to General Harmon and General Emmons. Although these C-78s were no use when it came to training pursuit pilots, they would allow both generals to ship supplies and move themselves around their vast areas of operations.

Bomber aircraft were also a cause for concern in the Pacific. Already B-17s in small numbers operated in the theater (Japanese forces destroyed eighteen of them in their attack on the Philippines in December), but they proved inadequate for the theater as a whole. The B-17 was not suited for the war in the Pacific, despite planning efforts prior to America entering the war that sent them to MacArthur. The Japanese destruction of American forces in the Philippines, the Europe-first mentality, and sheer aircraft shortage prevented more B-17s from finding their way to the Pacific theater. The end result would see the entire Pacific theater equipped with the sturdier B-24s *Liberators* instead of the *Flying Fortresses*. The Consolidated B-24s held far superior range for the long-duration flights needed to fly over the open water of the Pacific. The B-17s already in theater would be returned first to Australia and then back to the United States for use as training aircraft for pilots in four-engine aircraft, primarily future bombardment officers. Some of these B-17s also arrived in North Africa.[42]

Bombers were not the only aircraft problem faced in the Pacific. MacArthur wanted industry in America to stop production of so many different types of fighters and focus on producing more on a single type. The memorandum recommended to Kuter: "It would be wise to remind them of the impossibility of converting existing production of types which they declare unsuitable to production of P-38s, P-47s, and P-51s since our aircraft production is so inflexible that the cutting off of one line of production of an unsatisfactory pursuit plane will result in an even more critical shortages [*sic*] of airplanes of any type." The answer was clear. The air forces around the globe would get what they would get and learn to deal with it. Ironically, in theater, shortages beyond aircraft and equipment were bound to become an even greater concern for Kuter in very short order, but for the time being, he displayed both calmness and resolve in dealing with the theater commanders. He ensured that Arnold's expectations were met and that the needs of the overall war effort came first.[43]

Kuter's levelheadedness benefited him greatly as a staff officer serving first George Marshall and then Hap Arnold. Even though he had to routinely and forcibly argue with officers senior to him in both rank and age, there is no account of Kuter ever losing his cool or his temper. Perhaps this is another reason he is so often overlooked; his self-control does not make for great writing. He did what needed to be done and never lost control. As he found out on future assignments, other officers did not share his proclivity for levelheaded reactions.

The calmness and reserve displayed by Kuter benefited any officer who worked for General Arnold as "no box fenced in Hap Arnold." Arnold would, as we have seen, often have the first officer he ran into drop what he was doing to work a particular problem, regardless of that officer's rank. He was very much a "line of sight tasker." It took a coolheaded man like Kuter to keep the staff functioning and determine who was doing what and just which officer might be working a problem after Arnold took a stroll down the hall. In fact, it was this unflappability that endeared him to senior officers, especially an officer like Marshall.[44]

Kuter's experiences in Washington essentially established him as an up-and-coming officer in the army air force. His experience at ACTS had refined his theories of and feelings about aerial bombardment and helped him author portions of Air War Plans Division–Plan 1, along with Hansell, George, and Walker. He also helped brief the plan up the chain through to the secretary of war. His organizational skills made him a sought-after officer in all his future commands, and his work setting up the army air force Air Staff brought him to the notice of Marshall and Arnold, both of whose trust he earned, a not insignificant feat in itself. He was instrumental in shaping the organization of the US Army Air Forces once it became coequal with the ground component. Finally, his promotion to brigadier general at the age of thirty-six made him, at least for a short time, something of a media darling and a recognized face throughout Washington.

As the overseas combat commands were gaining experience, Arnold started thinking about the experience level of the officers he surrounded himself with. He knew that, if those in his closest circle were going to have appreciable roles in a postwar air force or even be considered for more senior positions, both in theater and back in Washington, DC, as the war progressed they would each need seasoning in combat. He clearly recognized his own lack of combat experience during the First World War, and, while he never mentioned it, he ensured that the same would not be said of the best and brightest officers under his command.

In early 1942, Arnold began to post his most trusted officers to overseas posts, many of them in command of a combat organization. First to depart was Ira Eaker, followed shortly by Carl Spaatz and the young Haywood Hansell, all three to Europe. For a time, Kuter remained in Washington working directly for Arnold as a somewhat indispensable man, but Arnold knew that he needed the seasoning that only command in combat provided. As a brigadier general, he was already too senior to command a squadron or a group, and this hindered his combat experience. Squadron and group commanders led combat missions. Wing commanders oversaw the larger unit. Kuter's jump in rank effectively promoted him out of a pure combat job, but the command of a larger organization was important for his future development. Arnold had him report to his office in October 1942. He had been in Washington for just over three years, and it was time for him to move on. To that end, Brigadier General Laurence Kuter became slated for his first overseas deployment and command of a wing. There was one caveat. In his memorandums to both George Kenney and Carl Spaatz seeking a command for Kuter, Arnold added the stipulation: "I want him back."[45]

4

The European Theater of Operations

Kuter was finally free of the "maelstrom of Washington." The architects of the Air Corps Tactical School (ACTS) needed combat experience. Even Arnold knew that his most trusted subordinates needed combat missions on their records if they were going to be leaders in a postwar air force, independent or not. To that end, Kuter was shipped overseas in October 1942 to take command of the 1st Bombardment Wing (later the 1st Bombardment Division), 8th Air Force, Brampton Grange, England. When he assumed command, he found that he now led four understrength groups of B-17 *Flying Fortresses* operating separately.

To be blunt, Kuter's time in command of a flying wing was brief in the extreme—only a few weeks. One might wonder whether he had even fully unpacked before he moved to a different theater. An official air force biography stated: "He succeeded in welding the individual squadrons and groups into a coordinated fighting force. This was done on the assumption that the largest practicable combat unit over the target at one time provided more mutual fire support, saving lives and planes, and improve the probability of destroying the objective without having to repeat." It is difficult to say whether this is true. Kuter certainly prioritized his bombardment wing's training program, but just how successful he was at "welding the individual squadrons" into combat shape is honestly debatable.[1]

1st Bombardment Wing

Kuter took over the 1st Heavy Bombardment Wing on or about 1 November 1942. His immediate commander, Ira Eaker, assigned him four tasks: improve the in-commission rate of his bombardment squadrons (the number of aircraft in service and prepared to perform missions), decrease the rate of aircraft that aborted after takeoff and returned to base, improve target recognition and bombardment accuracy in each of his three units, and finally put in writing just what tasks a wing commander should accomplish.[2]

Kuter's headquarters was located at Brampton Grange. His personal room was a short walk away at the "Water Meadows" hunting lodge—which formally belonged to the Earl of Sandwich—which he shared with other officers, although, as the senior ranking member, he stayed in the master's suite. Life at Water Meadows would have been grand had there not been a war to fight. Still, Kuter did have two issues with accommodations. For starters, the servant's wing had central heating and modern plumbing. Kuter tried to move into the senior butler's room, but the staff balked at this notion and refused to allow "Brampton's American General," as Kuter was known to the staff, to live anywhere other than a true "gentleman's quarters." As an American, Kuter preferred the modern amenities over the traditional gentleman's room. The second issue he had more success resolving. A specialty of the cooking staff was brussels sprouts. Kuter was more than adamant this time; they would not be served in the house as long as he resided there.[3]

Kuter set about visiting each of his four groups: the 93d Bombardment Group under Colonel Edward Timberlake, the 303d under Colonel James Wallace, the 306th under Colonel Charles Overackers, and the 305th under Colonel Curtis LeMay. Obviously, of this group, LeMay went on to have the most notable career and crossed paths with Kuter many times in the future. Kuter knew each of his group commanders and attempted to learn something at each of the groups. If he discovered one overarching theme, it was that each group seemed to take on the persona of its commander and that each did one thing very well. The trick, in Kuter's mind, was sharing this knowledge between groups to raise standards throughout the wing.[4]

Bombing U-Boat Pens

From late 1942 through the spring of 1943, the 8th Air Force was sent against the German submarine pens (i.e., U-boat bunkers) located in St. Nazaire and Lorient. The historian Donald L. Miller has said that the bombing missions against the pens proved to be "a wasteful exercise." Not only were the bombers not destroying them; they were barely denting them. Kuter was severe in his criticism of bombing raids targeting those "damned submarine pens," which were, he knew, a lost target set. The pens as a target viewed from the air were small, significantly smaller than other targets the bombers could be sent against: power plants, refineries, or factories. He much preferred to use the bombers against submarine manufacturing plants in Hamburg. He called the pen bombing missions an "inexcusable waste of strategic air strength" and "a straight waste of men and aircraft."[5]

In addition to not destroying the pens, the antiaircraft artillery fire around the ports led to severe losses of American aircraft and aircrews. On eight separate missions, eleven B-17s were lost. Although this would prove to be a small number of losses in comparison with those incurred on future bombing missions, it was significant for the time. Most of the B-17s that returned home were decimated by the antiaircraft artillery and showed signs of extensive damage. Kuter noted that his pilots and bombardiers were smart men who recognized the futility of these missions but persevered in the face of adversity. Even when they were able to hit their targets directly, little damage was done. On one particular mission, the crews returned citing a direct hit with a two-thousand-pound armor-piercing bomb. The next day photoreconnaissance mission showed workers filling the resulting hole with more concrete over the reinforced steel structure. Even direct hits had very little effect.[6]

Kuter recalled these attacks thirty years later in a 1973 letter to Possum Hansell: "I would have added that those losses were the highest during those last months when all missions were directed against targets which the intelligent crews knew they would not hit, if they did hit they wouldn't hurt the targets and even if they could have been hurt, it wouldn't have mattered very much, those miserable reinforced concrete submarine pens. I have always rated the discipline and the morale of those crews far above the troops who were not to reason why but just thunder into the valley of death." In mute testament to their strength, the submarine pens remain standing today.[7]

Even very early on in the American bombing campaigns it became obvious that tightly packed groups of B-17s could not defend themselves against a determined Luftwaffe attack. This rapidly exposed the flaw in the arguments regarding pursuit versus bombardment at ACTS. Kuter stated years later that there was remorse for the marginalization of pursuit aviation at the hands of the bombardment proponents: "There were regrets. No one regretted it more than the bombers. Ken Walker . . . was killed in a bomber. Possum commanded B-17s; I commanded B-17s. . . .

No, we had deep regrets." Kuter, along with Spaatz and Jimmy Doolittle, addressed these regrets in the North African campaign to come, giving pursuit aviation a preeminent role in escort and attack missions.[8]

Kuter called the attacks against the submarine pens "futile and costly." In retirement, he would echo these sentiments, saying: "I have always maintained that attacks on the submarine pens were the outstanding misuse of air power in World War II." For proponents of strategic bombardment against industrial targets, the pen attacks were anathema. This use of heavy bombers was, however, better than the "still more futile, wasteful, and probably totally ineffective" use of heavy bombers hunting submarines in the North Atlantic. The fact that these same submarine pens stand today is a mute testament to the difficulties faced in the early stages of the strategic air campaign. When remembering the men who were forced time and again to go after the pens despite no chance of success and heavy losses, Kuter said: "I am still just at a loss to explain the loyalty, the devotion, the discipline that took those bomber crews and squadrons and groups into those targets time after time. I think that [in comparison] the Charge of the Light Brigade was a Sunday school picnic."[9]

It is important to note that, while Kuter was correct about the futility of bombing the submarine pens, he missed the mark on the contributions of heavy bombers hunting submarines. The missions were not "futile, wasteful, and probably totally ineffective." Kuter wanted to go after the submarine manufacturing yards, a position that demonstrated his adherence to strategic bombardment concepts. In reality, B-17s working closely with the navy made significant contributions in destroying the U-boats operating in the North Atlantic. As the historian Donald Miller pointed out: "It was the airplane . . . that became the U-boat's deadliest foe. B-24 Liberators hunted down the wolf packs far out to sea, and lighter aircraft, flying from escort carriers, finished them off." Kuter was wrong on this account, preferring to stand by air force doctrine over the results presented even years later.[10]

While carrying out orders to bomb the submarine pens, Kuter did what he could to push for improvements in the 1st Bombardment Wing. He found morale in his squadrons to be "neutral." Moving forward with his task of overall improvement of the wing and its bombing accuracy, he looked to join LeMay's group on a bombing mission, something he was not supposed to do. His conscience "squirmed" as he thought of his Ultra (i.e., wartime signals intelligence) oath of secrecy and the fact that he knew the German high command would probably recognize him as a senior war planner with significant access to information should he be shot down and captured. Weather, however, prevented the mission from taking off, something that would happen to him on more than one occasion. He walked with LeMay back to the latter's office, where LeMay fumed that canceled missions did more harm to the morale of his men than did the missions that flew, hit the target, and returned to base. Kuter recognized that it was often weather over the target that would cancel these missions. Rather than cancel such missions, Kuter looked to use them as training opportunities.[11]

Kuter's desire to use fully armed aircraft for a training mission was consistently rebuffed by Eaker, who viewed canceled missions as a chance for the crews to rest. On one particular mission, when Kuter received the call to cancel, he was also informed that Eaker was away from Bomber Command. He announced his attention to launch anyway for training. When the officer on the other end of the phone stated that Eaker had not approved such a use for the aircraft, Kuter responded that he was "not asking permission but announcing my decision." He knew he might get in trouble for the flight, but he believed that the gains outweighed the risks or the repercussions. In the end, the wing put in several hours of work tightening up their combat boxes, and, despite Eaker's displeasure, Kuter received no formal reprimand. These training missions were also where Kuter made another significant contribution to bombardment tactics, but this owed more to a subordinate of his than to Kuter himself; Kuter was simply the conduit for the tactics adoption.[12]

Kuter made one more change to training and tactics before he departed England that proved to have ramifications for the conduct of the aerial war. One of his squadron commanders, Curtis LeMay, started trying different formations for his B-17 units during training and bombing runs. He finally settled on a new tactical formation for his entire squadron. It was a combat box formation. A total of eighteen B-17s composed the box formation. LeMay placed his eighteen bombers into three groups of six. The first six aircraft were at a high altitude, followed by six more at a lower altitude and finally six more back at a high altitude. The pilots and bombardiers—the latter having control of the aircraft on the actual bombing run—were instructed to follow the lead aircraft straight over the target without maneuvering. LeMay's formation improved both formation flying and bombing accuracy. Kuter took note. He recommended to Eaker that each group in the 8th Air Force take up this tactic and expand it from squadron level to groups and then wings for larger bombing runs. He also told Hansell about LeMay's tactics. Eaker, through pressure from both Kuter and Hansell, instituted the formation as the new standard operating procedure.[13]

Kuter and others, including Hansell, began to see the ghost of World War I bombardment in their current operations. Similarities, at least in the eyes of the American commanders, were noticeable between Kuter's 1st Bombardment Wing and the 1st Bombardment Squadron from the First World War. It had been felt in 1918 that American flyers and aircraft had been rushed into combat over Europe, and now, in 1943, it was felt that the same mistake was being repeated. Kuter and Hansell often discussed how a mistake or a poor showing by the wing could set the American concept of air operations back twenty years. Late into the night, the two friends shared stories, ideas, and concepts—and bourbons—about how to improve the American effort. Ironically, although Kuter commanded the wing and Hansell worked for Eaker, it proved beneficial for the two friends to spend so much time discussing the operations of the wing because these problems soon passed from Kuter to Hansell. The bottom line seemed to be that too many American aircrews were being rushed into combat not fully trained to meet the threat. Although it was readily evident to everyone involved—most notably the British—that the American air effort needed to get going, it was at the expense of fielding ill-trained aircrews.[14]

Some authors—most notably James Parton—have criticized Kuter for his lack of combat experience and not flying as an observer on more missions. There are several reasons this should not be held against him. First, many of the missions he attempted to go on were canceled. Second, his time in Europe coincided with the very early days of the American bombing campaign, and he had more than enough to keep him busy executing Eaker's instructions. Third, he had at least a working knowledge of the top-secret Ultra program and, like anyone with knowledge of the program, was expressly forbidden from flying over enemy territory for fear of being captured alive and revealing its existence. Every time he climbed into a B-17 for a mission, he was essentially disobeying an order. Fourth, his short time in command—only a few weeks—allotted him a limited number of bombing missions to go on. Finally, as the historian Martha Byrd points out: "Officers of general rank were discouraged from taking part in combat for a number of reasons, a basic one being that their talents for high command were too valuable to risk." Byrd wrote this about Brigadier General Kenneth Walker, Kuter's friend, who was killed on a low-level mission in the Southwest Pacific after disobeying an order from his commander, General George Kenney, who had instructed him not to fly on any more missions. Ironically, MacArthur put him for the Medal of Honor for the mission he flew in disobeying the order.[15]

Little has been written about Kuter's being moved from Europe to North Africa after only a few weeks in command, but what been written is largely incorrect. James Parton, Eaker's biographer, noted: "Kuter had not gone on any missions out of England in his brief stint as commander of the 1st Wing, and that was no way to win Eaker's confidence." He indicated that this was the primary reason Eaker replaced Kuter with Hansell. It was apparent that Eaker recognized Kuter's intellect and organizational skills, but Parton did not think that Kuter had the wherewithal to be the combat commander that Eaker was looking for. He was wrong. Eaker wanted to keep Kuter where he was.[16]

In a letter to Major General George "Strat" Stratemeyer, Arnold's chief of staff, Eaker said: "It is now perfectly apparent that a bombardment group is as good or bad as its commander." Parton believes that this was a direct reference to Kuter. This is certainly not the case. It is important to note that Parton's book on Eaker was heavily biased, Parton having been Eaker's aide-de-camp. Parton was patently wrong in his assessment that Eaker fired Kuter because he did not fly on any combat missions. For starters, it was extremely difficult for early wing commanders to go on combat missions as they were organizing their groups as larger and larger numbers of men and materiel rolled into England, especially this early in the strategic air campaign and with the weather in England and on the European continent halting so many missions in the winter months. Parton's bias against Kuter was repudiated by Eaker himself in Kuter's officer evaluation reports.[17]

That being said, Eaker's assessment of Kuter was less than glowing and probably the worst of Kuter's career. While Eaker rated Kuter "excellent" in two categories, he marked him only "very satisfactory" when it came to knowledge of his profession. He also recommended Kuter for "staff work" instead of another command. Perhaps most damning his ranking Kuter twenty-fourth of thirty-five general officers. When compared against Kuter's other officer reports, it becomes clear that Eaker's was unique as Kuter was often ranked number one. General Arnold even ranked him number eight out of every general officer in the army air forces. Still, Eaker must be forgiven for Kuter's lower-than-normal evaluation. He really had no other option. Finally, Parton was wrong in another respect. Eaker had not sized Kuter up and decided that he wanted to get rid of him.[18]

Kuter commanded the First Bombardment Wing for a scant five

weeks before he was transferred to Spaatz's staff gathering in North Africa. The transfer was in actuality a promotion in billet, in responsibility, and in the amount of action occurring in North Africa at the time. Eaker met with Kuter shortly before his departure and reiterated that the transfer had taken place only over his strenuous protestations, which given the eventual report on Kuter does not initially make sense. If Eaker was so unhappy with Kuter as to rank him so low, it seems that he would be pleased with losing him to another theater. The best deduction is that Eaker wanted to keep Kuter in place to give him time to prove himself. Five weeks hardly seems enough time to fairly rate someone's performance, and Eaker cannot be blamed for ranking Kuter lower than he did his other general officers, who had served longer in theater. Eaker even wrote to Spaatz asking to keep Kuter in place. Spaatz retorted that he specifically needed someone with Kuter's organizational background and overruled Eaker. He brought Kuter to Algiers to coordinate the air units. From a certain point of view, this singular moment in Kuter's career can probably be characterized as unfair—to Eaker, to the 1st Bombardment Wing, and especially to Larry Kuter. On the other hand, that fact that Spaatz specifically asked for Kuter indicated the high regard in which he was held by senior air force officers.[19]

The replacement/promotion stung Kuter: "To be relieved of my command before any of my several efforts to improve our performance could produce measurable results was most disappointing." However, he knew that his wing would be in good hands as it was his good friend Hansell replacing him. He said: "If I had the entire [army air force] from which to choose I would have chosen Possum to replace me." Despite the perception, Kuter was not fired or relieved of command because Eaker did not believe in his abilities. Quite the contrary, it seems clear that Eaker hoped Kuter would remain in command and that Kuter was moved to North Africa only over Eaker's objections. Eaker also expressed hope to Kuter that he would return to lead a larger air division once North Africa had sorted itself out, and they parted on good terms. Years later, as part of the air force's oral history interviews of senior officers, Eaker was adamant that he had no control over the loss of Kuter and that Kuter—along with Hansell—was too valuable to Spaatz and Arnold to stay in one place for any length of time. He would supervise Kuter again later in the war.[20]

In January 1943, Eisenhower consolidated his North African air power into the Allied Air Force. Eisenhower placed Spaatz in overall command with the US 12th Air Force and the British Eastern Air Command under him. To help him organize the Allied Air Force, Mortensen notes: "Carl A. Spaatz summoned Brig Gen Laurence S. Kuter, currently commander of the 1st Bombardment Wing of the Eighth Bomber Command in England, to Algiers to help coordinate air units widely separated and weakly connected by centralized command."[21]

5

North Africa

In January 1943, orders came through officially transferring Brigadier General Kuter to North Africa. Initially, he was to command the Allied tactical air forces. This was part of a reorganization conducted at the behest of Eisenhower as the general attempted to create a cohesive command and also force the British and American forces to work together in a combined headquarters. In short, the command structure in North Africa was a complete mess. At this time, there existed no fewer than six separate air forces operating independently in Africa, each still reporting individually to the Mediterranean Air Command under Sir Arthur Tedder. Tedder commanded the North African Air Forces, the Royal Air Force (RAF) Air Command Malta, and the Middle East Air Command. The air forces operating in North Africa needed to be combined and streamlined so that only one commander reported directly to Tedder. The Allied Air Forces in North Africa included the British Eastern Air Command and the US 12th Air Force, the latter under the command of Jimmy Doolittle. In February, the RAF's Western Desert Air Force reached Tunisia and merged with the Allied Support Command from North Africa, which finally merged the forces and necessitated a name change. Lieutenant General Spaatz commanded the new Northwest African Air Forces (NAAF), and Kuter, at least for a brief time, served as Spaatz's deputy. Spaatz reported directly to Tedder and oversaw all the air forces operating in North Africa. On 18 February, Spaatz issued Headquarters NAAF General Order no. 1, which combined all the disparate aerial sections, including the tactical, strategic, coastal, training, and reconnaissance commands. Henceforth, they each became a subset of the NAAF as the Northwest African Strategic Air Force, under Doolittle, the Northwest African Tactical Air Force (NATAF), under Coningham, etc.[1]

In April, Spaatz issued a memorandum to each of his air forces stating that the Axis armies had been forcibly driven back and would begin the process of extricating as many men and machines as possible from the continent, back through the Mediterranean to Sicily or the Italian mainland. Spaatz told his troops: "The major responsibility for preventing this withdrawal will fall upon Northwest African Air Forces. . . . This is a great opportunity for the Air. There must be no DUNKIRK; the enemy must be ANNIHILATED."[2]

Kuter now moved from working directly for Spaatz down to become the American deputy serving under Sir Arthur Coningham in NATAF. "Mary," as Coningham was known, was "probably the most knowledgeable British officer on tactical air operations," according to Colonel William Momyer, himself destined to be a four star in the US Air Force. Pete Quesada—later to make general during the war and considered the father of American tactical air power—said of Coningham: "We didn't have anyone that could even come close to him." Coningham commanded NATAF, and Kuter moved over to serve as his deputy. As always with command relationships, people and offices changed hands often. At the time of Coningham's arrival, Kuter was technically Spaatz's chief of staff, although the office assigned to that position was already occupied by a British air vice marshal, Robb. Spaatz told Kuter that he would eventually find a permanent position for him, which was odd considering that Spaatz had requested him in the first place. When Kuter and Coningham met in January 1943, Kuter found Coningham to be "big, self-confident, forceful and . . . bellicose." These initial impressions eventually softened into a lifelong friendship.[3]

Kuter, an avowed member of the bomber mafia, now found himself serving as a deputy commander of a tactical air force. This force included not only fighter aircraft but medium and light bombers as well. It was a different kind of air force organization than he was used to, but it exposed him further to other roles and missions being performed by the growing American air arm. For the first time, he was no longer myopically focused on bombardment. His horizons were expanding.

Interestingly, early in the year, as Kuter was organizing the NATAF staff before the arrival of Coningham, he received a letter from Colonel Edgar Sorensen. Believing Kuter still to be in command of the 1st Bombardment Wing and not in North Africa, Sorenson wrote him regarding the future of air operations in the European theater and hoped to establish back-channel communications with him and the 8th Air Force. He noted: "After due consideration, my conclusion concurred in by General Fairchild and General Gates is that certain information to be passed to the Eighth Air Force can best be transmitted through you. This conclusion is based largely on our mutual understanding of certain problems, together with the position which you now occupy." It seems that Sorenson intended that certain information to be passed to Eaker should come not through the chain of command but through Kuter. Somehow, the letter found Kuter in North Africa despite having Hansell's current address on it.[4]

Sorenson went on to tell Kuter that, while both believed the strategic air war could cripple Germany, they "must concede the practical necessity of the presence of the strong ground forces of our own to take control, if not to fight, and to obviate the undesirable necessity of our occupation being taken over by our allies from farther east." In other words, from the perspective of the most ardent air power advocates, a ground invasion of the European continent was necessary if for no other reason than to ensure that Soviet forces did not themselves eventually occupy the land. Sorensen also indicated that he felt it was a good idea for a number of men from the War Department to come to the European theater to help with picking bombing objectives, which itself was bad enough. The real problem with this particular letter was the subtly dropped hints about how the air war was currently being conducted: "I have heard it said by an officer from the Eighth Air Force. . . ." Sorenson used this unnamed officer to question how the war was being run in Europe. Again, rather than bringing his ideas or concerns directly to the 8th's commanding general; he was suggesting that a subordinate act as a conduit. Kuter quickly washed his hands of the entire affair.[5]

Kuter passed the letter back to Hansell, telling him: "Dear Possum, This baby is in your hands now." He also warned Hansell that Eaker was no fan of Sorenson's and it was up to Hansell himself to explain the matter fully. The inherent problem with the letter was that Sorenson and, thus, certain elements inside the War Department were proposing new targets for the 8th Air Force to hit. Kuter knew, as did Hansell, that Eaker would not take kindly to such an attempt to suggest how he do his job, and, to make matters worse, the news was coming from a subordinate. Kuter suggested that Hansell not tell Eaker, write to Sorenson directly, and tell him to contact Eaker. The letter to Hansell was not all bad news. Kuter also sent his friend a gift—a crate of North African oranges.[6]

By way of conclusion, Hansell did reach out to both Sorenson and Santy Fairchild to ensure that his opinions on the matter were known. While he personally indicated no problem with receiving help from the War Department, he noted that any advice should go directly to Eaker rather than come from a subordinate. He also noted that the 1st Bombardment Wing's headquarters was some eighty miles from Eaker's 8th

Air Force headquarters and that it was simply not practical to bring any matters, including target selection and bombing accuracy, from his headquarters to Eaker.[7]

Larry Kuter turned his attention back to NATAF. Coningham officially arrived at NATAF on 18 February 1943. Kuter noted that he came in at "full steam" with his "blunt charm," and this might very well be the only instance in Anglo-American cooperation where the American officer was the more refined of the two (although Coningham's bluntness came from the fact that he was not an Englishman—he had been born in Australia and raised in New Zealand). The two worked well together and, along with the rest of the staff, set about running tactical air power in North Africa and assuaging any misgivings the ground forces had toward close air support.[8]

One of the more interesting confrontations between the Americans and the British occurred early in Kuter's time in North Africa and shortly after Coningham arrived. Sir Arthur Tedder called it "a major crisis in Anglo-American relations," and it would eventually be immortalized in the 1970 American film *Patton* starring George C. Scott. General George Patton—perhaps grieving the loss of his personal aide, Richard Jensen— added a line to a situation report noting that he and his troops were under continuous enemy bombardment and had a complete lack of air support from Allied air units. He also ensured that what was a routine situation report had a significantly larger receiving list than was routine, ensuring a wide readership. He was intentionally spreading discord. Reading it at Ain Beida, Kuter initially took the report with a grain of salt. He knew Patton personally and believed that this was another example of his attempting to inflame the passions of those around him, senior and junior in rank, to dive into the fight. Coningham, however, was not as relaxed about the situation as his deputy.[9]

Coningham was incensed that Patton dared cast aspersions against the combined British and American air arm. During the night of 1 April, he typed out a response and sent it to everyone who received the initial report from Patton. It was absolutely blistering in its critique: "On receipt of SITREP [the situation report] it was first assumed to be seasonal April joke. It is assumed that intentions was [*sic*] not to stampede local American Air Command into purely defensive action. It is also assumed that there was no intention to adopt discredited practice of using Air Force as an alibi for lack of success on ground. If SITREP is in earnest and balanced against above facts it can only be assumed the II Corps personnel concerned are not battle worthy in terms of present operations."[10]

Eisenhower wanted to throw water on this fire and immediately decided that the air commander and the ground commander needed to meet. Along with Coningham, Spaatz sent Sir Arthur Tedder and Kuter from the air side to meet with Patton and Bradley. Kuter said that the meeting started out tense, with Patton wearing his "fiercest scowl." If he was attempting to intimidate the air officers, he picked the wrong opponent in Mary Coningham. Tedder brokered the meeting. He faced Patton and admitted that Coningham's response was inappropriate but pointed out that the two needed to sort things out between them. Kuter still believed that Patton acted "like a small boy who had done wrong, but thought he could get away with it." Kuter was not the only one who felt this way. General Harold Alexandar called Patton and said that he had read both Patton's message and Coningham's and that Patton had gotten what he had asked for. Coningham and Patton agreed to meet again the next day. This time they met alone.[11]

The meeting between Coningham and Patton occurred behind closed doors, but Coningham gave Kuter a description of it later. Evidently, the two men sat across from each other, yelling and pounding on the desk between them, but eventually "concluded that they each enjoyed a good fight, shook hands and had lunch together, all smiles." Another Anglo-American crisis was averted after the two spent their energies. Their subsequent recollections of the meeting differed significantly, however. Patton recalled that it was Coningham who apologized profusely, noting: "It is always easy to be generous to a man who admits his mistakes." Coningham's account has more the ring of truth to it. Omar Bradley later replaced Patton as commander of the 2nd Corps for the final push across North Africa as Patton was slated to command the American forces moving on to Sicily, and Bradley's more even-keeled temper did not need the constant assuaging that Patton's did.[12]

The incident between Coningham and Patton was not quite over. Somehow, General George Marshall also received copies of Patton's original and Coningham's rebuke. Spaatz was forced to explain to both Marshall and Eisenhower how it was Patton's original situation report that caused Coningham's explosion. In the end, both sided with Spaatz's perspective, and Eisenhower, for not the first or the last time, was forced to chastise Patton in writing.[13]

General Kuter became the American deputy commander in the newly consolidated NATAF, and he arrived just as things were heating up for the Allied forces in North Africa. Still, Kuter's day-to-day dealings were not limited to preparing air forces for combat; sometimes his days were filled with the mundane issues all commanders face. He was still forced to deal with logistic issues of feeding and supplying an army in the field, including the men at the airdromes, which he found to be drastically short of "coffee, sugar, flour, cocoa, and condiments." He left no room for question when he told the 12th Air Support Command: "I consider this action . . . both impertinent and irrelevant and categorically state that this command is dissatisfied with the rations. . . . I feel strongly that no stone should be left unturned by all echelons of this command to provide our fighting personnel in the forward airdromes with rations at least equivalent to those by personnel in the rear." While mundane, logistics was vitally important, and Kuter's insistence that suitable rations reach the forward bases proved his understanding that the logistic chain often became logjammed, something he refused to allow.[14]

Kuter's day-to-day correspondence also demonstrated that he was deeply involved at all levels of command and was working hard as the intermediary between the forces in the field and Coningham and Spaatz. He also seemed perfectly willing to draft a memorandum, forward it to Spaatz, and recommend that it be forwarded to Arnold. On 5 April, for example, he argued that current doctrine, which called for antiaircraft gunners to abandon their posts in the face of a determined attack, was "obviously unsound" and had been "emphatically disproved" during combat, demanding that "a message substantially as follows be sent to Arnold."[15]

As the war in North Africa progressed, Coningham detailed the present situation in a report to his forces. As the Allies pushed the Axis forces across North Africa, he reminded his officers: "The value of North Africa [for the enemy] is very great, both from the aspect of containing large allied forces in the theater and also for the value that the remnant territory gives to his weak Italian ally. There is no doubt, therefore, that every effort will be made by the enemy to retain possession of the bridgehead for as long as possible." He also noted that the reverse was necessarily true for the Allies: "The quicker the enemy is defeated in North Africa the sooner will forces be released to hit the enemy elsewhere and thus speed the next phase of the war. The greater the annihilation of the enemy the less opposition will be available in a new theater. The object, therefore, is the complete destruction of the enemy forces in North Africa as rapidly as possible."[16]

As NATAF commanding general, Coningham firmly reminded his flyers: "Our air forces are intimately bound with the operation of the land forces." This proved to have a profound impact on Larry Kuter.

Since his days at the Air Corps Tactical School, he had focused almost exclusively on strategic bombardment. This exposure to army–air force cooperation on the battlefield fundamentally altered his perception of air power. While he remained a staunch proponent of what strategic air power could accomplish, he also began to argue more forcibly for what tactical air forces could provide to ground components at the battlefront.[17]

The dedication that Kuter brought to air-ground cooperation manifested itself in different ways as well. War Department doctrine at the time called for air units to be assigned directly to ground units at the corps level, a concept called *direct support*. This limited any given air unit's effectiveness as it required the ground commander to release "his" air support to participate in the fight in another area. Although the preferred method of conducting business by army commanders on the ground, it proved to be a terribly inefficient way to provide air power across a wide battle space since it caused air power to be anchored to a particular area along the front. This made air power in the region inflexible and unresponsive. It also allowed Rommel a corridor to move his forces in and out of North Africa and Sicily, causing the very thing that Spaatz and Coningham wanted to prevent, the movement of 150,000 German troops—1,000 per day—from Sicily and Italy into Tunisia, something that, on his arrival in the theater, Kuter worked very hard to prevent.[18]

Other senior leaders recognized that tying air power to a single lower-echelon ground commander prevented it from contributing elsewhere on the battlefield. Field Marshal Bernard Montgomery later said: "The greatest asset of air power is its flexibility, and this enables it to be switched from one objective to another in the theater of operations. Nothing could be more fatal to successful results than to dissipate the air resources into small packets placed under the command of army formations commanders, with each packet working on its own plan. The soldier must not expect or wish to exercise direct command over air striking forces."[19]

There were certain ground commanders—particularly those at the corps level—who opposed losing the direct control they exerted over air power. This was not so much an issue of keeping air power subordinate to the ground commander as it was a ground commander not wanting to give up a certain aspect of control he had learned to count on. As an example, Kuter remembered: "It was anathema to George Patton to suggest that [air force] units in his Corps area were not subject to his instant and absolute authority."[20]

Years later, in 1954, when General Kuter was commander of Air University, he spoke to the young captains attending Squadron Officer School. His audience was too young to have served in World War II, and he spoke of the changes that occurred in North Africa as American air forces entered sustained operations: "The unsound doctrine under which the air forces were fighting a losing battle in Tunisia was published in War Department Field Manuel 31-35. In its opening, this manual announced its gross built-in error: It was entitled 'Aviation in Support of Ground Forces.' In two of its worst deficiencies it failed to recognize that air forces must be commanded and employed as an entity and that the first take of the air force is to win the air battle."[21]

Operation Flax and the Palm Sunday Massacre

As the war in North Africa progressed, Kuter continued to implement Coningham's orders and have forces attack both the Luftwaffe and German ground forces. As the Germans began to pull their forces out of North Africa, he directed attacks against shipping and German aerial movements. Attacks on shipping used heavy and medium bombers as well as fighter aircraft. If the use of air power is always contextual, the particular context of the North African campaign was a perfect moment of circumstances and geography allowing air power to ply its trade. Since freighters left Tunis and sailed north to Sicily, Allied air power stood a good chance of intercepting them along the route of travel. Since the area was also heavily mined, this effectively prevented the navy from attacking the ships in transit, but there was no aerial mine-field to prevent attacks from on high. Between January and April, Allied aircrews caught and sank the *Saturno,* the *Vercelli,* the *Ines Corrado,* and the *Monti,* all in open waters, but this record paled in comparison to the forty or more ships sunk in port by both Doolittle's strategic forces and Coningham's tactical forces. Doolittle's heavy bombers also "worked over" the airports and seaports in Italy. Strategic and tactical air power destroyed the large merchant vessels and forced the Germans to resupply their forces with smaller Siebel Ferries and Kriegstransport-ers. These smaller vessels proved adept at avoiding both air power and submarines but could not carry the necessary weight to keep the German military reinforced. The Germans slowly found the logistics of holding North Africa impossible. The German general Hans-Jürgen von Arnim called the situation "catastrophic." Taking such a heavy toll, German forces decided to try another means of moving men and equipment into the region.[22]

As Allied air power sunk Italian shipping in the Mediterranean, the Germans began flying larger aerial transport missions to move in supplies and reinforcements. Kuter wanted to use his tactical air power to attack this aerial bridge. Thanks to new radar stations along the coast as well as intelligence-gathering operations, Kuter knew when these regularly scheduled flights took place and went to Coningham and Spaatz asking for permission to hit them with overwhelming numbers. Spaatz approved the mission. It was given the code name Flax.[23]

The first Flax operation was scheduled to take place on 21 February, but it was pushed back owing to the debacle at the Kasserine Pass, which began on 19 February. It would take until 5 April—shortly after the incident between Patton and Coningham—for Flax to get airborne. It quickly became an aerial rout. The first wave of P-38s from the 1st Fighter Group intercepted and shot down eleven J-52 transports. By the end of the first week, NATAF shot down hundreds of German transports and fighters. The German transport fleet was so badly damaged that the Luftwaffe pressed ME-323s into service as low-altitude transports. The ME-323 was a massive four-engine aircraft and the largest transport built during the war. On Palm Sunday, American aircraft located a virtual aerial bridge of the ME-323 transports headed into Tunis. The historian Chris Rein noted that the hundred or more transports attempted "to sneak into Tunisia before sunset" but were caught over the open water by the 57th and 79th Fighter Groups. With a call of "Tallyho," the fight was on. Kuter remembered the scene:

> I watched the fight over Tunis on our radar scope and heard it through my head set. All was excitement. All conversations were in the clear. Code names of units and targets were forgotten. Colloquialisms and profanities over the air identified New Zealand, Australian, English, and American pilots as they demanded room in "the bloody air space" to get in on the kill. From my electronic view the scene resembled the feeding frenzy of our Atlantic coast blue-fish. By dark the Tunis harbor was littered with some floating air cargo, ditched aircraft and small rescue boats. On Palm Sunday our claims totaled over 100 transports and ten fighters.

The "Palm Sunday Massacre" was a devastating defeat for the Luftwaffe. Despite the heavy losses, the Germans were forced to try again the next day, but this cost them an additional twelve transports.[24]

Operation Flax proved a resounding success and effectively ended Germany's ability to withdraw its troops and supplies from North Africa. The historian Robert Ehlers noted the effectiveness of these aerial operations: "The Luftwaffe was defeated, and German troops were running out of fuel and ammunition as the final Allied offensives began." In the month of April, Allied air power decimated the Luftwaffe's transport capabilities. Air power destroyed between two and three hundred transport aircraft as well as other escort fighters. Flax continued throughout the spring and summer months and ended with more than two thousand enemy aircraft destroyed. Kuter's plan helped hasten German defeat and surrender in North Africa.[25]

The losses highlighted a significant strategic problem: the German forces were simply spread too thin and fighting in too many places to be decisive. While they could provide effective resistance, they could not defeat the Allied armies in North Africa and hold off the Russians in Eastern Europe at the same time. By spring of 1943, the die was cast, but it was certainly not obvious to the men leading the Allied campaign. As far as the Luftwaffe was concerned, Germany could replace the aircraft, but there was no way for them to replace the trained pilot corps that flew them. Conversely, now that American industry and military training facilities were reaching maximum output, the Allies could replace both aircraft and aircrews as needed.

On 14 April, General Eisenhower visited the forward area to discuss the final drive to capture the remaining German troops now stuck in Africa. He brought Mark Clark with him and asked Patton, Bradley, Alexander, and Spaatz to meet him for a conference. Tooey's plane made a forced landing, and he missed the conference, meaning that only Alexander was present to represent the views of the air arm when the ground commanders demanded control over air assets in their sections. Alexander, of course, argued against the parceling out of air power, and Eisenhower agreed with him.

Spaatz finally arrived that evening to go behind closed doors with Eisenhower, Clark, Patton, Bradley, and Kuter. Eisenhower said that he was "Goddamned tired of hearing that ground forces had to have control over air forces," settling the matter once and for all. In the coming climactic battles of North Africa, air power operated as an independent force, wreaking havoc on shipping and the Luftwaffe, while also providing support to the ground commanders when requested.[26]

As Bradley replaced Patton as commander of the 2nd Corps, Kuter spent time as near to Bradley's headquarters as possible to ensure that air-ground cooperation was meeting the offensive commander's needs. Bradley told Kuter that he was "wholly satisfied" and that there were no improvements he could think of. It probably helped that Bradley's headquarters was a din of constant noise as the NATAF fighters flew to the front directly overhead. By this point in the campaign, Allied air power had ensured virtual air supremacy over North Africa. Air-ground cooperation proved to be a deadly combination, and the Allied forces executed a blitzkrieg of their own across North Africa. On 6 May, more than two thousand sorties flew in support of a move to open the road to Tunis, impressing Bradley; that kind of operation was something he made use of again in his Cobra offensive as part of the breakout that ended the Normandy campaign the following year. But Kuter almost missed the end results of all his cooperative efforts.[27]

Although Kuter had made great contributions in two wartime theaters, his days in North Africa, much like his days in command in Europe, were numbered. For starters, he knew about Ultra, and this limited his ability to go on bombing missions. Of course, as a NATAF deputy commander, he should not have been going on missions anyway; his responsibilities lay elsewhere. Some officers—most notably Jimmy Doolittle—ignored the edict that those with knowledge of Ultra should not fly over enemy-held territory. Doolittle later noted: "I disagreed with this policy and continued to fly missions. I felt the effect on morale of my being up there with my boys far outweighed the theoretical possibility of revealing intelligence information." Because he was a proponent of strategic bombardment and now tactical air power, it proved impossible for Kuter to actually conduct these bombing missions, something he regretted. Perhaps more important was the fact that his organizational skills were in demand elsewhere. He had already served in Europe and North Africa. During the Tunisian campaign, General Arnold, commanding general, army air forces, directed that Kuter be released from the Mediterranean theater and returned to Washington effective the day General Rommel surrendered. The order came down on 27 April.[28]

Eisenhower sent Marshall an "eyes only" telegram on 28 April 1943 that read: "Until the Battle of Tunis is finished, departure of Kuter would be worse than unfortunate. Therefore I am taking advantage of your verbal authority to me to ignore orders of the kind when needs of battle are involved. For your information, our Air Force has destroyed a minimum of 275 hostile planes during the past week. Kuter is a key member of the team which is doing this work." Curtis LeMay called Spaatz's headquarters with a message from Arnold directing Kuter to pack his bags. Arnold wanted Kuter back in Washington. The message was worded strongly enough that Spaatz replied: "Kuter will clear this theater on May 18."[29]

Kuter had two more memorable experiences. He flew a small aircraft to observe the attack on Tunis, remembering later: "The entire landscape seemed to be squirming with long lines of our troops moving forward. In striking contrast, the roads in the enemy territory appeared to be totally deserted." On 10 May 1943, he climbed into an open-air car with Alexander, Bradley, and Coningham for a ride through the streets of Tunis, during which he noted how intact the city remained despite the conflict. More impressive, however, were the several German units of the Manteuffel and Herman Goering Divisions that they passed marching smartly along as they looked for the proper officer to surrender to. Even in defeat, the German soldiers kept their bearing.[30]

Directly before leaving North Africa, Kuter wrote to Arnold about the "organization of American air forces." It was both his after-action report and his declaration of what he desired to work on after his return to Washington and the Air Staff. He began by stating: "The organization of the air units in North Africa for the support of ground forces from November 1942 through February 1943 proved to be unsound in battle. During that period the failure to achieve a satisfactory degree of success in fighting in the air, on the ground, and in concert was due to a considerable extent to the unsound air-ground organization and its effect on air support operations." He was again attacking the command relationships that subordinated air power to a ground commander at any echelon below that of the theater commander. He went on to request that Arnold—or he himself when he returned to Arnold's staff—immediately "direct the revision of all army air force publications to delete the statement, inference, or implication that any air force unit except reconnaissance squadrons can normally be expected to operate under the legal command or practical control of any surface force commander."[31]

Kuter went on to lay out all the instances in which the "unsound organization and operational concept" of subordinating air units to ground commanders in the direct support role hindered the overall campaign because the air units became incapable of responding to unfolding combat operations. He noted that, because of this, 150,000 German soldiers moved into North Africa when there were American air units stationed only eighty miles from the ports. He did recognize that "each ground commander naturally and properly viewed the ground (and air) operations on his immediate front as of paramount importance and insisted that *his* air support forces be employed on *his* front." While all commanders of ground forces believed in the importance of gaining air superiority, that particular battle "should be fought by someone else's air force." Kuter also pointed out that each ground commander wanted an "umbrella" of friendly fighters over his own troops at all times and that the fear of a Stuka attack was being blown significantly "out of proportion." In short, he viewed the relationship developed after the arrival of Coningham as the proper method to employ air power in all theaters.[32]

During the campaign in Tunisia, Kuter and Coningham worked together to generate new tactical air concepts that allowed army air force regulations to be revised accordingly. The basic changes reflected in them are still the principal doctrinal basis for the present tactical air power concept of the US Air Force. Kuter used his memorandum to Arnold as the basis for his work on further air-ground doctrine. One of the first things on which he set to work on his return to Washington was FM 100-20. He was ready to codify his operational experiences into doctrines that improved combat effectiveness.

As initially a proponent of strategic bombardment, Kuter had his views on the proper employment of air power modified during his time in North Africa. He became more rounded in his experience and exposure to what tactical air power provided in combined arms battle. He was not the only air power leader who had his views changed. Spaatz also changed his opinion, stating later: "The correct use of air power was . . . air superiority and interdiction operations." Both still believed in the efficacy of strategic bombardment, but both now recognized the importance of integrated air and ground cooperation. As Robert Ehlers noted: "This reminds us that US senior airmen were pragmatic in the current fight even as they maneuvered for independence in the long term."[33]

Although Kuter's time in North Africa was brief, it proved important—for both Kuter himself and for the army air forces as a whole—and he once again demonstrated a keen organizational skill that certainly aided in getting results in combat. Spaatz praised Kuter as he returned to Washington: "The Northwest African Air Forces deeply regret the departure of one its most outstanding and distinguished general officers. I wish to commend you for the courage, foresight, intelligence and sound judgement you have demonstrated. . . . [Y]our achievement in integrating the American components with the tactical Air Force, and in obtaining effective coordination with the other elements of the Northwest African Air Forces, was in no little measure responsible for the triumphant conclusion of the campaign." Kuter also received the award of the Legion of Merit, the citation reading in part: "His executive efforts meant the difference between inadequate fighter support of the ground forces in the Tunisian campaign, and the present ever increasing efficient aerial activity." Other awards came from Allied nations, including a Chevalier de la Legion D'Honneur by the order of the general of the army, commander in chief of the French forces in French West Africa and French North Africa. Kuter returned to Washington with combat and leadership experience that he could not have gained by staying at Arnold's side throughout the war.[34]

6

Back to Washington and Hap's Stand-In

The unpublished autobiography that Kuter later worked on ended with his departure from North Africa, but his arrival back in Washington allowed for a separate and equally rich paper trail to be developed. One sees his hand in much of what comes out of the Air Staff in 1943, most prominently in his work on FM 100-20, *Command and Employment of Air Power*. Kuter's service in both the European and the North African theaters now garnered him new respect, exactly what Arnold intended in sending him overseas.[1]

In May 1943, General Kuter returned to Headquarters Army Air Forces to become assistant chief of staff for plans and combat operations, a position that put him in daily contact with General Arnold. He spent only a few short months overseas, less than a year in total, as the 1st Bombardment Wing commander and deputy commander to Coningham as part of the Northwest African Tactical Air Forces (NATAF). Though brief, these stints in command and leadership positions gave him a keen grasp of how the war—and not just the air war—was going overseas. They also presented him with very developed ideas about just what the Air Staff should be focusing on in Washington, DC. During his tenure there, he worked extensively on *Command and Employment of Air Power* and also stood in for Arnold at the Yalta conference. He spent the majority of his time during the remainder of the war working directly for Arnold, but the jobs he handled routinely saw him traveling overseas to the different theaters of the ongoing war.

On his return to Washington, Kuter issued a press release covering the action in North Africa. "The function of the tactical air force is one of working in partnership with other components of air power," he noted, continuing: "[The word] support has now so many old fashioned and wrong implications in the public mind that it is much better not to use it." On 25 May 1943, he also sat for an interview with the assistant chief of staff for intelligence. While the subject of the interview was what went right and what went wrong in North Africa, it allowed him an opportunity to express his more esoteric views on air power. He wanted air power to support ground forces, but not in the way traditionally understood by the ground element. He was perfectly happy with air power providing firepower and attack functions, as long as these were centralized under an air commander and codified in sound doctrine. On the latter point, he was about to get his wish, but not before arguing the finer points of attack aviation with George Kenney.[2]

Air Power in the Pacific

It was generally understood that there were two army air force officers whom you did not want to show up at your door. Lauris Norstad was one, and Larry Kuter the other. Their presence clearly indicated that Hap Arnold was taking more than just a benign interest in your operations, but Kuter's world travels would have to wait as he currently had more than his fair share of problems awaiting him in the capital, the first of which was a confrontation with George Kenney over the Southwest Pacific.

It should be no surprise that two individuals such as Kuter and Kenney would clash with each other. George C. Kenney was "MacArthur's airman." In modern parlance, one might call him an innovator or an outside-the-box thinker. He used every means necessary and available to him to improve his situation, including unique fixes to in-theater problems. At the time Kuter returned to Washington, Kenney was laboring away in the Southwest Pacific. They were separated not only by age and temperament but also by an important aspect of geography that always plagued military men in wartime. Kenney's view of the war was that of the war fighter, myopically, but not wrongly, focused on what he saw in front of him. Kuter's view took in the larger global picture, but he was also the man not actively involved in combat operations. Kenney's biographer, Thomas E. Griffith, said: "Though Kenney did not personally produce every new or innovative idea, his focus on improving methods and a willingness to jettison established routines encouraged innovation in his command." He demonstrated a preference for attack aviation going back to the Air Corps Tactical School (ACTS), where he led that department. Therefore, the two were bound to clash.[3]

In June 1943, Kenney wrote to Arnold regarding what he called "attack aviation." Though the letter is lengthy, a segment of it and some of Kuter's equally lengthy retort are worth quoting in their entirety. Kenney wrote to Arnold:

> Speaking of attack aviation, how about putting these words back in the Air Corps dictionary? The tactics of attack aviation are still sound, we have proven them effective and they are more in evidence every day all over the world. We have yet to lose a plane with low altitude work against shipping and it is not because we have no opposition. The secret is high speed approach and exit under cover of a lot of forward gun fire. What I would like to have you do is put attack aviation back on the map and as soon as I get these groups fixed up for this type of work let me organize an attack command. . . . It would be a popular move and I believe it would be much better than breaking the Bomber Command into two or more wings when there are too many groups to handle under one command control.[4]

Kenney's letter was interesting several respects. First, his statement that he had yet to lose a plane at low altitude was patently false. He had even lost a B-17 on a low-level bombing mission and, with it, Brigadier General Kenneth Walker. Second, he should have known that what worked in one theater or even on one mission might not translate to the air force as a whole. Arnold asked Kuter to draft a reply.[5] To say that Kuter held nothing back in his response would be gross understatement: "Your proposition that the words, 'attack aviation' be put back in the Air Corps dictionary is a bit confusing. Surely you are not talking about your own personal dictionary, since you have never asked any one's approval of your extraordinary vocabulary before. The enclosed press release confirms my belief. Quite evidently you already have an 'Attack Group' and 'Attack Squadrons.'"[6] Kuter went on to state that the term *attack aviation* was incorrect and redundant for two reasons. First: "Attack tactics have *definitely not* as you state proven sound 'every day all over the world.'" Kuter pointed out that an attempt by Eaker to use B-26s in an attack role resulted in a loss of eleven of eleven aircraft and that changes in German tactics had made attack tactics below sixty-five hundred feet completely prohibitive in the European and Mediterranean theaters. He was not entirely accurate here as "skip bombing" proved effective in both the Mediterranean and the Southwest Pacific.[7]

Kuter's second point was that it was Kenney's tactics that were different from those employed in the other theaters, not that he had developed a unique form of aerial warfare necessitating a new classification. He pointed out that Kenney was simply using bomber and fighter aircraft in a unique manner and that it did not matter whether these aircraft operated at "high, medium, or low altitude"; their fundamental application did not change. He closed his eviscerating letter: "Lest there be any doubt, however, you are perfectly free to continue using your own unexpurgated vocabulary."[8]

While this letter initially seems to indicate an extreme antipathy between Kuter and Kenney, nothing was further from the truth. The two had known each other for years—since the early 1930s—and were actually on quite friendly terms. In fact, when Arnold first wanted to send him overseas in late 1942 to get combat experience, Kuter initially wanted to serve under Kenney in the Southwest Pacific. Before Arnold decided to send Kuter to Europe, he had sent Kenney a message on his thoughts about having Kuter serve under him. Kenney's response was "glad to have him." Kuter's abrasive letter seemed to be the kind of gruff, toughly worded letter that Kenney would have expected to come from Washington. Kuter was not being rude; he was simply speaking Kenny's language.[9]

Field Manual 100-20

In 1983, William Momyer sat down with air force historians to discuss the air war during World War II. About Kuter and FM 100-20 (*Command and Employment of Air Power*) he said:

> Kuter came back at the time from North Africa, as you will recall, and made that the basis of the writing of the [Field Manual] 100-20. The 100-20 was really the emancipation proclamation, I call it, of air power, at least of tactical air power. It was the first time it was really set down in unequivocal terms as to the priority of missions. The first priority was to gain and maintain air superiority. The second priority was to isolate the battlefield. The third priority was to support the ground forces. That, I think then, you can say kind of summed up what came out of the North African campaign. Those three elements. For the first time, I think we had a doctrine that you could talk about in for-

malized terms and people could now see that this was the way it was going to be employed.[10]

Kuter departed North Africa in May, as we have seen, and returned to work on the Air Staff shortly thereafter, except he now worked in the recently opened Pentagon. The War Department published FM 100-20 on 21 July 1943. It is probable that the publication was in an advanced draft form or even in production before Kuter returned from North Africa. The historian David Mets certainly believed so. He called the contents of FM 100-20 "corporate property," ideas that existed prior to Kuter deploying overseas. This may be true, but Kuter pushed these concepts into the public sphere on his return.[11]

The manual was concise enough, a scant fourteen pages, its content self-explanatory and not inflammatory, and Mets is probably correct that the ideas found in it were common knowledge and accepted in the air arm all the way back to ACTS. But this should not lessen its importance or Kuter's contributions in promoting it. The most important line in the document was the following: "Land Power and Air Power are co-equal and interdependent forces; neither is an auxiliary of the other." Even if this principle was accepted among air officers prior to or during the war, its codification in an official publication was extremely important. Air officers now had it in writing that their branch was "co-equal" to the land component. Land commanders also had to accept this as codified doctrine now, which, after their experiences in North Africa, most of them did.[12]

Even if Kuter did not personally write FM 100-20, there are a lot of experiences from North Africa found in the document, which is why his name has been linked to it for the past seventy plus years. The organization and employment of air forces in combat closely mirror the organization and operations he helped establish in NAAF before becoming Coningham's deputy in the NATAF. FM 100-20 called for each war-fighting air force to be composed of a strategic air force (for strategic and deeper targets) and a tactical air force (for ground support) in addition to air defense and air support forces. If Kuter did not write FM 100-20, his fingerprints were all over it and his DNA found within it.[13]

The War against Japan and the B-29

The planning for the overall air offensive against Japan reached a new level of importance in 1943. The war in Germany with the B-17 and the B-24 was finally under way in a meaningful manner, and the Air Staff turned its attention to the bombing of Japan. Beyond missions being flown from China, planners set their sights on air attacks from other directions. It was time to organize a strategic army air force in the Pacific. Arnold oversaw the establishment of this command from his office in Washington, and Brigadier General Kuter served as his chief of staff and deputy chief of staff plans. Kuter set about organizing this aerial effort in the hope of playing a more meaningful role in the war than he had in Europe. He wanted a combat command in the Pacific. The basis for this effort was the 20th Air Force and, when it moved into the Pacific, the 8th Air Force. These units later formed the US Army Strategic Air Force, Pacific.

In August 1943, Kuter's assignment involved determining how quickly strategic and tactical air forces could pivot from Europe to the Pacific. If Germany collapsed in 1944, the air war could be further prosecuted as early as 1945 despite current guidance stating that no full war against Japan would begin until 1947. Clearly, planning statistics current in 1943 assumed that the war in Europe was going to continue for as many as five more years. In a private letter to Arnold on 9 August, Kuter argued that Japan could be defeated no sooner than 1946 and, only then, if "large numbers of B-29s and B-35s can be operational in the face of final desperate Japanese opposition."[14]

In this letter, Kuter pointed out that aerial combat over Japan was likely to include "heroics" on the part of the Japanese involving their aircraft colliding with the bomber force—something that would indeed come to pass in the Pacific theater—and that the B-35 should be properly armed to prevent their destruction in this manner. The fact that the B-35 was actively being planned for indicated just how long military planners believed the war was going to last.[15]

Despite being considered one of Hap Arnold's indispensable officers, Kuter was by no means what one could call a yes-man. Not only would he argue with Arnold, but he would also ensure that his objections made it into written form. A particular incident in August 1943 demonstrated the extent to which Kuter would go to indicate his disagreement with the senior air force commander. Arnold, returning to his office after a meeting of the Joint Chiefs, took umbrage with a report indicating that the German air force was actually increasing its production of aircraft despite the hits taken as part of the strategic air campaign. Kuter wrote to Arnold that the numbers were, in fact, true and represented the best data from both American and British sources. He noted there was no way around the facts: the German fighter force was increasing rather than decreasing. Still, he made it plain that he was perfectly willing to allow Arnold to accept the production numbers or not: "It is very clearly the prerogative of the Commander to throw that advice away and place [i.e., use] any figures which he may choose." Kuter was not afraid to stand up to Arnold.[16]

Victory through Air Power

Kuter and Arnold also disagreed on another matter, but this divergence stemmed from Arnold's personal animosity for Alexander de Seversky, author of the book—and the star of the Disney film of the same name—*Victory through Air Power*. Seversky and Arnold both shared a deep and unending enmity for each other, although Seversky counted Kuter as a close friend. Kuter thought the same of Seversky, calling him "Alec" and "Sasha." While personal and professional disagreements could often be overcome, there was little chance of Kuter getting Arnold to agree to anything if Seversky was going to be involved. Seversky's story bears telling here as prelude to a personal conflict that eventually embroiled Kuter as well.[17]

Alexander Prokofiev Seversky was born in Russia (in the present-day Georgia) in 1894 to parents of noble ancestry. He attended military school and eventually the Russian naval academy, from which he graduated in 1914, just prior to the beginning of World War I. During the war, he transferred to the flying service. On his first combat mission in 1915, he was shot down by antiaircraft fire during a bombing run against a battleship. His plane hit the water and exploded, and Seversky lost his right leg in the process. This in no way deterred the intrepid young aviator, and, after more than a year off, during which time he worked in aircraft production, he returned to flying status, eventually becoming an ace and shooting down a total of thirteen German aircraft. During one mission, "he was shot in the leg—although now he required the services of a carpenter rather than a doctor." His gallantry in combat earned him multiple awards, including the Cross of Saint George, the highest military award of imperial Russia. Later in the war, he was sent to the United States as part of the Russian naval mission, an assignment from which he would never return. As the Bolsheviks took control of Russia, Seversky (now de Seversky owing to a mistake made when he entered the country) elected to stay in the United States.[18]

Seversky spent his early years in America moving from place to place and employed in various jobs. It was while living in New York as an aircraft inspector that he met the army air corps officer and advocate Billy Mitchell. At this time, Mitchell was attempting to show the world the efficacy of air power by sinking surface ships from the air. Seversky claimed years later that it was he who suggested to Mitchell the idea of dropping bombs next to ships—not on them—to cause a "water hammer" effect that would open gaps in the side of the vessel below the waterline. No matter who proposed the idea, it worked, and Mitchell used it in 1921 when he sank the German battleship *Ostfriesland*. Seversky later moved to Ohio, where he worked with the army air corps on various assignments. Perhaps the most revolutionary of these assignments was an air-refueling device that was used on the "Question Mark" mission in 1929. Question Mark proved conclusively that air refueling was an achievable goal as it enabled the air corps to keep a plane in the air for seven consecutive days.[19]

In 1931, Seversky organized the Seversky Aircraft Corporation. At the time, many of his employees were fellow Russian expatriates. The company had modestly successful dealings with the US War Department and in 1936, competing with the Curtiss Aeroplane Company, won a government contract. Thus, the Seversky P-35 became the first all-metal, enclosed cockpit, fighter interceptor procured by the US Army Air Corps. Sadly, despite its many attractive features, the plane was nearly impossible to fly, and many were lost in accidents. Even though the P-35 had retractable landing gear (also a first for the air corps), "there was no way for the pilot to tell whether it was down and locked in place." The crashes that resulted from the landing gear problem proved that the overall design an inadequate. As a result, most of the aircraft were converted to trainers, though a few still flourished on active duty, thousands of miles from the continental United States. Of those still on active service in 1941, most were destroyed when the Japanese invaded the Philippines.[20]

While Seversky was designing and building aircraft, he was also busy pestering the chief of the US Army Air Corps, Major General Henry Arnold. At this time, Seversky was a proponent of escort and pursuit aircraft, and he lost no time in making his thoughts about the validity of pursuit aviation known to Arnold. Arnold's response to the criticism is not my subject here; however, it is known that he intervened with the board of directors of Seversky's company, which was already facing financial hardships and needed nothing more to tip the scales against Seversky. Geoffrey Perret described Seversky's removal this way: "Seversky was no business executive. Seversky Airplane Company was run haphazardly, according to its founder's whims and idiosyncrasies. He'd also earned the antagonism of Arnold. Seversky kept telling him he was going to have to build thousands of long-range escorts. Arnold didn't want to believe, didn't want to hear it. In October 1939 Seversky Airplane Company, under pressure from Arnold, ousted dynamic, colorful Sasha and was reorganized as Republic Aviation."[21]

Seversky was furious at Arnold for the intercession and never forgave him. It would be a contentious feud that remained heated throughout World War II. As far as Seversky was concerned, anything that went wrong with the US Army Air Corps and the US Army Air Force over the following decade inevitably fell at the feet of Arnold. As the historian Phillip Meilinger noted: "For the next several years, de Seversky blamed Arnold for every deficiency—real or perceived—that he found in American airpower." Unfortunately for Arnold, the ouster did not solve his Seversky problem; in fact, it inadvertently made it far worse. Now free of the restraints of running a company Seversky had nothing but time on his hands, time he used to write.[22]

After being ousted from his aircraft manufacturing company, Seversky turned his attention to writing and in 1942 released *Victory through Air Power*. The book was an instant hit. *Reader's Digest* released a condensed version, which gave the work an even wider readership. It is estimated that, by the time the film version was released, an estimated five million people had read *Victory through Air Power* and that fifteen million more knew of Seversky's perspectives on and theories of air power.[23]

Seversky's thesis was self-evident from his book's title. Seversky argued that victory, not just in World War II but in any war, could be won only through the use of long-range strategic air power. Unlike many other authors writing at the same time, he warned of dire consequences for not taking immediate action: "A realistic understanding of the new weapon, of its implications in terms of national security, of its challenge to America, is not a matter of choice. It is the very condition on national survival." He also called for the army air force to be reorganized into a separate and independent service, calling the action *emancipation*. The same word was being used inside the Air Staff at this time, especially with regard to FM 100-20.[24]

Once the book was released, two camps developed: those who were intrigued by Seversky's ideas and those who were opposed. The historian Charles Beard was quoted on its cover as saying: "In my opinion this book is more important to America than all the other war books put together." However, this was not a universal opinion, and those who would seem at first glance to be proponents of Seversky's were actually his biggest detractors. The US Army Air Force—and Hap Arnold especially—was less than thrilled with the book. There were those inside the air force who wanted independence, but wartime was not the right time to have these discussions. Seversky put the discussion into the public sphere, something Arnold wanted to avoid. Arnold's reluctance does not preclude the possibility that Arnold already had an agreement with General George Marshall about the creation of an independent air force and that he therefore felt that Seversky's making waves might disrupt things.[25] In any case, Arnold went on the offensive. The historian Russell Lee had this to say about Arnold's attacks:

> Arnold wrote to General George V. Strong, head of Military Intelligence, describing Seversky's accusations. His comments were tolerable in peacetime, Arnold said, but during a war "a serious situation is created when anyone breaks down the morale of the people of the United States, builds up in them a lack of confidence in the equipment that our fighting forces use, have sisters, mothers, and wives of aviators protest against their brothers, sons, and husbands flying inferior equipment." Arnold added ominously, "I think this is a matter for drastic action." Seversky's statements might actually aid the enemy, Arnold continued, and the charge of treason was a real possibility. However, by protesting the publicist's accusations, the general validated some claims.[26]

Arnold also unleashed Brigadier General Paul B. Malone on Seversky. Malone went vicious from the start: "I want to correct De Seversky's statements. . . . I think that De Seversky is a near subversionist. He is doing a lot of harm . . . completely disrupting the organization, both of the Army and Navy." However, he went one step too far, questioning Seversky's military record as well as his knowledge and understanding of American air power. While it is not unusual to see retired officers criticize each other, it is unusual for attacks to sink to the level of questioning someone's military record, especially someone as decorated as Seversky. Malone was also apparently woefully unaware of Seversky's contributions to the design of aircraft being flown by the army air force, which made Seversky an eminent source on American air power.[27]

The attacks by Arnold and others did very little to stem the readership of *Victory through Air Power.* If anything, they only further exasperated the efforts to discredit Seversky by giving him a wider audience and making more people familiar with the flamboyant Russian. Perhaps the biggest reason the army air force could do little to stop Seversky was that he was outside the operational chain of command. Even though he technically held the rank of a major in the reserves, this was more of an honorarium. He was therefore untouchable, unlike his predecessor and self-described mentor Billy Mitchell, who had faced a court-martial over similar issues.

Not all the military powers rallied against Seversky. In January 1943, Brigadier General Claire Chennault—the former commander of the Flying Tigers and now the head of the China Air Task Force, having exiled himself to the Far East for disagreeing with fellow air corps officers at ACTS—wrote the publisher disagreeing with the theory that the "bomber will always get through" and prescribing long-range fighter escort, which placed him in stark contrast to the dominant paradigm of long-range strategic bombing. He thanked the Simon and Schuster people for the copy of *Victory through Air Power,* and he took the occasion to express his opinions of Seversky and the current leadership of the army air forces. The historian Russell Lee described Chennault's thoughts this way: "According to Chennault, many American military leaders were responsible for the poor state of air readiness when war began. The general now hoped that 'proper weight will be given to air power now to insure early victory and minimum losses.'"[28]

This was where Larry Kuter also figured in the story. In 1942, prior to his deployment to England and North Africa and while working for Arnold and the new Air Staff, Kuter and Brigadier General Harold George renewed their acquaintance with Seversky; George and Seversky had known each other since 1920. The Seversky biographer James K. Libbey said that Kuter and George "both belonged to the camp of officers who believed de Seversky, despite his criticisms, correctly championed the quest for air power and an independent air force." A lifelong friendship developed between the three men.[29]

Both George and Kuter believed that Seversky was better as an ally than as an adversary, and they wanted to heal the rift between Seversky and Arnold. (Kuter did admit that doing so would be difficult because Seversky had "two hates"—"the Republic Aircraft Corporation and Gen Arnold"—and Arnold "was never noted for his restraint or tolerance in matters involving Seversky.") After the Battle of Midway, when Arnold expressed frustration with the US Navy, George saw his chance. The two officers scheduled a "peace talk" meeting between the air chief and the author in Arnold's office. Kuter remembered that Seversky was currently reaching a "big audience" with his writing and that he and George wanted Seversky to take a "much kinder view" toward Arnold. Things did not go well.[30]

When it came time for the meeting, George and Seversky entered Arnold's office, Kuter staying behind, but Arnold shouted out to Kuter: "You come in here, too." There followed minutes of dead silence as Arnold and Seversky stared at each other. Arnold, who was willing to discuss problems with the air service with his closest advisers, refused to discuss anything critical of any service with Seversky. Finally, Arnold broke the silence by asking Seversky: "So what?" Seversky shouted back: "So what? What so what?" Arnold went on the offensive: "You don't know what the hell you are writing. You have no information. You are writing something that has nothing to do with reality or fact. You are writing about things you cannot possibly know about unless there is a leak in this office." After uttering this, Arnold shifted his gaze to George and Kuter, who "both stiffened" in their seats.[31]

At some point during the meeting, Kuter and George either asked to leave or were kicked out of the room by Arnold. Arnold and Seversky continued shouting at each other as Seversky limped out of the office. It was the last meeting between the two for three years. Kuter and George now dropped the idea of converting Seversky into an Arnold ally, but Seversky refused to go away and was about to become an even bigger thorn in Arnold's side thanks to the interest shown in the Disney version of *Victory through Air Power*. Kuter would get pulled into the battle again.[32]

By the time Walt Disney came across the book, it was estimated that 5 million people had read *Victory* and another 20 million, out of a population of 130 million, knew of Seversky and were familiar with his ideas. Sometime in late 1942, *Reader's Digest* sent a copy of *Victory through Air Power,* along with several other short stories, to Disney in the hopes that he would be interested in producing them as educational and family-oriented films. While the collaboration never came to fruition, *Victory through Air Power* struck a chord with Walt Disney. This was the chance he had been waiting for. This was the opportunity for the company to contribute something original to the war effort and, just as important, something outside government control. The book was also heavily laden with futuristic concepts, which appealed to Disney's fascination with technology. He immediately set about securing the rights to transform the book into a film version.[33]

The motivation for making a film about air power was about more than just a love of technology or a desire to do something outside government control. Disney strongly believed in the ideas behind the book. However, in making *Victory through Air Power* into a movie, he would be producing a purely topical film that would have little life beyond its initial production, as opposed to his other feature films, which he had always envisioned as being timeless. As Richard Shale said: "After the war the film would be virtually useless." Or, as Leonard Maltin put it: "For a man whose financial standing was rather shaky, and whose studio was thriving on military assignments, it was a bold move." Nevertheless, Disney had committed himself fully to this bold new project, and, once he made a decision, nothing could change his mind.[34]

Victory through Air Power was filmed in late 1942 and early 1943 while Kuter was in England and North Africa. It premiered that summer. Outside military and government circles opinions were mixed. William Randolph Hearst and Nelson Rockefeller praised the film. The film critic James Agee felt: "I was sold something under pretty high pressure, which I don't enjoy, and I am staggered by the ease with which such self-confidence, on matters of such importance, can be blared all over a nation, without cross-questioning."[35] The *New York Times* reported:

> On purely cinematic terms "Victory through Airpower" is an extraordinary accomplishment, marking it as it were a new milestone in the screen's recently accelerated march toward maturity. Mr. Disney has adroitly blended the documentary technique of presentation with his own highly skilled cartoon form of infectious humor. The result is a delightful and stimulating combination entertainment-information film. . . . If "Victory through Air Power" is propaganda; it is at least the most encouraging and inspiring propaganda that the screen has afforded us in a long time. Mr. Disney and staff can be proud of their accomplishment.[36]

On 23 June 23 1943, Larry Kuter broached the topic of Seversky with Arnold for the first time in more than a year. He placed a memorandum with an attached article from the *Los Angeles Times* regarding the Disney *Victory through Air Power* in the general's daily mail. The review not only praised the movie and Seversky's work, saying that everyone in America should see the film, but also noted that recent victories in Europe "have been through air power." Devoid of any personal animosity, the film was, in fact, very pro–air power. Kuter assured Arnold that the Disney version had "been stripped of all personal prejudice." This tentative olive branch received a brusque response, the single handwritten word "Noted." Kuter knew better than to press the matter further at this point.[37]

Arnold was otherwise mute on the subject. When the film previewed in August, he remained silent while many members of his senior staff actually praised it. At the Quebec conference, Churchill convinced Roosevelt to see the film, and Arnold was forced to have Kuter procure a copy. There is a legend that, against his own wishes, Arnold called Kuter, who was back in Washington, told him to procure a plane and a copy of the film, and get to Quebec as quickly as possible. It is difficult to know whether this is true. Kuter was an air planner at the conference but when discussing the conference then or later never mentioned anything about the film or having to get a copy of it. The president watched the film once with Churchill and then had the Combined Chiefs of Staff watch it. While Arnold made no overt statements on the film, it is clear that he no longer felt that it was a good idea to attack Seversky publicly, especially now that he seemed to be aligned with Walt Disney.[38] Russell Lee described Arnold's options once the film was released: "Despite his concern, Arnold . . . took no official position on the making of *Victory through Air Power.* Assuming the film mirrored the publication, [the army air forces] could not promote it, yet dared not oppose it openly. The popular backlash sure to result from attacking an entertainment icon like Disney could permanently damage political support for the [army air force]. Their public image was no match against Disney."[39]

Seversky remained in touch with Kuter after the incident, sending him at least one more letter, and asking to be provided a comprehensive air strategy. Whether the previous meeting between Seversky and Arnold had anything to do with Kuter's feelings toward Seversky is not known. Kuter drafted a reply to Seversky, but it is marked "not sent." Close to the same time he did send a memo to Arnold regarding air strategy against Japan in which he called on Arnold to form a committee of "avowed civil air power experts," swear them to secrecy, and present the plan and current strategy for the defeat of Japan. He then wanted these experts—including Seversky, Bill Ziff, and Al Williams—to be sent to Maxwell Field and have them help create an air-only plan to defeat Japan. He proposed included civilians in the planning because he recognized that it was possible for military officers to overlook things that the civilians would not. This plan never gained enough momentum to be pursued further.[40]

Kuter did not waste any more time on the Seversky issue. He knew Arnold well enough to know when he wanted something dropped. He turned his attention back to the Pacific and the development of the B-29. In a 15 September 1943 memorandum to a Major Wildman on a proposed test of the B-29, he indicated that he wanted "the test to simulate in all practicable items an attack on Tokyo by 100 B-29s from a base in the Changsha area." Furthermore, the flight should have as "much practical realism as can be foreseen should be inserted in this first test."[41]

On the same day that Kuter was working on the B-29 project, he was also dealing with issues of overwork of the Air Staff personnel. He had personally visited the Pentagon at 11:00 P.M. on a recent Saturday to find more than twenty members of the staff working on an "all-night program planning job." He noted that, even though the country was at war, this had to stop as one member of his staff was "believed . . . to be in a psychopathic ward at Walter Reed Hospital as a direct result of overwork." He sent as many officers home as he could and tried to get a semblance of work-life balance instilled at the Pentagon. It is clear that he recognized that a burned-out staff did not serve the needs of anybody: he himself, Arnold, or the air force as a whole.[42]

Cairo Conference

In November 1943 Kuter, accompanied General Arnold to the Cairo Conference. He departed with Arnold and another twenty general and flag officers on board Admiral King's flagship, the *Dauntless*, on 11 November. A few hours later, out in the Hampton Roads portion of the Chesapeake Bay, they transferred to the battleship *Iowa*. The other army air force officers who boarded the *Iowa* with Arnold and Kuter were Generals Hansell and Emmitt "Rosie" O'Donnell. At 9:00 the next morning, President Roosevelt arrived on his yacht, the *Potomac*, and came on board along with Admiral Leahy and the presidential adviser Harry Hopkins, and the battle group set off across the ocean.

The transatlantic voyage was not without its terrors. With so many general and flag officers, not to mention the president, held as a captive audience aboard the *Iowa*, the navy crews put on a display of gunnery practice and torpedo exercises for the benefit of their guests. In the middle of the display, Arnold pointed over the side of the ship and shouted: "What is that?!" A torpedo was heading directly for the *Iowa*. Now the guns that had been trained skyward kicked up bits of ocean as everything was turned on the incoming torpedo. The assembled guests stared in disbelief as it approached. It was a tense few moments, but eventually the torpedo slipped behind the ship and exploded in its wake with a deafening roar that shook the ship as if a "heavy door had been slammed."[43]

It was later determined that an inexperienced crew on the USS *Dewey* had fired the errant torpedo. Since Admiral King had just explained to the assembled guests how accurate the new torpedoes were, Arnold wasted no time in ribbing him: "Ernie, you tell us that these sonic torpedoes can't miss. That *Dewey* was only 500 to 600 yards away and missed this great big target. What's the matter with your sonic torpedoes? It went off astern back there." The mission continued with Arnold poking King for the duration of the crossing. The president and the rest of distinguished visitors made port in Oran on 20 November, and from there the group motorcaded to the airport for the flight to Tunis to meet Eisenhower. After a day of briefings, the president, with the dozens of generals and admirals in tow, flew to Cairo.[44]

The conference itself went smoothly. Roosevelt met with Chinese president Chiang Kai-shek and British prime minister Winston Churchill and discussed the future of the war with Japan. Stalin did not attend the conference since this could have triggered the Japanese to declare war on Russia, although at this point in the war none of the major powers felt that the Japanese Empire could realistically fight the Soviet Union. This was Kuter's first interaction with Generalissimo Chiang Kai-shek, but it would not be his last.

The trip was not all work, and traveling with General Arnold apparently had its perks. On 5 December, Arnold's entourage flew to Luxor and visited Tutankhamen's tomb and the Valley of the Kings. The next day, they flew to Tel Aviv to visit Jerusalem and Bethlehem. Kuter noted that the group was "vastly disappointed by the shoddy, commercialized scene of the birth of Christianity in contrast with the magnificent splendor of far more ancient Egyptian pagan culture at Luxor."[45]

1944

In 1944, Laurence S. Kuter became one of the most traveled men in the US military. January found him still in Washington, DC, attending dinners and parties with Ethel, and catching up with old friends, including Possum Hansell, while serving on Arnold's staff. His travels had only recently ended—with his return from the Cairo conference—but they paled in comparison to what was to come. In the meantime, he continued to work the needs of the army air force in advance of the coming invasion of France.

Brigadier General Kuter, now the assistant chief of staff for plans under Arnold, forwarded a copy of the report "Air Operations in Western Europe in 1944" to Lieutenant General Spaatz. Although he knew for a fact that Brereton and Eaker had copies of the report, he did not have confirmation that Spaatz, who was actually overseeing air operations in Europe, did: "As I have no way of knowing whether you yourself have ever seen it . . . I am forwarding it to you personally." One wonders, however, why Arnold's wartime commander in the European theater would not have a copy of the plan that Arnold produced in the first place.[46]

The report, compiled by Kuter and signed by Arnold himself, set forth the Air Staff's guidance for the specific tasks, targets, and steps to be taken in the lead-up to the invasion sometime in the spring or early summer of 1944. This included first and foremost the "Defeat or Neutralization of the enemy air forces in the assault area" by attacking German aircraft assembly and engine factories in Germany and the destruction of existing aircraft in the air and on the ground or at least their containment in order to keep them away from the assault area. Following the attainment of air superiority was defense of the surface assault force, defense of the shipping lanes, isolation of German troops in the combat zone, preventing reinforcement of the beachhead, and, finally, the direct support of the troops coming ashore, gaining and maintaining a hold on the continent, and moving inland.[47]

Arnold's report noted that, by this point in early 1944, the POINT-BLANK directive and combined bombing offensive was already seriously degrading German aircraft production. Although Germany would continue production throughout the war, it was not the bombing offensive that was having the biggest effect but, unbeknownst to Arnold, the fact that it was losing qualified fighter pilots faster than they could be replaced. As previously noted, Kuter had already informed Arnold that aircraft production in Germany continued to increase.

In his opening letter, Kuter called Spaatz's attention to Tab A of the report—labeled "Top Flight"—which was the portion of Overlord preparation dedicated to the destruction and dislocation of the Axis transportation system. The report noted that rail traffic accounted for 75 percent of Axis freight movement and passenger travel. Arnold wanted all rail capacity destroyed, including "marshalling yards, railroad and highway bridges," and, finally, "trains and truck conveys in motion." The report then detailed all rail lines, their routes between major cities, and the associated bridges to be attacked. The key marshaling yards were Antwerp, Liege, Dusseldorf, Cologne, Ehrang, Saarbrucken, Strasburg, and Paris. Although the strategic air war against Germany continued, Air Staff planners recognized the necessity of preparing the close-in battle space for the coming invasion.[48]

Kuter's own opinions on the use of strategic bombardment forces prior to the D-Day landings were, again, pragmatic. He later recalled that he still wanted the 8th and the 15th Air Forces to attack petroleum, oil, and lubrication targets, but he was not wedded to their exclusive use against those target sets. As far back as the Air War Plans Division–Plan 1, strategic bomber forces were expected to be used in direct support of invasion "if it should prove to be necessary," and, although Kuter did not personally believe that their use was necessary prior to the D-Day invasion, he did not argue openly against it. He called the deeper strategic targets the "proper targets" for the heavy bombers but never once argued against their use to support ground forces in the attacks on the transportation network. Kuter and Spaatz might have both believed that a strategic air war was the proper use of heavy bombers, but those attacks against the railroads and bridges prior to D-Day paid dividends. German supply routes were significantly degraded prior to the invasion to allow the Allied forces to gain a foothold and push inland. The Wehrmacht did not have the logistics necessary to hurl the Allies back into the sea.[49]

Trip around the World

On 22 February, Kuter departed Washington, DC, during a driving rainstorm for a thirty-two-thousand-mile trip around the globe. His mission was a series of briefings with the major commands. General Marshall wanted each service chief to brief as many commands in person on the "thinking of the combined chiefs-of-staff," and each service chief picked a trusted adviser. Arnold chose Larry Kuter. From Washington, the group traveled to Bermuda, then to Casablanca via the Azores (25 February). From Casablanca they headed to Algiers and a conference with Ira Eaker and General Spaatz (27 February). (Kuter was back in North Africa for the third time in one year.) They moved on to Cairo, Baghdad, and the Persian city of Abadan (1 March), next Bahrain and Karachi (3 March), then Jodhpur, Delhi, Agra, and the Taj Mahal (6–8 March), and then eastern India in preparation for a flight "over the hump" into China. On 11 March, Kuter and the rest of the party crossed the hump and landed in Kunming, where they were met by Kuter's old flying friend and ACTS instructor Major General Claire Chennault.[50]

Here in China, the group met with Chennault and Stratemeyer and visited American combat units actively engaged against the Japanese. The respite, if it could be called that, was brief. They departed from Kunming on 15 March, arriving the next day in Calcutta, a city marked by "heat, squalor, congestion, starving Bengalese, burning ghats and other unpleasant aspects of India." The next few days proved to be a confusing back-and-forth between Calcutta, Columbo, and Delhi (to meet with Stratemeyer again). From Colombo, the group ventured out into the Pacific for the "longest flight in world navigation," a thirty-two-hundred-mile jump to the Exmouth Gulf in northwestern Australia (25 March). This was followed by the "dullest flight in world navigation," a twenty-five-hundred-mile trip directly across Australia with a late-night arrival in Brisbane. Arrival in Australia was another welcome respite from flying. There, Kuter met with General Kenney, General MacArthur's chief of air operations.[51]

Kuter was supposed to meet with General MacArthur, but MacArthur's chief of staff, Brigadier General Richard Sutherland, stonewalled him and sent him directly to Kenney without allowing him to pay MacArthur a courtesy visit. Kuter, again speaking on behalf of Arnold, met with Kenney to explain that he still would not receive any B-29s for use in the Southwest Pacific. The new bombers, operating out of Tinian, Guam, and Saipan, would be used against the Japanese homeland rather than the Philippines. Kenney's biographer, Thomas Griffith, noted: "Kenney paid little attention [even after Kuter explained the situation] and returned to his sales efforts." But Kuter remained "unimpressed." Kenney recorded in his diary: "I remarked that I hoped no one expected me to cheer either decisions or the beliefs that he had voiced." He grudgingly accepted the reality that no B-29s were coming to him and that arguing with Kuter was just as useless as arguing with Arnold.[52]

The third phase of this trip was a further tour of the Southwest Pacific theater that included Townesville (29 March) and Nadzab (30 March), both in New Guinea, and then Guadalcanal (31 March) and Tarawa (1 April). These hops included flights around Japanese-controlled islands and meetings with various staff and command elements, including the 5th Air Force. The trip was nearing its end. From Tarawa the group headed to Johnston Island and then to Hickam Field in Pearl Harbor for a meeting with Admiral Nimitz and, finally, to Long Beach, California, and the final flight. Kuter landed back in Washington, DC, in heavy rain on 6 April. If he hoped for a few months of stability away from flying, he was soon to be disappointed.[53]

In late February, at the very beginning of his around-the-world trip, Brigadier General Kuter was promoted to major general. On the night of 3 March, Ethel received a telephone call. This caused a "flutter of fear" since she knew Larry was traveling. However, the news was good. On the other end of the phone were the Hansells, the Fairchilds, and the rest of the plans division informing her that General Arnold had nominated her husband for promotion. Ethel was thrilled, but she did not know whether Larry knew. Once she took a minute to think, she realized that she was not even sure where Larry was. At that moment, there were several places he could have been. As it turned out, 3 March found Kuter on the island of Bahrain en route to Karachi.[54]

D-Day

Kuter's time back in his office was short-lived. He remained in Washington for just over a month before Arnold told him he was headed overseas again, this time to observe the invasion of Normandy. All the US chiefs of staff planned to be in England shortly after the invasion. This served the dual purpose of actually being there for the big event but also being able to directly support Eisenhower should something go terribly wrong. Arnold wanted to send Kuter on ahead as a member of the advance party. This created a slight problem. There was no good reason for Kuter to be out of the office, and his attachment to Arnold would indicate that something was up should he fly to England. This was also true of the other members of the advance party, but more so for Kuter since he had just returned. The departure of any senior staff members from Washington was always of interest to the press, and, if a group of senior officers from each service departed at the same time, it would certainly make the papers the next day. Some way had to be devised to secret the advance party out of the capital without anyone knowing it.[55] The advance party included two general officers, a navy flag officer, two bird colonels, and a navy captain: Kuter and Colonel Fred Dean from the army air force, Major General T. J. Handy and Colonel George Lincoln from the army, and Rear Admiral C. M. Cooke Jr. and Captain D. R. Osborn from the navy.[56]

Each officer was given a "cover plan" to explain his absence. Kuter's proved easy enough. Having just returned from the trip around the world, it was only natural for him to have a break. General Arnold "ordered" him away to rest, relax, and catch some fish. This story also served to put off anyone looking for signs of the invasion since it was highly unlikely that Arnold would send Kuter away if the invasion was imminent. Kuter departed for his "fishing trip" on 28 May. The other officers rendezvoused at Washington National Airport and boarded a DC-4 parked in a "remote corner" with its entrance door facing a hangar that was unlikely to draw attention. The aircraft departed with only ten men aboard, allowing them to travel "under conditions of considerable luxury." As it turned out, "luxury and security this time went hand-in hand."[57]

Kuter and the others were originally head to Stephensville, Newfoundland, but found it closed by weather and headed to Goose Bay instead. Since they were traveling under heavy security, the troops at Goose Bay were quite surprised when so many senior officers deplaned on their runway. Staff cars replaced the initial jeeps, and a satisfactory dinner was produced. Most importantly, "the keys to the bar were finally located." From there it was on to Prestwick, Scotland, for fuel and, finally, Bovingdon, thirty miles northwest of London.[58]

Kuter and the other staff officers arrived and set to work preparing for the arrival of their bosses, but, for Kuter, that chore had to wait until after the welcome dinner with General Spaatz. The following morning, Kuter secured the necessary arrangements for Arnold and started making the time-honored commitment of office calls, including one on General Eisenhower and his chief of staff, Lieutenant General Bedell Smith. It is important to remember that, although Eisenhower and Kuter were separated by only two stars, Eisenhower was still fifteen years Kuter's senior. (Kuter had turned thirty-nine the day he departed for England.) Both officers expressed confidence in the invasion plan but showed a reserved hesitation, particularly when it came to the impending drop of the American and British airborne troops. Kuter also spent much of the next week visiting American aerial units of all kinds—fighter, bomber, and transport—to get a sense of their preparedness for the coming operation. Prior to departing Eisenhower's headquarters, he met a final time with the other members of the advance party, and all agreed to find a way to participate in or observe the invasion. Since their senior officers were not scheduled to arrive until after the invasion, and since all the necessary arrangements had already been made, there seemed to be no good reason why they should not find somewhere to observe the invasion that was as close to the front as possible. Kuter, as the senior airmen, had a better chance than the others of getting an overall view of the actual landing zones.[59]

In visiting the fighter and bomber units, Kuter noticed an "indifference" to the coming invasion. He found the explanation quite simple. When it came to the ground armies, many soldiers were entering combat for the first time. However: "This air crowd had been fighting its battle day in and day out for a couple of years. Its role in connection with the actual invasion was only a little more of the same, except this time against very much softer, less-heavily defended objectives." The tremendous casualties suffered by the strategic bombing units of the 8th Air Force throughout the war are often forgotten. More than twenty-six thousand men of the 8th Air Force alone lost their lives in the skies over Europe.[60]

In the early morning hours of 6 June, Major General Larry Kuter departed in a B-17 flown by Major General R. B. Williamson, the commander of Kuter's former unit, the 1st Bombardment Wing. It was the lead ship in the mission to strike the Normandy beaches prior to the assault ships landing. Despite later criticisms that Kuter never "proved himself in combat," he was on that morning in one of the largest aerial armadas ever known to man—eighteen hundred heavy bombers heading for the French coast on a mission to blanket the beaches with iron, a bombardment ending only five minutes before the first landing craft beached and discharged their men. He was a prime target for the Luftwaffe should it chose to engage, but he was not going to miss this opportunity.[61]

Kuter watched "that enormous swarm of heavy bombers proceed steadily across a solid unmarked overcast ceiling to an invisible point in space where the bombs were released to fall into the solid clouds below as the bombers turned right and proceeded in their enormous vast column along the prescribed route of withdrawal." The crews experienced light antiaircraft artillery fire from the German forces below, but no Luftwaffe fighter appeared.[62] The lack of Luftwaffe presence surprised Kuter: "If Goering and all the meteorologists of the Luftwaffe had prescribed ideal weather to permit the German Air Force to operate most effectively against our invading fleet they could not have set up more favorable conditions for them than weather which actually existed from the center of the channel to the invasion beaches on D-Day."[63]

After returning to the airfield at Brampton Grange, Kuter drove back to the headquarters of the Allied Expeditionary Air Forces and met with General Vandenberg, who assuaged his worry about the Luftwaffe: "It was quite some time before I could believe his statement that no Luft-waffe aircraft—fighter, fighter-bomber, or bomber—had as yet appeared on the scene. . . . The total failure of the Luftwaffe was a wholly unex-pected contribution of the greatest magnitude to the success of the cross-channel invasion." Kuter was certainly aware but still struggling to believe that, by June 1944, the Luftwaffe was unable to put up any mea-surable defense of France. Its destruction—primarily its loss of pilots—at the hands of Allied fighters now ensured virtual air supremacy.[64]

Kuter spent the rest of D-Day with Vandenberg in the Allied Expedi-tionary Air Forces headquarters monitoring the progress of the invasion. Buried deep underground, the headquarters nevertheless had excellent connections to the ongoing fight, and Kuter felt that "no Napoleon had ever had an opportunity to watch his forces in the minute detail and pre-cise detail that the Air Commander in Chief had on his control board." This might be true, but not every commander agreed. The commander of the 9th Fighter Command, Pete Quesada, felt that he received too little information that day; eventually, "had had enough" of the inability to know what was going on and took matters into his own hands.[65]

General Arnold arrived along with the rest of the Combined Chiefs on D+3, 9 June. From then on, Kuter joined him in a series of brief-ings with everyone from the prime minister on down. Arnold even met with the King George VI, but Kuter was not in attendance. Arnold, with Kuter in tow, met with Spaatz to discuss the employment of the strate-gic air forces from this point forward. Now that the invasion force was safely ashore, attacks on the industrial heartland of Germany resumed. On 11 June, the Combined Chiefs and their entourages boarded a ship and headed to the beachhead. As they made their way across the chan-nel and into the artificially created harbor, Kuter could not help but let his service get the better of him. He noticed that several ships had been sunk to help create a harbor. Here, he wrote: "Never again can it be truthfully said that no practical use has been found for a battleship. They make peachy breakwaters when sunk." The group debarked onto the Normandy coastline and was met by General Bradley.[66]

From here, it was another series of meetings with senior command-ers, including Quesada. Afterward, Kuter, along with Arnold, traveled to Italy. Kuter and Arnold both noted the destruction of the German ground forces and the complete absence of German aircraft. Arnold noted that as many as ten thousand vehicles of various sizes from Tiger tanks down to small trucks sat damaged or destroyed. Kuter saw "at least seven hun-dred wrecked and burned-out German trucks, armored cars and tanks at congested points in the highway and more particularly at the approaches to the bridges." Here, he learned that the current tactic involved Allied fighter bombers first blocking the roads and then destroying the vehicles caught in the resulting traffic jam. Kuter noted: "It worked. It worked well." This trip had a profound effect on both Kuter and Arnold, but it was Kuter who passed the experiences and current tactics back to Quesada and training units back in the States.[67]

Taking notes the entire time, and recognizing that none of the in-theater commanders had the time to do so, Kuter dispatched back to the Air Forces School of Applied Tactics a series of reports on the Allies' ever-changing tactics and techniques that were meant to inform the curriculum. This represents another example of his being a true architect. Even during the war, he continued to use his own position to strengthen the structure of the air force and codify new tactics even at lower levels and in the rear echelons. His experiences at ACTS in the 1930s continued to affect his thinking throughout his career, and he wanted to ensure that future air force leaders received the most up-to-date information possible. He, Marshall, and Arnold then left for North Africa and Italy to get updated on the conduct of the war in the Mediterranean.[68]

As the group made its final approach into Caserta, General Marshall decided that he wanted to view the landing from the copilot's seat. Since no one was going to tell him no, that is where he was sitting when a P-38 flew dangerously close in front of the C-54. On disembarking the aircraft, the normally taciturn Marshall exploded at General Vince Meloy that a P-38 "very nearly cut the nose off of our transport!" Meloy, not missing a beat, apologized profusely about the irresponsible French pilots flying around with a complete lack of aerial discipline. This seemed to placate Marshall as Kuter stood uncomfortably nearby. Later, Kuter was able to separate Meloy from the crowd and told him that the French were not flying any P-38s. Meloy knew that, and so did Kuter, but both agreed that there was no reason for Marshall to know that.[69]

One thing became clear to Kuter in his travels in Europe, North Africa, and Italy. The Luftwaffe was a broken organization. Its ability to defend the German homeland might still be a real and dangerous one, but its ability to reach the front line in the ongoing war was significantly decreased, if not nonexistent. The bulk of the American aerial fighting force at the army's front was concentrating on finding German troops and transports on the ground and destroying them. Through the strategic bombardment of aircraft production factories and shooting down of those fighters that existed, the army air force deprived the Luftwaffe of planes and trained aircrews. Kuter noted: "The fight with the Luftwaffe was over. It had been won."[70]

Marshall, Arnold, Kuter, and the rest of the staff departed for the United States on 20 June. Their aircraft lifted into the air, circled the erupting volcano Vesuvius, and made a short stop in Casablanca before heading across the Atlantic. Somewhere over the ocean, Arnold began to talk to Marshall about their current schedule, noting that they were set to arrive in Washington early enough in the day to report in to the secretary of war and, in all likelihood, the president as well. Arnold continued that they would probably also have to return to their offices to start going through all the paperwork that awaited them, concluding: "The prospect was horrible to behold." According to Kuter, Marshall was "reasonable about the whole thing." On landing in Newfoundland, Marshall and Arnold took the base commander, Colonel H. H. Maxwell, aside for a private discussion. In short order, Maxwell produced all the equipment, including "waders, hip boots, rain jackets, sweaters, gloves, wool socks and other paraphernalia," necessary for a morning of fly-fishing. In those icy waters, Marshall, Arnold, Kuter, and three others caught six Atlantic salmon. After completing a very successful fishing expedition, the group returned to base, changed clothes, and headed out to board the aircraft. The base commander met them with a going-away gift of five dozen Newfoundland lobsters already secured and stored onboard. The group boarded the C-54 and proceeded to Washington, landing just after sunset.[71]

Return to Staff Work

Not everything that Larry Kuter came in contact with had serious implications for national security or the future of the army air force. The problem was that too much unimportant staff minutiae continued to filter up to the higher echelons of the organization. On 12 October 1944, Kuter had a telephone conversation with General McFarland in an attempt to gain a "general reduction in the trivial papers that come to the chiefs." Sadly, there seemed to be no way to stem the unending tidal wave of paperwork needing the approval of one or more of the Combined Chiefs.[72]

In November, Kuter displayed his unswerving belief in strategic bombardment over everything else in a memorandum to the undersecretary of war regarding the mining of Japanese harbors by the 20th and 21st Bomber Commands. The undersecretary, Robert Patterson, wrote to Kuter in October, saying that, while he recognized that there existed "plenty of other targets for our B-29s," he wanted assurances that the mining of Japanese harbors was being given due attention. It is doubtful that he felt reassured by the response he received. Kuter explained that the two units would "achieve the most significant progress if concentrated against the Japanese aircraft industry." He continued to feel that the use of bombers for anything other than strategic bombardment was a waste of the aircraft's full potential. While this demonstrated his adherence to air force doctrine, it proved to be shortsighted. Kuter was one among many army air force officers who simply refused to see air power assets used in any role other than strategic bombing. He noted that attacks against Japanese shipping were a priority already agreed on but intoned that they still should not divert strategic aircraft away from their current mission of destroying Japanese industries. Echoing what was a continuing refrain from strategic bombing advocates throughout the war, Kuter said: "This headquarters is of the opinion, however, that the limited scale of effort available to the Twentieth Air Force should not be diverted from its primary mission."[73]

The aerial mining issue did split into two camps. LeMay, Stratemeyer, and Chennault all liked the idea. Kuter, Norstad, Hansell, and Kenney did not. The latter group were soon proved to be wrong. As part of Operation Starvation in 1945, the aerial mining of Japanese ports did exactly what its name implied. Not only did it significantly drop the caloric intake of the average Japanese citizen; it also brought to a stop the movement of materials to Japan's war-making industries. The historian Kenneth Werrell pointed out that aerial mining accounted for 63 percent of sunken Japanese merchant ships from March 1945 until the end of the war. Kuter's later writings do not indicate whether he ever recognized the significant contribution the aerial mining operations played in the defeat of Japan and that he was, in fact, wrong on this issue. This also shows that, even within the army air forces of World War II, not all senior leaders were in lockstep when it came to doctrine and tactics.[74]

An Airman at Yalta

When General Arnold became suddenly and seriously ill after another heart attack, it was Major General Laurence S. Kuter who was designated to sit in for him at the upcoming Yalta conference. In a letter to his wife, Bea, Arnold stated that he had reservations about his replacement:

"I am not sure that Kuter has obtained a stature or the size to fill the bill." While he recognized Kuter's flair for organization and his superb staffing abilities, he worried that, as a major general, he would be over-shadowed and outmuscled by officers senior to himself in age, rank, and position.[75]

As Arnold's representative at the Yalta and Malta conferences, Kuter indeed found himself a relatively junior officer among four-star generals and the civilian leaders of the Allied cause, an experience that he detailed in *An Airman at Yalta*. If there is one major flaw in his description of events, it is that more often than not he referred to himself in the third person, for example: "On this occasion the fact that General Arnold was represented by a junior deputy reacted to the advantage of the Deputy. Stalin had one hamper [containing vodka and caviar] presented to the Deputy and one to be taken to General Arnold." He did not mention whether the "deputy" took the extra caviar and vodka back to Arnold: however, Ethel did indicate in a letter to Larry's parents that he returned home with a large quantity of vodka, Russian cigarettes, and caviar.[76]

The Yalta conference took place between 4 and 9 February 1945, immediately following the meetings held between the Americans and the British, along with Roosevelt and Churchill, at Malta. Kuter arrived at Malta in January 1945. On the last day of the month, Prime Minister Winston Churchill invited Major General Kuter and the rest of the lower-level staff planners to a dinner. The American two-star air force officer was met and welcomed to the party by two British five-star field mar-shals, Churchill having "turned out his first team" for the evening. On seeing Kuter, the prime minister disengaged himself from a conversation and greeted him warmly: "Larry, how well you look and how good it is to be together again." Kuter was impressed that the prime minister could so easily recall his name considering the limited amount of time they had spent together in the past. It meant a lot to him that Churchill remembered him. After several minutes of reminiscing, the prime minis-ter pulled closer and whispered conspiratorially: "Larry . . . what name do you call General Hull, your Army planner?" On receiving a reply, he headed for Hull, saying: "Ed, how good it is to have you with us." Kuter and the rest of the officers departed for Yalta a few days later.[77]

Initially viewed as an amazing success, Yalta soon came to repre-sent the subsequent conflict between the Western powers and the Soviet Union, but that turn of events could not be expected at the time. Kuter's aircraft, flight no. 10, also carried Generals Marshall and Somervell. The separation of rank quickly became apparent as beds were present for only two of the officers. Kuter decided to fly up front on the flight deck. He arrived at the Yalta conference with one goal: preserving the strategic bombardment against Germany and preventing any other mission from diverting the air assets in another direction.[78]

The Yalta conference officially began on the afternoon of February 4. The American delegation at the table consisted of President Roosevelt, Secretary of State Stettinius, Admiral Leahy, General Marshall, Admiral King, and, representing General Arnold and the army air force, Major General Kuter. Approaching the table, at which everyone else was already seated, Kuter hesitated in taking his seat, not sure whether it was meant for him or for a member of the Soviet delegation. A photographer captured the moment, an image that was later jokingly circulated throughout the Air Staff with the caption: "There is really nothing like standing up while everyone else is sitting down."[79]

The delegations broke into two camps: political and military. Over the next several days, the two groups debated the future war effort. For the European theater, Kuter asked for coordination between the American, British, and Russian flying arms. He knew at this point that cooperation was unlikely. The failed Operation Frantic bombing missions—which involved American crews taking off from England and recovering in the Soviet Union—ended in September 1944 and proved the Soviets' "genius for obstruction." At Yalta, as the militaries closed in on Berlin from two directions, the target areas in Germany grew ever smaller, and the possibility of fratricide in turn increased. With regard to the ongoing air war in the Pacific, Kuter sought basing rights in Siberia for the B-29s.[80]

The senior military leaders decided that the aerial delegations of each nation would break off to meet in a smaller group. The group included Marshal of the Royal Air Force Sir Charles Portal and Marshall of the Red Air Force Khudyakov along with several more junior assistants. Against these two five-star officers stood Major General Laurence Kuter with four other one- and two-star American army air force generals. Khudyakov wanted each airman to be frank and speak his mind. There was no need for stilted diplomatic language among aviators. Kuter led off the discussion with a request for coordination in aerial attacks against Germany. Khudyakov wanted, he said, to approve the concept, but he was forced to obtain concurrence from "the General Staff and from the Marshal [Stalin]." The Russians asked for assistance in bombing oil and transportation targets in eastern Germany, including the city of Dresden, but the Russians refused to accept overall coordination and the creation of a bomb line running between "Stettin-Berlin-Ruhland-Dresden-Brno-Vienna-Maribor-Zagreb."[81]

For the next several hours, Kuter went back and forth with the Soviet air marshal. Finally, the discussion turned to the strategic bombing campaign in Europe. Khudyakov asked the Americans to prohibit attacks against targets near the Soviet front. Here was the eventuality that Kuter had been sent to ensure did not happen. The strategic bombing campaign against Germany must not be restricted even if a bombing line could not be agreed on. The US Army Air Force could not bow to pressure from any front, internal or external. With the bombing finally beginning to bear fruit, it was up to Kuter to ensure that nothing halted it.[82]

The final conference between the air marshals and the American delegation was held on 9 February. By Kuter's account, it was short. The Soviet air force would not coordinate bombing operations or agree to a bombing line. The Americans and British therefore planned to continue bombing operations unabated even if missions approached the Soviet front line. Kuter and the army air forces secured what they had come to Yalta for; the bombing campaign against Germany continued.[83]

Any hesitancy Arnold felt in sending Kuter in his place was overcome by his performance. Despite being a junior not only in rank but also in age, Kuter acquitted himself well. His dual performance—representing Arnold and also serving as the senior representative for the air force—greatly impressed the ailing air force chief. Arnold wrote to Kuter that had he "undertook the two most difficult assignments" and did "a superb job throughout." He went on to state unequivocally: "On Air matters, the position and views of the Army Air Forces were clearly, thoroughly and forcefully presented to the US and British Chiefs of Staff and to the Soviet Military Staff. On broader questions involving policy and strategy and military matters outside the air sphere you employed, in my opinion, the best military judgement in the action which you took. I do not know of anyone who could more ably have represented me and I am proud of the work you did and the contribution you made to these meetings." He also praised Kuter in his postwar book *Global Mission,* saying that he did a "wonderful job." It is extremely significant that Major General Larry Kuter led the American air delegation when one considers the other three-star generals who might have been asked to do so. Arnold's trust in Kuter to represent the US Army Air Forces was unwavering.[84]

Kuter departed with the rest of the American delegation from the airport at Saki on the morning of 11 February 1945 aboard one of the thirteen C-54 transports that had delivered them there. Obviously, so young a general officer still made for great press, but the Kuter family, and especially Ethel, went to great lengths to keep Larry's location and actions a closely guarded secret. Having seen two military wives (Mrs. Clark and Mrs. Doolittle) get into hot water for inadvertently revealing top secret information, Ethel wanted to ensure that she too did not disclose anything. She went so far as to move into the guest bedroom when Larry was home to avoid overhearing late night phone calls, which were frequent. However, the same was not true of Larry's parents.[85]

Larry's mother turned up in the press under the headline "Mother Keeps Kuter's Secret." Ethel was furious. She typed a letter to Minna Kuter but decided in the end not to send it. The letter is worth quoting at length to show the pressure that Ethel, still in her late thirties, felt she was under not to release any information about her husband:

> This letter is not going to please you. . . . It is very simple to explain to the newspapers that General Kuter is in such a position that NO PUBLICITY should be released to the news that has not been cleared through the War Department Public Relations. In that way Larry will be protected and so will you. . . . Apparently you did not understand that Larry's request for NO PUBLICITY released personally, by him or by our families, was a very serious request. The thing that is hard for me to understand is your basic modesty which is irreconcilable with the intimate, personal admissions that appear in print. Two women here in Washington have made fools of themselves by giving out public publicity concerning their husbands and both have been reprimanded.[86]

Planning the Pacific War and the Postwar Air Force

In early March 1945, Larry flew down to the air force hospital in Miami, where Arnold was still convalescing. He also took three days of leave himself and spent the time fishing, something he had not done since the Newfoundland stopover. On returning to Washington, he worked closely with Lauris Norstad on setting up the postwar air force and establishing the strategic air forces in the Pacific. This latter organization would continue the bombing raids against Japan but at a drastically increased level once the war in Europe ended and senior air force officers moved into theater. Kuter hoped to include himself in that group.[87]

In the meantime, Meilinger notes: "Larry Kuter, Arnold's assistant chief of staff for plans, formed a Post War Division within his office, headed by Col Rueben C. Moffat, to look at the matter as well. Maj. Gen. Lauris Norstad replaced Kuter in the spring of 1945. These four men—Davison, Kuter, Moffat, and Norstad—would plan the future of the postwar air arm." Kuter and Norstad both were aware that the atomic bomb was being developed, and this knowledge affected their perception of how a postwar air force should be organized and equipped: the focus should not remain solely on strategic bombardment but broaden to include the delivery of atomic weapons.[88]

Once Norstad replaced Kuter as chief of air plans, Larry was freed up for an assignment in the Pacific theater, and he received orders to depart in the middle part of May. However, before he left the States, a series of events significantly affected the Kuter family. On 12 April, President Roosevelt died. At almost the same time, Roxanne's friend Carol Young also died. The Kuters attended Carol's funeral, at which Larry served as a pallbearer. A few weeks later, Larry developed a "facial disturbance" that turned out to be Bell's palsy. He initially thought that he was the victim of a stroke. The disease forced him to travel to Miami for a stay at the same hospital recently occupied by Arnold.[89]

On 13 May, Major General Larry Kuter returned to Washington, where Arnold presented him with the Distinguished Service Medal, both officers looking significantly worse for wear. The war's toll showed on them both. Ethel remembered that the event demonstrated "the beating that these two planners had taken." Larry Kuter—still ill but refusing to be sidelined in the United States as the war moved into its final phase—departed Washington for the Pacific on 16 May for service in the Pacific theater. As far as he knew, he was headed to another combat command and a hand in using the B-29s. These plans quickly changed, and the next few months fundamentally altered his perception of the air force and his career as a whole.

After earning his wings, Kuter was assigned to the 49th Bombardment Squadron at Langley Field, Virginia. Kuter is in the back row, third from right. (US Air Force Academy Special Collections.)

Larry Kuter flew various aircraft during the early years of air power development, including the B-9 bomber. Of it Kuter said: "[If you] jammed down the rudder and looked back at the fuselage, you could see the monocque twist." Note the P-26 in the background. (Photo courtesy US Air Force.)

Perhaps even more than West Point, Larry's attendance at the Air Corps Tactical School (ACTS) altered his way of thinking and his understanding of what air power could do. After his student days at ACTS, he stayed on as an instructor and became chief of the bombardment section. ACTS became a breeding ground for air power doctrine. The lessons taught there heavily influenced the air plan for the Second World War. (US Air Force Academy Special Collections.)

After becoming an instructor at the Air Corps Tactical School, Larry, Ethel, and Roxanne moved into Quarters 267. Here is the house in 2016. (US Air Force Academy Special Collections.)

In February 1942, Kuter was promoted to brigadier general (skipping the rank of colonel) and, at age thirty-six, became the youngest general officer in the US Army. (US Air Force photo.)

After a brief stint commanding the 1st Bombardment Wing in England, Kuter found himself transferred to North Africa, where he eventually served as the deputy commander of the North African Tactical Air Force. His experiences in North Africa shaped his thinking on tactical air power but did not alter his strict belief in the efficacy of strategic bombardment. Here, he stands with his immediate commander, Arthur Coningham, and Carl Spaatz and Arthur Tedder. (US Air Force photo.)

Kuter spent much of the Second World War working for General Henry Arnold. Although the two were not friends, they had a deep mutual respect for one another. (US Air Force photo.)

Kuter's longtime friend Alexander de Seversky caused a rift between Kuter and Arnold. Here is Seversky being congratulated on receiving the Harmon Trophy in 1947 with Secretary of War Robert Patterson and Seversky's wife, Evelyn, looking on. (Photo courtesy Michael Barrier.)

In early 1944, Kuter was promoted to major general. Here he is in his official photo taken around the time of that promotion. (US Air Force Academy Special Collections.)

This is Ethel Kuter in a photo taken around the time Larry was promoted to major general.

This is Roxanne Kuter in a photo taken around the time Larry was promoted to major general.

Major General Kuter with President Roosevelt and senior staff members, including King, Leahy, and Marshall, at the Malta conference in 1945. (National Archives and Records Administration photo.)

Kuter represented the ailing Henry Arnold at the Yalta conference. In this famous photo of the "Big Three," Kuter can be seen in the background.

As Arnold's representative at the Yalta conference, Kuter became momentarily wary when he did not know whether he should take a seat at the table lest the spot was reserved for a member of the Soviet delegation. This photo later circulated throughout army air forces headquarters with the caption: "There is really nothing like standing up while everyone else is sitting down."

Kuter was Arnold's indispensable man. Although many others worked closely with Arnold throughout the war, including Muir Fairchild, seen here with Arnold and Kuter in 1943, none had the confidence of Arnold as much as Kuter did. (US Air Force Academy Special Collections.)

Larry on leave in 1952 with the bear that nearly (and prematurely) ended his career. (US Air Force Academy Special Collections.)

As commander of the Far East Air Forces, Kuter came into contact with many of the leaders of the region, including Chiang Kai-shek, seen here after awarding Kuter the "Medal of the Cloud and Banner with Grand Cordon." (US Air Force Academy Special Collections.)

The full general Larry Kuter as commander of the North American Air Defense Command. For an officer who started his career in the field artillery and learned to fly in canvas biplanes, he now commanded a binational command responsible for the defense of Canada and America against the Soviet Union and composed of radar sites and interceptor jets. (US Air Force photo.)

Kuter flew in an F-106B like the one pictured here. An in-flight emergency nearly killed him. He jokingly said: "It's fun to fly in hot aircraft." (US Air Force Academy Special Collections.)

The stone lantern that the Kuters brought with them from Japan. It now sits in the backyard of the superintendent's house at the air force academy a few miles from where General Kuter is buried. (US Air Force photo.)

The General Laurence S. Kuter trophy is presented to the winners of the US Air Force Academy–University of Hawaii football game. (Photo courtesy University of Hawaii Athletic Department.)

7

The Pacific, War's End, and Air Transport Command

Kuter moved from staff work to an operational theater one more time. With the war in Europe having just ended, attention turned in full to the Pacific theater. Kuter spent considerable time in his last Air Staff assignment working on establishing in the Pacific a strategic air force in which he hoped to play a large role. He departed for the Marianas Islands on 16 May 1945 to become deputy commanding general for the US Army Air Forces, Pacific Ocean Area and to help operate the US Army Strategic Air Forces in the Pacific. The 20th and 21st Bomber Commands were to be combined into the 20th Air Force, which would control the 8th Air Force on its transfer from the European theater. Kuter's immediate commander was Barney Giles, also recently in the Pentagon, now the commanding general for the Pacific Ocean Area. Thus, Giles and Kuter were to oversee the ongoing bombing of Japan. Because the organization was initially established inside the Pentagon and controlled by Hap Arnold, Giles and Kuter also carried the position titles chief of staff and deputy chief of staff out of Washington and into the Pacific. It took Kuter nearly two weeks to arrive, and he began his final wartime assignment on 1 June 1945.[1]

The move to Pacific Ocean Area proved short-lived. Two newspaper headlines spaced a few days apart demonstrated this: "Curt LeMay arrives in Guam"; "Tooey Spaatz Arrives in Guam as Commander of All Strategic Air Forces." The arrival of these other officers had a cascading effect on the available positions. Curtis LeMay became Spaatz's chief of staff, forcing Giles into the position of deputy chief of staff. And, when the reshuffling stopped, it was Larry Kuter who was left without a position. He was also essentially homeless—as was Giles—as Spaatz and Lemay moved into the houses they had been occupying. It is an interesting aspect to this story that, had Spaatz and LeMay not moved from the European theater to take over bombing operations in the Pacific, the names Giles and Kuter, still relatively obscure, would have held responsibility for the dropping of the atomic bombs.[2]

Here was another example of the architect being replaced by the builder. Kuter spent a considerable amount of time during his Washington assignments managing the B-29s and establishing the strategic picture in the Pacific. Then, at what seemed to be the last minute, he was denied a role in the culmination of all his efforts. This had nothing to do with his abilities or the role he played in organizing the units in theater. He simply became the low man on the totem pole with the surrender of Germany.

Kuter was not the only one to lose a job in the Pacific. Arnold fired Haywood Hansell as commander of the 20th Bomber Command and replaced him with LeMay. Ironically, Kuter had a hand in Hansell's firing. Arnold wanted to step up the bombings against Japan and became frustrated with Hansell. Norstad and Kuter prodded him to make a decision. When he announced his decision to relieve Hansell, both men recommended he fly to Hansell's headquarters and break the news personally. Instead, he sent Norstad.[3]

A clearly distraught Kuter wrote to Ethel: "A few days ago it became clear to me that I shall be ordered away from here . . . to any other place without much regard to function as long as it is away from the Strategic Air Forces in the Pacific." This was an extreme blow personally and professionally. He had spent much of the previous two years planning for this very organization. This posting was also his chance to get one more combat tour under his belt prior to the end of the war. He wrote that he was "deeply disappointed in being excluded from [the Pacific strategic air force operations'] fruition." The only consolation was that Spaatz asked him where he wanted to go. Sadly, no matter what the assignment was, it probably would not be a combat command.[4]

At this point—on 5 July 1945—Ira Eaker, now serving as the deputy commander of the army air forces and chief of the Air Staff back in Washington, reached out to Lieutenant General George Stratemeyer, commander of the US Army Air Forces in the China theater, to see whether there was an opportunity to place Kuter there. Strat discussed it with his commander, General Wedemeyer, but, while Wedemeyer "admired Larry very much and at one time would have liked to have had him assigned to his theater," there was unfortunately "no position in China for his assignment."[5]

Two days later, on 7 July, Wedemeyer received a message from General Marshall asking for a spot for Kuter. Apparently, senior leaders in

Washington felt that, having sent Kuter to the Pacific for a command, they were now responsible for his lack thereof. Wedemeyer called Stratemeyer, but both felt it not "worth while [sic] to break up the team" despite Larry's "brilliant staff ability." Left with no option in the strategic air forces in the Pacific, and rebuffed by China, Kuter was still sitting without a job.[6]

Kuter made a career-altering decision at this point—whether in anger or sadness we cannot know—and sought to be separated from the bomber mafia that for so long nurtured his career. His old planning friends, Harold George and Possum Hansell, were now heading the Air Transport Command (ATC). Kuter wanted to join them. Kuter put it this way: "My philosophical view is that my last two years on USASTAF [US Army Strategic Air Forces] are now completed. The staff work was my exclusive responsibility and I have had an opportunity to help get it started in the field. . . . It may prove to be advantageous for me to round out my experience and duties by getting into another new and essential element of Air Power—Air Transport."[7]

Hal George was only too happy to have him, and, on 25 July, he received orders transferring him from the strategic air forces in the Pacific to the ATC. Barney Giles threw him a farewell dinner and pinned the Bronze Star on his chest. Ethel later remarked that this curious turn of events was in fact a blessing in disguise: "What seemed to be a heartache, a dismissal, became the opening and beginning of a whole new plan; that would develop in peace and war." Kuter departed the next day and headed for the recently captured island of Okinawa.[8]

Kuter was now officially back under the command of an old friend. George was the same officer he had served under when writing the Air War Plans Division–Plan 1 before the United States entered the war. H. L. George took command of ATC on 1 July 1945. Kuter moved over to serve under George, but his time in the Pacific was over, or at least so he believed. ATC headquarters was back at the Pentagon, so Kuter hopped a flight and headed back to the States. However, his route took him west, not east, which would have been quicker. Since he was already in theater, George wanted him to become acquainted with the organization and units of ATC. His orders called for him to make stops at ATC bases along the way and visit theater commanders. Kuter departed from Guam in an aerial convoy of "war-weary" C-54s and "beaten" C-47s. The war in the Pacific ground on, with most military men seeing no end in sight—the atomic bomb was still a closely guarded secret—and preparations continuing for an invasion of the Japanese homeland.[9]

Kuter's new assignment was predicated on the war with Japan continuing and an invasion of the Japanese mainland in the future. Kuter also felt that, in rather rapid succession, the bombing would end and that "air transport was just beginning." He was, without a doubt, making the best of the new situation. He arrived in Okinawa, where he met with General Jimmy Doolittle, General Joseph "Vinegar Joe" Stilwell, and Ennis Whitehead, the commander of the 5th Air Force. He found Okinawa crowded and living conditions there grim. From there it was off to the Philippines.[10]

Kuter's travels throughout the Pacific while making his way back to the Washington also allowed him to continue his disagreements with George Kenney over the use of B-29s. The two previously exchanged a series of messages, if not personally critical, certainly edged with resentment. Then again, Kenney was a notoriously difficult man to get along with. As he himself noted: "I remarked I hoped no one expected me to cheer either the decisions or the beliefs that [Kuter] voiced."[11]

Kenney also labeled Kuter one of the "Young Turks," the group of younger general officers with whom Arnold surrounded himself and who would take on more senior positions of leadership in a postwar air force. Kuter and Kenney could not have been more different. The two must have presented an almost Laurel and Hardy appearance standing next to each other, although the two seemed to have a good working relationship and Kenney had hoped to have Kuter join him earlier in the war in the Southwest Pacific before Arnold decided to send him to Europe. One could not blame Kenney for wanting someone with Arnold's personal stamp of approval to serve with him.[12]

The US Army Air Force was truly a global operation now. Leaving Guam, Kuter had, as we have seen, flown to Okinawa and then the Philippines. He then crossed China, headed to Kunming and then Chungking, flying the hump for the second time on 1 August 1945. Ironically, he was joined on this flight by Stratemeyer, and the two conversed about Kuter's new assignment. After a stop in India, it was on to Cairo, Tripoli, and Tunis, cities familiar from his earlier experiences in North Africa. His party continued its westward travel from 31 July through 13 August. During this time, the strategic air forces in the Pacific dropped the two atomic bombs on Hiroshima and Nagasaki. Finally, Kuter arrived in Frankfurt, Germany, where he expected to travel through the country inspecting the ruins caused by the bombing campaign. However, an office call at Eisenhower's headquarters redirected him to Paris.[13]

In Paris, Kuter was met by Brigadier General Gordon Saville with sealed orders from General Arnold. Kuter was to turn around immediately and return to Pacific with all possible haste. The surrender of Japan was imminent, and Kuter, the senior ATC officer in theater, or at least the closest by proximity, was to establish an aerial bridge to move General Douglas MacArthur's troops onto the mainland of Japan. The war in the Pacific was over. Kuter and his aide-de-camp, Captain Humphrey Doulens, were given rooms at the Ritz Hotel in Paris for the evening. After checking into the hotel and falling into a seat in his room, Kuter shocked his aide by jumping to his feet: "Hell, I want to see Paris." In short order, he dragged Doulens to the Tuileries Garden, the Place de la Concorde, the Champs-Élysées, the Arc de Triomphe, and the Eiffel Tower before taking in a show at a local theater. After a brief sleep, they awakened at five the next morning to see more of Paris on foot. Kuter maximized his brief few hours in the City of Light.[14]

Kuter and Doulens boarded the C-54 that ended up being their home for the next three weeks. It was while he was in the air en route back to the Pacific that Japan surrendered. Doulens remembered it this way: "As the sun rose [on 14 August] over the wastes of the Persian Deserts we learned through our radio that the war was over, that the Japs had capitulated. Our celebration was in our hearts." Forty-one hours later, on 17 August, Kuter landed in Okinawa.[15]

Kuter found himself on the leading edge of a massive aerial armada, C-54s and C-47s from across the globe converging on the Pacific theater to move the conquering American army into Japan. His orders were to join MacArthur in Manila and move from there back to Okinawa and on into Japan. He arrived just in front of the Japanese delegation and was present for the surrender negotiations. He was back in Okinawa on 23 August to oversee the two hundred C-54s moving the American troops into Japan. He himself never set foot on the Japanese mainland. A typhoon marooned him on Okinawa, and, by the time that cleared, he received orders once again sending him back to Washington, DC.[16]

Kuter directed operations for less than a month. Again, as had been the case many times before, as soon as he established and organized the flow of men and materiel, he was pulled from theater. From Europe, North Africa, and now the Pacific at war's end, he had established an organization only to be directed away from it before it was fully engaged. Since his arrival in the Pacific in May, when he was to be a part of the strategic air forces, he had been reassigned on three different occasions, been made part of two different commands, flown halfway back to Washington, turned around, completed his assignment, and flown out again. His final night in theater was 27 August, when he was the guest of honor at a dinner hosted by Barry Giles and attended by Tooey Spaatz, Nate Twining, and Curt LeMay. The next morning, he departed the Pacific, heading this time east through Hawaii. On 1 September 1945, he once again landed in Washington, DC.[17]

Kuter's remarkable fitness reports continued during his time in the Pacific. Contrary to Eaker's earlier report on Kuter—the one he signed in May 1945 before Kuter departed for the short-lived deputy commanding general job—could not have been more different from the one reporting on his spring 1943 performance. Eaker praised Kuter's "thorough, hard, and brilliant work" during his time in Washington.[18]

Arnold's appraisal of Kuter during this period found him even more praiseworthy: "General Kuter is an experienced young officer, who is a keen, brilliant thinker capable of rapid analysis of a problem with resultant sound decision. Untiring in his efforts towards the defeat of our enemy, he never wavers from extreme emotional soundness. A polished individual with intimate friends in all walks of life. . . . Always a leader, though young in years, he is mature in experience and a great asset to the Army." Lieutenant General Giles rated Kuter first among his eight general officers. Major General Laurence Kuter was forty years old.[19]

Kuter received several appraisals in a short amount of time: one before he left Washington, one when he transferred over to ATC, and another from George after his brief stint moving assets into Japan. Perhaps it could be said of him that no other general officer had so much said of him by so many other general officers in such a short amount of time. George also called Kuter "a highly intellectual, energetic, versatile leader with imagination, initiative, and broad professional knowledge."[20]

Kuter's time in the Pacific might have been limited, but his time flying around was not. From his initial departure from Washington in May 1945 until he returned as a member of ATC in September, he flew a remarkable amount. In fact, among his trips were two circumnavigations of the planet. His earlier "trip around the world" at the behest of Arnold or Marshall already granted him membership in the "Circumnavigator's Club," but it was because of these two trips that he was later invited to give a keynote address in January 1950. Kuter recalled some five years later that his trips around the globe were "unique even in the annals of The Circumnavigators":

This double compound circumnavigation started by a flight from Washington to Paris and back to Washington and then from

Washington westward through Hawaii and Guam. From Guam I was instructed to return to Washington through the Philippines, India, the Middle East and Europe. Arriving in Paris, one global circuit was closed. However, upon reaching Paris, my instructions were modified substantially and I turned around in a hurry and flew back across Europe, the Middle East and India, to Manila, Okinawa, and finally back to Guam. From Guam I was instructed to return to Washington across the Pacific, thereby completing two circumnavigations with two trips around the world meeting in Paris, although the origin of this double compound circumnavigation was Washington, D.C.[21]

The return to Washington, DC, meant another new assignment. Kuter was losing track of all the organizations he had been assigned to in the previous four months. Hal George preceded him back to Washington and met him at the airport. He took him back to ATC headquarters and told him that he was going to command the Atlantic Division of the ATC. To do this, and in the course of the next year, Kuter needed to consolidate three ATC divisions into the Atlantic Division, ATC. After learning what his future held, Larry Kuter headed "home" to Ethel at the Westchester Apartments, no. 539, a building he had never seen before.[22]

There was great pressure placed on Kuter in this new position. Far from it being simply an aerial transportation job, with the war over there was "a great rush to bring the boys home." Although hundreds of thousands of men traveled by ship, there was still a great need for significant aerial transport as well. Kuter's official headquarters was in Fort Totten, New York, but Ethel remained in the Washington, DC, apartment, while Larry commuted back and forth. This proved to be a difficult time for her. From her perspective, now that the war was over, they should be living together. She noted: "I didn't know what my status was, where I belonged." Larry, apparently hoped that the assignment would be short-lived and that he would return to the permanent address in Washington.[23]

Kuter had five wings—divisions in the wartime air force—under his command: the North Atlantic, the Caribbean, the South Atlantic, the Azores, and Rio de Janeiro. His old friend Possum Hansell returned from overseas and commanded the Caribbean wing. Since the war was over, basing rights, landing permits, and aerial routes all had to be reestablished for peacetime operations. This was true for civilian airlines as well, and Kuter represented the air force at the US-UK Bilateral Air Conference in Bermuda, a meeting of military and civilian aerial leaders. He also participated in negotiating an agreement with Portugal for the postwar US Air Force use of Lajes Air Field in the Azores.[24]

February 1946 saw the departure and retirement of air force general Henry Arnold. The service to his country of Larry's longtime mentor and the father of the air force was finally at an end. Spaatz stepped into Arnold's shoes as the head of what was still the US Army Air Forces. The Kuters attended the going-away dinner. As much as Arnold had an impact on Larry Kuter's career, the same was true of Bee Arnold's impact on Ethel. Ethel wrote to her saying, as she reported later, that, next to her mother, "she was the most influential woman in my life."[25]

Kuter was also being seriously courted by the airlines at this time. With his leadership, planning and organizational skills, and operational experience, not to mention his relative youth compared to his peers, he was sought out and offered significant salaries. For example, he was offered a vice presidency with American Airlines, and the Peruvian airline offered him a presidency. These were serious offers for a man in his position to give consideration to, not to mention the pay. In the end he decided that "he liked what he was doing" and stayed in the military.[26]

Ironically, Kuter's time actually wearing a uniform ended for a while during his next assignment. Along with the establishment of new air routes and the expansion of air travel, a new international civil aviation organization was created to oversee this massive expansion. This international organizational meeting took place in Montreal, and the result was the creation of the International Civil Aviation Organization (ICAO). In September 1946, President Truman appointed Major General Larry Kuter as the US representative to the "Interim Council of the Provisional International Aviation Organization." Kuter transferred—rank and all—to the Department of State. Congress passed a law to allow this to happen, and President Truman issued an executive order giving Kuter the State Department rank of minister. His official title became "the Honorable Major General Laurence S. Kuter." Kuter was reappointed by presidential order as the US representative to the newly established and permanent ICAO. Despite being part of the State Department and not actively serving in the air force, he found that his need to travel had not been lessened. The newly created international agreements for aviation saw him participate in major civil aviation conferences around the globe. He returned to London and Cairo as well as making first-time visits to Lima and Rio de Janeiro.[27]

The job was not without its challenges and, by no stretch of the imagination, purely diplomatic. The major issues facing Kuter included creating global—not just American—standards for the rapid advancement of technology: for example, ground control approach radar and the instrument landing system. These replaced the rapidly aging systems used during the Second World War, primarily in the European theater. Kuter's time at ICAO also saw the establishment of English as the official language of aviation. This was the biggest confrontation with which he dealt during his time in Montreal. He recalled: "French had been the language of aviation." The secretary general of ICAO, one Monsieur Roper, was, as Kuter noted, "a strong, able French administrator." He was joined by "the representative of France, Henri Bouchet—an able politician and a zealously patriotic Frenchman." As he summed up the situation: "I knew they were going to fight and die for the French language. They fought and almost died, but it's English. When you fly over a French airport, they have got to answer you in English."[28]

The acceptance of English—and specifically American English—as the official language of aviation did lead to one unintended consequence. It required certain reports to be listed in inches rather than in metric measurements. Kuter admitted that this caused some interesting math to be done in the cockpits by anyone other than American flyers: "We made some mistakes. . . . We should have gone metric."[29]

It is worth noting, and also somewhat ironic, that Kuter was serving as the US ICAO representative when he officially became Major General Laurence S. Kuter, US Air Force. He left no record of his thoughts on the US Army Air Forces becoming the US Air Force. He was asked years later about his contributions to the creation of the independent air force, but he declined to answer. He indicated that his work toward air force independence was done during and shortly after the Second World War. For a man who was so much a part of the movement for air force independence and whose organizational skills could be found in the DNA of the US Air Force, he was conspicuously absent from its official birthday. Serving in Montreal at the time, he sent a letter the assistant chief of staff regarding the forthcoming promotion board and noted that he was the only officer serving at his station and therefore could not attend the festivities. In a way, he was like a father absent at the birth of his first child.[30]

Kuter survived his first political appointment but not his second. President Truman nominated him for the chairmanship of the Civil Aeronautics Board (CAB). This indicated the regard that his name now held inside the War Department and the political administration. Fortuitously, he needed to be in Washington the first week of January 1948 for his annual physical. No longer having a residence there, Ethel having joined him in Montreal, he contacted his old friend Lauris Norstad, now a lieutenant general. Norstad secured lodging for him at Fort Myers, telling him that the reservation was in the "Visiting General Officer's Quarters Dog." Larry got the joke. It was not the first time he found himself in the dog house in Washington, DC.[31]

Kuter arrived and went to his physical, but it was while he was with the doctor that the routine trip took a turn toward the bizarre. An officer in the Pentagon reached him by phone and told him that it was urgent that he come to the building as soon as possible. He departed and arrived at the Hoyt Vandenberg's office, who took him to Secretary of the Air Force Stuart Symington's office, who finally told him that President Truman wanted to see him and that he needed to make his way up the White House immediately. Symington refused to give him any indication as to why, but Kuter did insist that Symington accompany him.[32]

It turned out that Truman was pleased with Kuter's work on the ICAO and wanted him to head the CAB. He needed an "honest, disinterested authority," and Kuter was his man. The president gave Kuter a day to think about it. Kuter returned the Pentagon and talked the issue over with Symington, Spaatz, Vandenberg, and Norstad. They all agreed that it was a good move, and Kuter returned to the White House the next day and told the president: "I will do my very best for you as Chairman of the Civil Aeronautics Board."[33]

The US Senate had other plans in mind that required a great personal sacrifice on Kuter's part and one that he was not willing to make at the time. Several military figures had recently been appointed to high civilian positions. Marshall was secretary of state, Bedell Smith was a senior assistant on the Department of State, and Omar Bradley ran Veteran Affairs. General Eisenhower had also recently emerged as a possible political figure, although it was not known at the time whether he was a Republican or a Democrat. The Senate Armed Services Committee refused to confirm the nomination of another military man to another civilian position. To them, it looked as if Truman was placing only senior military officers into top positions. This was viewed through the dual lenses of graft for services to the nation during World War II and, more seriously, crossing the civilian-military divide. The committee indicated that it would be necessary for Kuter to resign from the service before accepting the position. Kuter preferred not to resign and asked Symington to ask the president to withdraw his nomination. For an officer who joined the military not knowing whether he would make a career of it, Larry Kuter could no longer imagine a life not in uniform even if staying in uniform meant losing a significantly more lucrative civilian position. Symington told Kuter that the issue was out of either of their hands and that the president planned to meet with members of the Senate committee. He also told Kuter that it was "fifty-fifty chance," as far he could tell. Kuter never heard anything officially. The president did meet with Senate members, but no one called Kuter to tell him what transpired at the meeting. The problem solved itself when Secretary of Defense James Forrestal appointed Kuter to command the newly created Military Air Transport Service (MATS). Kuter's name was never confirmed by the Senate, nor was it ever officially withdrawn.[34]

MATS

Within a month, Kuter was named commander designate of the proposed MATS. This was the first "integrated" military service or what later became known as a *joint* command, composed of members of two or more services. It became both a predecessor to *functional* commands and an early example of a *combatant* command. Despite being multiservice, the command did not come with a third star. Kuter became responsible for its charter and organization. MATS was devised to merge, or at least oversee, the navy's air transport service and the air force's air transport service. When MATS activated four months later, on 1 June 1948, Kuter became its first commander.

Kuter called it a "shotgun marriage," but he went to work with his normal organizational aplomb. He had helped build the army air force during World War II and was instrumental in establishing US Air Force independence. He certainly felt capable of organizing this new unified command. To this end, he wanted to keep senior leaders in the command aware of what was going on and set out to write a series of letters. As he later noted: "I wrote [the letters] trying to keep that global command of MATS oriented—and how the command was doing, what we were thinking about, what our objectives were, and an effort to make this Navy and Air Force organization into some form of cohesive, single command."[35]

In his first letter to his subordinate commanders, dated 1 September 1948, Kuter noted: "This organization consists of 54,000 uniformed men and women of the navy and the air force serving under 730 separate commanders, at bases all over the world." Of course, by the time he sent this out, the Berlin Airlift, or Operation Vittles, as it was known in the United States, was already under way. MATS proved its organizational soundness and its operational capability in its first six months of operations when its global resources were directed into the operation of the airlift. Operation Vittles was a purely air power operation, but, contrary to the teachings of Douhet and Billy Mitchell and to a lesser extent the instructors at the Air Corps Tactical School, including a young Lieutenant Larry Kuter, it was a conflict to be won by aerial lift and not bombardment.[36]

The Berlin Airlift

The Berlin Airlift developed slowly over the course of spring 1948 during a series of moves and countermoves between the Western powers and the Soviet Union over access rights to the city of Berlin. General Lucius D. Clay, US Army, began relying more heavily on air-delivered supplies as early as April. This continued until late June, when the Soviets cut off access to the city by rail and river. Clay had two choices: drive an armored column toward Berlin and risk a shooting confrontation with the Soviets to open the land routes or bypass the ground routes and use only the already agreed-on aerial routes, which would make the Soviets the aggressors if they interfered. The agreed-on air routes into the city proved to be significantly more complex for the Soviet Union to shut down without escalating tensions into a shooting war. US Air Forces in Europe (USAFE), commanded by Curtis LeMay, responded by slowly increasing the air traffic flying into Berlin to deliver supplies to the beleaguered city. To keep the operation up, USAFE needed men and aircraft from MATS. It established the Airlift Task Force with Major General William H. "Bill" Tunner commanding. Tunner therefore had to report to both LeMay for airlift operations and Kuter since the bulk of the airlift assets belonged to MATS.[37]

Undeniably, Kuter's biggest challenge during his time commanding MATS came during the Berlin Crisis. His second biggest challenge probably came in the form of one of his deputy commanders, Bill Tunner. Tunner later argued that Kuter "blithely took off for an inspection tour of MATS operations in the Pacific, leaving me to mind the store and fret about Berlin." Nothing could be further from the truth. It is also apparent from the letters exchanged between Kuter and Tunner that Tunner did not seem to be piqued at all. The two wrote each other continuously during the early months of the airlift operation, and at no time did one or the other indicate anything other than cooperation.[38]

Kuter also worried about sending Tunner to Berlin in the first place.

LeMay was a notoriously—some might say legendary—tough-nosed individual, and there was no doubt that a commander in one theater would resent an officer from a different theater, and in this case not a war fighter, being sent to take charge of an operation. Kuter knew this: "There was not a good feeling there at all. Will didn't generate a great deal of friendship wherever he went. He was good, but he was a boss man; he didn't persuade; he ordered. And LeMay is not noted for his warmth of person either. . . . So there was bound to be trouble. So there was organizational competition."[39]

It would be all too easy to get bogged down in a retelling of the story of the Berlin Airlift, but Kuter's portion of the event focused exclusively on the relationship between MATS and the airlift itself, which was a USAFE operation. Therefore, the discussion here is more about the relationship between Major General Kuter and Major General Tunner, two men of the same rank in the same organization with different perceptions as to how best to handle the airlift. MATS provided aircraft and aircrews for the operation, but it was not by any stretch a MATS operation.[40]

While his later recollections could be as circumspect as Tunner's, Kuter recalled the beginning of serious airlift operations this way: "When I was in Shanghai, I got a message that Berlin had been blockaded and had to be supported by air and to come back to Washington fast." He returned and began planning with his staff:

> I met with my people in MATS headquarters and, within hours, I concluded that this had to be a MATS operation. Nobody else had the lift; we did. My deputy for operations ought to go over there and run it, Brig. Gen. William "Bill" Tunner—that we should support him. Throughout the command, we assembled crews and, in accordance with the guidance from the Joint Chiefs, scaled down other lifts to provide that lift. That was the national objective. Bill was on his way. We were in the airlift in just a very short time.[41]

Kuter later remembered that, while MATS received very little credit for providing the critical components necessary for the operation to get up and running, Tunner had no problem with personally accepting praise:

> I was a bit piqued myself and registered it two or three times, because MATS was rarely credited with that operation. We had built a huge training school out at Great Falls, Montana, around

an exact duplicate of the airlift. We trained hundreds of crews to fly the airlift. Every airplane got its heavy maintenance in MATS facilities back in the states, hauling something. . . . MATS did the right thing; we provided all of the support; we did all of the work. We got the talent there, and we supported them, and we kept them there. It was a MATS operation and a good one.[42]

While MATS played a prominent role in the airlift, perhaps even the dominant role, Kuter did not fully support the operation despite what he remembered. The historian Dan Harrington pointed out that Kuter held serious reservations about committing too much of the MATS force to the airlift project. This was a perfectly understandable position because supporting the airlift did not alleviate his responsibilities to provide MATS transport everywhere around the globe. He was caught in a catch-22. He had only so many aircraft at his disposal to provide airlift, be that in Berlin or anywhere else, and taking aircraft from one sector and funneling them into Europe for Vittles inevitably left him with fewer aircraft to perform day-to-day operations. Providing air support to Berlin did not obviate MATS' other responsibilities, and it would be irresponsible if the organization failed somewhere else because its assets were all tied up in Berlin. It was, of course, correct for Kuter to keep his eye on worldwide operations while Tunner more myopically focused on Vittles. This became a back-and-forth conversation between Kuter and Tunner but one that remained cordial despite their disagreements.[43]

Tunner wrote his first preliminary report to Kuter in early August after having been in the region long enough to make a detailed account of the operation as it currently stood. In his opinion, the entire operation came down to one issue: "The key to the whole problem is big airplanes and lots of them." In this instance, he indicated, C-54s were the aircraft needed if Vittles was to succeed, as many as 225 of them. He later noted that General Clay was going to ask for more airplanes: "I get the impression that he is a man with big ideas and that, however much tonnage we can give him, he will want more."[44]

Kuter wrote to Tunner: "MATS will wind up in a very strong position if you have . . . all troop carrier C-54s when VITTLES terminates. On the other hand, as a global air transport agency, MATS will in fact have been destroyed if we wind up with our resources in VITTLES and the troop carriers doing the global job." He acknowledged the need for more aircraft, and told Tunner they were working on getting him the 225 aircraft he requested, but warned: "The withdrawal of this number will very nearly put us out of the global transport business." Again, he approached the Berlin Airlift from a holistic perspective. Simply because MATS aircraft participated in the airlift did not alleviate his responsibilities elsewhere. He finally told Tunner to keep up the good work: "The eyes of the world are on you. You may be sure the whole MATS organization has the very keenest interest in your show . . . [and] hopes for your continued success." After this, the airlift settled, more or less, into routine, at least as routine as an operation of that magnitude could ever settle into. Kuter continued to support Tunner, and, although the two had disagreements, relations never turned hostile. It was not until years later that Tunner made undignified and uncalled-for attacks against Kuter.[45]

During the Berlin Airlift, there were turf fights, not just between Kuter and Tunner, but also between the leaders of all the commands involved. Tunner resented being under USAFE control. In his opinion, this was a MATS operation and, more importantly, a MATS operation under his command. Brigadier General John K. Cannon, LeMay's replacement as the USAFE commander, did not see it this way. As far as Cannon was concerned, this was his airlift, and Tunner was just there to help organize and run the operation. It was a classic case of what the historian Dan Harrington called "poor command relationships." Tunner wanted this to be a purely MATS operation under his own command, and, as he explained later, he strongly believed: "I knew best how the job should be done." LeMay, and later Cannon, knew that, as commander of USAFE, he was ultimately responsible for the success or failure of the airlift. Kuter was more of an outside observer in all this. Tunner technically belonged to him, as did many of the aircraft, but it was not his operation to run.[46]

In January 1949, while the airlift was at its full operational tempo, Kuter spoke to the Institute of Aeronautical Sciences. The airlift was the focus of the majority of his comments. He noted that, at full strength, the airlift task force under USAFE operated more than 225 C-54s, 25 US Navy R5Ds, and more than 100 aircraft flown by the Royal Air Force. He reminded his audience that this was an airlift force that operated even as they sat enjoying their dinner. He sounded as much the advocate for the airlift as he used to sound like an advocate for bombardment: "For the first time in peacetime history, air transport—strategic air transport—has become a conspicuous expression of American air power, peace power, and an effective weapon of diplomacy."[47]

In the end, it did not matter who received the credit, although many of the participants, Kuter included, spent years remembering the event from their own particular perspective. Airlift proved to be both an indispensable and a strategic part of air power. It also allowed the Western powers to paint communism in an ever more unflattering light. Kuter's contributions to the Berlin Airlift were minimal, but they were impossible to ignore. If nothing else, his ability to provide support to the airlift and keep MATS going proved him to be a capable commander on a global scale.

Commanding MATS

The numerous disconnected units of MATS necessitated that, as the commander, Kuter either bring his units' leaders to him or travel to see them. In a way he did both. Early on, he often took trips to visit his field units, as noted so blithely by Tunner. However, as the senior commander, this was precisely what he was supposed to do as a geographic and functional commander: delegate authority to subordinate commanders while maintaining focus on the overall health of the entire organization.

His early travels brought Kuter into contact with a variety of world leaders. This included the president of Saudi Arabia, Abdul-Aziz ibn Saud. One of the MATS units was located at Dhahran Air Base. As Kuter later reported: "[The president] didn't like American Ambassadors, even our best ambassadors. On the other hand, he like generals, good, bad, big or little, but especially big." This worked out well for Kuter, who was six-two. Kuter also learned on visiting the base that ibn Saud had been a guest of President Roosevelt's in the aftermath of the Cairo conference in 1943. The cultural formalities of the Bedouin king meant that he felt a strong connection to the American president, one that did not end with Roosevelt's death and the transfer of power to Harry Truman. As far as ibn Saud was concerned, he was still a close, personal friend of the American president.[48]

The first meeting between the king and the general was nothing short of terrifying for Kuter. Despite his extensive travel through the Middle East, he had never been without the comforting support of a group, nor had he ever been the most senior leader present. He entered the king's presence only to discover a room "occupied by grim weather-beaten Bedouins all wearing drab brown burnooses and cradling long curved swords in gold encrusted scabbards." Worse, there was no way of knowing precisely which one was the king. An interpreter, a graduate of the University of Southern California, collected Kuter and took him to the king.[49]

The king wrongly assumed that Kuter, one of Roosevelt's generals, was very close to the "seat of power," that is, the president. In audience, Kuter was told (through the interpreter) that "his friend the president would always do what the King wanted if one of the president's generals told the president whereas ambassadors only wrote notes to somebody in the capital and never told the president what the king wanted." This was typically done in front of the ambassador, much to Kuter's discomfort. Luckily, the ambassador, James Reeves Childs, knew to expect this. He later told Kuter that there was no point in arguing with the king or attempting to explain to him how the American political and military establishments worked. Kuter and Childs developed a routine where, on each visit, Kuter listened to ibn Saud, took notes, and then passed them on to Childs, who forwarded them up through the proper political channels.

April 1950 found Kuter, along with most of the other general officers in the US Air Force, at Ramey Air Force Base, Puerto Rico, for the second commanders' conference. It was a time for these senior leaders to "let [their] hair down and see what the problems are and see if [they] can get some of them solved." This was certainly a mere metaphor, although General Vandenberg did allow them to change out of uniform into sports clothes. These meetings became routine in later years under the name *corona*. Even from a modern perspective, sometimes the best way to let an organization know what its missions and priorities are is to get all its senior officers in the same room at the same time. Kuter believed that meetings like this one helped the postwar air force plan for both the near- and the long-term future. It was the same way he operated as commander of MATS.[50]

Not all aspects of commanding MATS involved diligent and difficult work. The other way Kuter led the organization was to frequently bring his commanders to him. As he noted: "It was essential that the many busy operating Major Commanders, stationed separately at distant points on the globe, be brought together with reasonable frequency in order to have some interest and understanding of the capabilities and the limitations of the other components with which they had to cooperate and, more basically, to know each other." Kuter wanted to duplicate the commander's conference he was a part of at Ramey Air Force Base. He believed that face-to-face meetings were one of the best ways to make his intentions to his commanders known.[51]

Kuter made a point of gathering his worldwide commanders together once a quarter, but he did so in a unique way. He directed that two of those meetings each year be held at MATS headquarters at Andrews Air

Force Base. The other two were "off-sites," held at other MATS locations around the globe. Kuter had several bases available to him for those other meetings. These included multiple locations on the East and West Coasts of the United States, Hickam Air Force Base, Hawaii, and stations in both Europe and Asia. While Kuter mentions calling his commanders together in Hawaii and Texas, there is no indication in any record of Kuter's or in the MATS histories that a meeting was ever held in Dhahran, Saudi Arabia. Some locales were simply better suited for meetings than others.[52]

These meetings, while still occurring in many military commands, would probably not be tolerated as part of official business by the air force today, at least not to the degree that Kuter's excursions mirrored an officially sanctioned vacation. One of these meetings bears mentioning here because it helped engender in Kuter a love for hunting, an activity that nearly cost him his life later. In the fall of 1950, he and nine of his most senior commanders met at the MATS headquarters element located in Wiesbaden, Germany. After a full day of discussions and meetings, the group boarded a train on which the staterooms "might well have read, 'Himmler' or 'Goebbels' or 'Eva' slept here." From there, Kuter and his small group moved to Garmisch, where the group broke up, some to ski, some to golf, and some to hunt. Kuter admitted to not being a golfer yet in his life. He also confessed: "Some folks may really like downhill skiing in the Alps—I am the sauerbraten, kartoffelsalat, and Munchener beer type." That left hunting.[53]

Early the next morning, Kuter and a small party drove out to meet their German *Jägermeisters* (master hunters), who were responsible for the party. Despite a life in uniform, the physicality of climbing the three thousand feet up the mountain trail winded Kuter and the subordinates who had also chosen hunting. They reached the top of their mountain and looked across to the Brenner Pass. Now they prepared and sat in wait for the Hirsch, a cousin of the American elk. In the end, Kuter only sighted a Hirsch through his scope, but it was too distant for the *Jägermeisters* to give permission to fire. However, something about the event kindled in Kuter a desire to hunt more, and he did not have to wait long, although with more of the same results.[54]

After the hunt for elk failed to produce results, Kuter and the rest of his MATS subordinates took part in "Royal Hunt." Kuter recalled that his hunting party did not look the part: "Each was dressed differently and between us we produced the full line of Sears Roebuck, L. L. Bean, and Army Quartermaster in variated old, worn, middle grade hunting hats, coats, jackets, straight trousers, cuffed trousers, rubber boots, field shoes, paratrooper boots, etc." He admitted to being envious of the German *Jägermeisters* in their official hunting uniforms complete with trophied feathers. His contingent was strategically placed in hunting stands at the exit to a forest, and the German *Jägermeisters* and "beaters" drove the game to them by charging through the forest with hunting dogs while making loud calls and beating the trees with sticks.[55]

The hunters were expected to kill any game, large or small, that escaped by running into the open field. The *Oberjägermeister* implored the party to shoot only once the game had fully exited the forest, and thus not to shoot in the direction of the forest, and to avoid shooting "the beaters, their dogs, the jägers or themselves." As the commanding officer, Kuter was given the "premier platz" from which to shoot. Of course, this was the spot that offered the best chance of shooting the game, and, as tradition would have it, it also proved to be the least active spot. Kuter shot nothing that day, but his men bagged enough game for a magnificent dinner. He wistfully remembered that the next day it was back to the "humdrum responsibility for running air transportation, communication, weather, and rescue service around the world."[56]

Two years later, the same MATS global resources were operating across the Pacific Ocean in support of the fighting in Korea. At the same time, Kuter's command brought the air evacuation of troops into extensive and effective operation. Kuter's time as MATS commander ended, three years now being more than enough time for a commander to stay in the same command billet. At least this time Larry and Ethel did not have to move far, as now Lieutenant General Kuter was selected to return to the Pentagon as the air force deputy chief of staff for personnel.

8

Air University

The position of deputy chief of staff for personnel (DCS/P) came with a promotion. In April 1951, Kuter was promoted to lieutenant general a few months before being posted to his next assignment. He returned to the Pentagon for the first time since the end of World War II and, in a career that saw many Pentagon assignments, for the final time. There is no question that this was a purely staff officer position, even for a senior officer. Kuter reported directly to the air force chief of staff, General Hoyt S. Vandenberg, the second man to hold that position after General Carl Spaatz. Kuter's career had reached the point that, while he still commanded units, he was far removed from the day-to-day leading of airmen. His world revolved around policy decisions now, but important ones. He delved into decisions and organizations still affecting the air force, including the creation of the US Air Force Academy (USAFA) and the accreditation of Air University.

Despite being a prolific writer throughout his career, Kuter left very little information on his time as the DCS/P. In only one letter written as he was departing the job in 1953 did he tell his family that it was "[his] business to arrange for the manning of all key positions in the United States Air Force, or at least to know all the intentions of the Chief of Staff." Only two major events stand out during his time back in Washington. The first was the establishment of the USAFA, and the second was a hunting trip where Kuter did his level best *not* to be killed by a rampaging bear.[1]

The USAFA

Lieutenant General Kuter spent a considerable amount of time as the DCS/P working on the establishment of the USAFA, including the selection of the staff and faculty members as well as which courses would be included in the curriculum. He noted that, even before the war, when an independent air force was discussed, there already existed plans for the creation of a separate air force academy.[2]

Kuter, and by extension his staff inside the Pentagon, insisted that the academy's faculty members all be uniformed service members. (West Point was only beginning to experiment with credentialed civilian instructors at this time.) It was his belief that the "high standards of morale, esprit, tone, attitude, and discipline" could come only from uniformed faculty and not "from purely academic types." He insisted that only "fighting men" instruct the cadets. He wanted those instructors to be all rated pilots. His tone softened in later years, and he admitted in 1974: "I would not take those positions as strongly now."[3]

As a West Point graduate, Kuter also reviewed the history and traditions at both West Point and Annapolis for possible structural incorporation in the new air force academy. He said that he wanted to "pick the good things and eject the stupid things." Among the "stupid things" were rifles and swords, which would he thought make the new academy too much like West Point. He had support in this measure because there was "unanimous opposition." The problem was that no one could come up with any other solutions, especially when it came to marching and parades. The rifles and swords stayed. Kuter also worked with other senior leaders to ensure that there was to be a durable system for the freshman, such as the one he experienced, and a strict honor code: "I wanted a strong, plebe system concept that was strictly from West Point. I wanted kids picked up and 'shaken' vigorously into shape."[4]

There is one element to the development of the USAFA for which Kuter did not receive approval. He felt strongly that the academy should be subordinate to Air University. Although he found it natural to organize the air force education system hierarchically, many did not agree with him, including Harold Talbott, the new secretary of the air force. Talbott and Kuter did not see eye to eye on many issues, the organization of the academy being one of them. Their inability to find common ground could also be a reason Kuter was never considered for either the vice chief or the chief of staff position. In this instance, Talbott won out, but having two separate institutions within the air force functioning as colleges would cause problems later on.[5]

The Bear Hunt

On 12 June 1952, Kuter traveled to Anchorage, Alaska, for a meeting with the commanders of the Alaskan theater. He also flew separately out to the air force station at Cold Bay on the tip of the Alaskan Peninsula. Once there, he changed out of his uniform and into civilian attire. He was now on leave and headed out on a hunting trip. He flew north to a small lake in the Left Hand Valley and met with his friend Walt Abbey. From there the pair hiked two miles to a small camp in the valley where they met other hunting parties and their guide for this trip, Mike Utecht. At 3:30 the next morning, the hunt for Kodiak bears began.[6]

Utecht hiked his charges through the valley and up along ridges in search of the bears. Along the way he explained the vision and hearing limitations of the bears but also the extraordinary sense of smell that meant that hunters had to stay upwind of them. If the wind conditions were not correct, the bears would lift their heads, sniff the air, and shamble off out of harm's way, something Kuter and Abbey experienced that day. Utecht also used this time to assess his guests and determine whether they possessed the mental stability required to hunt bears. Although bears rarely attacked hunters, preferring to get away from danger, they had been known to do so, and Utecht was very particular about whom he allowed to get into a firing position.[7]

In the course of their hike to a secondary hunting cabin, which served as their base of operations, Kuter and Abbey saw dozens of bears, but never under such conditions that their guide allowed them to take a shot. Arriving at their destination, the trio discovered that bear cubs had broken into the cabin and ransacked it. Kuter remembered that Utecht was visibly furious that his hunting partner had failed to secure the door correctly. The bears had not only destroyed the sleeping bags and the cots but eaten all the prestocked provisions as well. The cabin was "knee deep in feathers, Kapok, canned goods, coffee grounds and bear droppings." The group cleaned the cabin as best they could, rolled out what remained of the sleeping bags, and got what sleep they could trying not to think of the cabin's previous occupants.[8]

They awoke early the next morning, ate breakfast, drank "brown fluid identified as coffee," and headed out to stalk their prey. Utecht told them that two large bears, a male and a female, were not too far away and that the wind conditions were favorable for an approach within firing distance. They marched out and within an hour had crawled to a vantage point from which they could shoot, only to discover that a second large male had joined the group and that the males were currently fighting over the female. Kuter, Abbey, and Utecht were only one hundred paces from the fighting bears (a distance they later measured off). Utecht arranged Kuter on the left and Abbey on the right and assigned them the bears they were each to fire at. The bears batted, pawed, and roared at each other as they continued to fight, slowing ambling in the direction of the shooters. Utecht needed to get them up on their hind legs to give his charges better shots at the bears' massive hearts.[9]

When all was ready, Kuter and Abbey in position and ready to fire, Utecht jumped up and shouted. Their adrenaline already up, the bears broke apart and rose to their full height. Utecht told his companions to shoot. Kuter could see nothing in his scope but thick brown fur. He pulled the trigger. The bullet's impact tore through the bear's heart with 3,450 pounds of pressure. The impact knocked the bear end over end, but he came up fighting. Kuter remembered that the bear then charged in his direction. Utecht would tell him later that it was probably just trying to escape to the safety of the tree line behind the shooters, but all Kuter could see was a bear headed directly for him. He fired again. The second round spun the bear around, but it continued to move forward. Kuter fired a third shot and then a fourth: "His final viciously aggressive action, with eyes blazing violence in my direction was to open his great jaws, gather up a craw full of stone and gravel which I could hear him grind in his last living movements." The massive bear lay dead no more than seven steps from Kuter's position.[10]

Kuter snapped back to the reality of the moment with Utecht shouting at him. Locked in battle with the first bear, Kuter completely forgot that there was another bear, Abbey's. It was still moving and also attempting to escape into the alder bushes, but, with two hunters now firing at it, it dropped just short of the tree line. Utecht later recounted to Kuter and Abbey that the first shots should have dropped both animals on the spot, but that the adrenaline already pumping through their systems while they were fighting each other only increased when he started shouting to get their attention. Both animals were in peak fighting condition when the hunters opened fire.[11]

The hunters returned to the cabin and collected their knives and Kuter's Kodachrome camera. The sun broke through the clouds, allowing them to get the necessary pictures, "hunter with trophy, hunter with guide and trophy." The photograph of Kuter and Utecht showed a truly colossal bear turned on its side, claws clearly visible with a smiling Kuter sitting behind his hulk of a kill, both hunter and guide dwarfed by the dead animal. After that, the rest of the day was spent skinning what turned out to be two enormous bears, both possibly of record-setting size. The skins were eventually packed away to be sent to a taxidermist and turned into rugs. The hunters salted the meat, placed it into barrels, and loaded the barrels onto a boat piloted by one of the Utecht's associates to be shipped downriver. The skulls eventually found their way to the American Museum of Natural History in New York, where the Boone and Crockett Club measured the heads. Kuter's bear officially measured in at $28^5/_{16}$ inches, just shy of the world record. Kuter said: "I shall forever maintain that mine was a very big bear with a relatively small head and some other lucky trophy hunters had located lesser bears with oversized heads." He called it a thrilling hunt but a once-in-a-lifetime experience that never needed to be repeated.[12]

Air University

Kuter stayed in his position as the DCS/P until April 1953, when he assumed command of Air University at Maxwell Air Force Base, Alabama. Kuter actually lobbied for this position. In his own words: "Ethel and I liked Montgomery. . . . I have had a strong professional interest in officer education since that date and I was the principal staff officer under Arnold who worked with my good friend, the late great Muir S. Fairchild and established the concept of Air University." It was no secret among his Pentagon colleagues that he hoped to return to Maxwell: "I announced at every possible opportunity, after becoming the Deputy Chief of Staff, Personnel, that naturally I would follow in Idwal H. Edwards' [Edwards was his DCS/P predecessor] wise footsteps and move from this assignment back to Maxwell." He received his wish.[13]

The idea of an air force university for professional officer education predated the war. Kuter recalled: "Before the war, Santy Fairchild and I had drawn up a lot of futuristic charts of a separate Air Force, and there always had been an Air Force Academy in it. There always had been an Air Force professional educational system, the concept of the Air University." His time as an instructor at ACTS was at least influential enough for him to want the education of officers—particularly flyers—to be greatly expanded after the war. He said that he felt that ACTS "had made a very great contribution to the country and the defense system." He also undoubtedly wanted an air force institution that rivaled the army's Command and General Staff School.[14]

When it came time for Lieutenant General Edwards to retire, it was Kuter's job as the personnel chief to make official recommendations to General Vandenberg as to who should replace him. On 15 January 1953, Kuter entered Vandenberg's office with two names, neither one of which was his own. Vandenberg then informed Kuter that it was actually his intention to name him to the position. There was also the very strong possibility that Secretary Talbott wanted Kuter as far away from himself and the Pentagon as possible. Kuter's next assignment found him making the homecoming that he and Ethel ardently desired. To date his longest posting had been his time as a student and instructor at ACTS. He was now returning to Maxwell Air Force Base as the commander of Air University.[15]

Kuter's longtime friend Rosie O'Donnell replaced him as DCS/P, and Kuter found several officers in the Pentagon expressing disappointment that he was not staying around to take a fourth star and a job as either the vice chief or the chief of staff. His name did come up later for consideration as a possible candidate for these positions, but he was competing at that point with more senior officers. Kuter was also demure, but premature, in a letter to family members saying: "It is sure that I will not be promoted." In the same letter he stated: "For the confident and personal information of my friends and my family, I do not now or ever want to be Chief of Staff or the Vice Chief of Staff." This was because he did not want to deal with the problematic relations between Congress and the military, a result of the then-prevailing political climate, apparently a problem as old as civil-military relations period. It is also possible that he simply could not see himself working for Secretary Talbott, and the reverse was probably true as well. Kuter had no choice but to leave Washington, but it was to go to an assignment that he very much wanted.[16]

On arriving at Air University, Kuter moved forward with obtaining funding for the as-yet-unbuilt library and securing degree-granting rights for the Air Force Institute of Technology, a subordinate of Air University. His goal was to have Air University operate like an actual institute of higher education. To that end, he also initiated an annual air power symposium to which were invited the best minds from around the country in the fields of business, government, and the military. Forty to fifty individuals assembled at Maxwell each year and distributed throughout the seminars of the relatively new Air War College. It was at one of these symposia that Kuter allowed the university to take credit for an up-and-coming doctrine: "Massive retaliation was the philosophy, I believe initiated and I know developed at the Air University at about that time. As I remember it, it preceded by about two years John Dulles' use of the phrase. I believe John Foster Dulles attended one of our airpower symposiums. I know Allen Dulles participated in all of them as an active member."[17]

Beyond these symposiums, Kuter did not have much luck in developing further air power doctrines. Air University was a great place to discuss and develop doctrine but not to test it or put it to practical use. Kuter envisioned, perhaps naively, an organization where the air force's newest doctrines could be created, debated, and then flown and tested from the base, exactly the situation he experienced at ACTS. When asked years later what happened to the concept of the Air War College actively developing and testing new doctrine, he replied: "It drifted away."[18]

As the Air University commander, he was expected to address each of the classes, including both the captain's course, called Squadron Officer School (SOS), and the more senior course for majors at the Air Command and Staff School (ACSS). (ACSS was the successor to ACTS.) His first speech to an in-residence class, probably on 15 September 1953, was delivered to SOS, a course for midgrade captains that varied in length from six weeks to three months. (The length of the course changed often.) Very few of these officers would have been veterans of World War II, but a significantly higher proportion would have served in Korea. Kuter wanted each and every one of them to make a career of the air force: "I believe that you should find considerable assurance in my conviction that no Air Force officer in good health is ever going to be involuntarily separated if his effectiveness reports show . . . that this officer is a leader in thought and action."[19]

In November, he spoke to SOS again, and the old ACTS instructor came out. He informed the students that there was no way his speech would take less than seventy minutes and told them to grab "a cup of coffee": "Coffee helps to keep some people awake, even after a heavy lunch." The remarks that followed revealed that the development of doctrine and the role of Air University in that development were very much on his mind: "Officially, the Air University is responsible for drawing up the doctrine of the United States Air Force . . . for drafting progressive changes required to keep our doctrine alive and valid . . . for assuring that Air Force doctrine is understood throughout our armed services." It was clear that he continued to envision an Air University that functioned like ACTS. His experience as a student and instructor there had been so defining of who he was as an officer that he wanted to replicate it for this next generation.[20]

This proved to be a bridge too far. While ACTS students could take classes one week and then conduct an exercise in those early bombing and pursuit aircraft, giving the Air University students the same opportunity proved to be impractical at Maxwell Air Force Base during Kuter's time there. ACTS was, in a sense, lightning in a bottle. The years Kuter spent as an ACTS student and instructor and the core of officers surrounding him were unique to their time and particular circumstances. Beyond that, technology was also moving beyond what Maxwell was capable of providing or at least what the air force wanted it to provide. The jet aircraft of which Kuter spoke so fondly needed special infrastructure and specialized ranges. The implementation of doctrine in the form of tactics, techniques, and new procedures moved from Air University to testing and training bases, including Nellis, Hill, Eglin, and Tyndall. Air University became a facility focused on the education of students. Testing and tactics moved to other bases, and Maxwell became a sleepy hollow. This disappointed Kuter, but he still managed to help build Air University into a thriving, if not entirely academic, environment. To his credit, no officer in the US Air Force who demonstrates potential for advancement and promotion is capable of avoiding at least one year of service at Maxwell Air Force Base.

On 17 December, Kuter spoke again to ACSS. He wanted these students to know that, unlike the situation that prevailed during the Second World War, there was currently unlikely to be the time necessary to build up large forces or to make the kinds of early mistakes the air force made in 1942 and 1943: "In World War II there was time . . . but in the Jetomic Age there is no bank of time to draw on. . . . In the Jetomic Age there is no tolerance for gross mistakes about air power." He continued: "Air Power, they insist, has done nothing but extend into the air the ways of combat that surface forces have always used. Scarcely a day goes by that we do not hear that the wars of the future will always be settled by the slugging soldier on the ground, by inference, in hand-to-hand and man-to-man combat."[21]

Kuter found it useful to quote Admiral Arthur Radford, a navy man and incidentally the chairman of the Joint Chiefs of Staff, when defining *air power:* "Airpower is the dominant factor in war. It may not win a war by itself alone, but without it no major war can be won. As far as we are concerned, it is a primary requirement, both offensively and defensively, and in support of other forces."[22]

As previously mentioned, a problem arose while Kuter commanded Air University with regard to confusion between the university and the air force academy; that is, the press kept confusing or conflating the two. During one visit to his command, he later recalled: "Some members of the national press were visiting the Air University. They were surprised and impressed by the work that the officers' wives were doing. They wrote up a substantial story correctly but some headline writer put the Air Force Academy headline on it. Talbott had me on the phone instantly for damaging his Academy." Kuter was actually forced to form a committee to try and determine a new name for Air University, but either no new name could be settled on, or the committee simply disappeared with Talbott's resignation in 1955.[23]

Numerous international officers also wanted to attend the courses at Maxwell Air Force Base, notably ACSS. Kuter remembered an unusual practice he observed: "At Maxwell it was not unusual for visiting members from senior air forces in the Orient to present inscribed portraits when they called on the Commander of the Air University. Not being very bright I just thought they were insufferably egotistical whereas they were paying great respect according to their custom."[24]

As the commander of Air University, Kuter elevated the standing of both ACSS and SOS. These were important changes affecting the quality of education offered at the university. While this was still long before professional military education courses became degree-granting institutions, it was certainly a move in that direction. Kuter also brought Air University closer to its original concept as a university with a university staff and faculty to handle all levels of professional military education in the US Air Force. This concept has been adopted by the air forces of several foreign countries.

Kuter's career was still ascending. In 1955, General Nathan F. Twining, now the air force chief of staff, called him to Washington and informed him that he was headed to the Pacific theater to take over the Far East Air Forces, headquartered in Tokyo. The new position also came with a promotion to full general. Kuter protested both the job and the promotion. He was of the opinion that his work at Maxwell was finally bearing fruit, and he wanted to stay until it was completed. Twining was slightly shocked. The vice chief of staff, General Thomas White, told Kuter: "No one turns down a four star promotion." And Kuter did not. Just shy of twenty-seven years of service, he was promoted to four-star general.[25]

Ethel and Larry "bade farewell" to Maxwell Air Force Base on 14 May 1955. They would return there many times in the future, either for Kuter to give speeches at one of the schools or as a member of the Air University's Board of Visitors during his retirement. Although they lived in other locations longer, they always felt a special attachment to Maxwell. Ethel later called it "the happy home of our heart." Major General Dean C. Strother took "acting command" of Air University. Kuter trooped the line, walked from the stage, and stepped into his car, where Ethel was waiting, and the two drove away from the heart of Dixie to the West Coast. There they boarded a plane to Hickam Air Force Base and beyond that Tokyo, but the new command proved more complicated than initially anticipated.[26]

9

Fixing the Far East Air Forces and Creating the Pacific Air Forces

While in flight over the Pacific Ocean on his way to Tokyo to take command of the Far East Air Forces (FEAF), Lieutenant General Kuter was promoted to full general at 12:01 A.M., 29 May 1955. As an officer whose first flight was in a biplane, he surely did not miss the importance of assuming this final rank on a transoceanic flight. During his career, the US Army Air Corps had transitioned to a truly independent air force capable of global operations, but it was also flying Kuter rather comfortably to his new assignment. The air force had, like Kuter, fully matured and reached a pinnacle thought impossible as little as a decade before. Kuter had grown with this air force, molding it, organizing it, shaping it, and giving it the ability to span the globe. The promotion took place in the air as a matter of prestige. The outgoing FEAF commander wanted to ensure that the new commander arrived a full four-star general and would not have to go through a promotion ceremony with the local populace and dignitaries. He felt it would be better if Kuter exited the aircraft in Japan already wearing four stars.

It is easy to forget just how large an area Kuter was now responsible for. As he pointed out: "It is as far from Tokyo to Manila as it is from Winnipeg to Miami. Farther from Bangkok to Tokyo than it is from Salt Lake City to Honolulu." He was expected not only to manage his disparate forces but also to visit them and the heads of state of their respective countries as well. His time as commander of both FEAF and the Pacific Air Forces (PACAF) offers insight into the geopolitical realities of Southeast Asia and the Pacific region as a whole during the Cold War era. Korea cleared the front page of the press after the conflict ended in 1953, but Kuter's excursions throughout the region provide insight into the global struggle against communism in this particular part of the world.[1]

Kuter took command of FEAF on 2 June 1955 and promptly moved into the commander's "home," owned by the Tajima family, but administered by the government of Japan. Once in command, he immediately realized that he was faced with a major problem: there existed two masters of air power in the Pacific, and he was only one of them. Pacific air units were split between FEAF and PACAF, in Hawaii. On paper, Kuter controlled PACAF and had a staff that worked there. However, he did not have the authority to move his air units from one command to the other without the permission of two theater commanders—those of the Pacific Command (PACOM) and the Far East Command (FECOM)—or the Joint Chiefs. Kuter became determined to fix this problem and unify all air assets in the Pacific under one commander.[2]

What the new commander needed was the ability to rapidly deploy units from either command to meet threats, but the separation of powers between FECOM and PACOM hindered this. Kuter immediately made a long-term recommendation that change needed to be enacted. His strenuous objections to the divided command system were sent forward in a formal recommendation to the chief of staff, US Air Force, at this time General Nathan Twining. Kuter was not the only one making waves over FECOM and PACOM. The Joint Chiefs of Staff of all the services examined the issue as part of the Unified Command Plan reorganization of 1956. Kuter's position was also the US Air Force's official position. The navy agreed with the air force, but the holdout was the US Army. Army chief of staff General Maxwell Taylor took the opposite approach and called for the expansion of FECOM to include Taiwan, Indonesia, and the Philippines. Unable to come to a decision, the Joint Chiefs referred the matter to the secretary of defense, Charles Wilson, for arbitration. Wilson sided with the navy and the air force, paving the way for the consolidation of the two commands and the establishment of the single Pacific Command.[3]

The new plan, approved on 21 June 1956, was to go into effect on 1 July 1957. On 30 June 1957, Kuter, the most senior members of his staff, and local dignitaries held a small ceremony at the airfield. Larry Kuter, Ethel, and the rest of the former FEAF command staff departed Tokyo on 30 June at 11:45 P.M. And, at midnight, 1 July 1957, FEAF ceased to exist—*disestablished* in military speak—and Kuter became the commander in chief of the newly established PACAF with his headquarters at Hickam Air Force Base in Hawaii.[4]

As was customary in Japan, when Larry and Ethel were packing their belongings in preparation for the move to Hawaii, the owners of the Tajima house asked them to pick a gift from the furnishings of the house to take with them. Ethel chose an ancient stone lantern. The lantern eventually went on a journey all its on, but that story will be shared later. A bonus to moving into the larger home at Hickam Air Force Base was that the Kuters could have household goods held in storage at Maxwell shipped to the new home. However, when those goods arrived, it was discovered that things were missing and damaged. While this was an expectation among military families around the world, it was a bit more than the Kuters were used to accepting. Larry wrote: "During the storage and shipment in the States nothing was pilfered, except the expensive items. They were looted expertly. No furniture was broken except the good furniture. Eleven crates . . . were missing from the Maxwell inventory. This was the worst move ever. All damages added up from all the previous 30 years of moves resulted in less than this one."[5]

FEAF headquarters was outside Tokyo at Fuchu Air Station. Kuter found it to be a fifty-minute ride from his residence to the base. He spent the time in the car dictating notes to his secretary, who also rode with him. For his first two years in the Pacific, the Kuters lived at the Tajima house, a survivor of World War II. Along with whatever personal items he brought, Kuter came to his new assignment and home with old prejudices: "It was hard for me to understand how these same people managed the Death March in the Philippines, in which I lost a number of classmates. I was no friend of the Japanese when I moved in there; they had killed friends. It was hard for me to associate those atrocities with their character as it appeared to me when I arrived."[6]

The consolidation from FEAF to PACAF and FECOM to PACOM took the better part of Kuter's first two years as FEAF commander, but there was a lot more going on the Pacific region than just doctrinal and organizational changes. Kuter also spent his first two years in the Pacific dealing with problems unique to FEAF. His command was one in which monotony and crisis were interspersed. His time in the Pacific also provided unintended lessons in politics, diplomacy, and the subtle art of saying what needed to be said without doing so bluntly.[7]

Kuter's lesson in understanding the Japanese people began shortly after his arrival. On 11 June, Kuter attended an award ceremony for Brigadier General Roger Ramey. During the war, Ramey led the hundreds of B-29 *Superfortresses* over the city of Tokyo in the nighttime incendiary bombing that killed more than eighty thousand Japanese. Eleven years later, the Japanese honored him with the Order of the Rising Sun on behalf of Emperor Hirohito. The presenter, Minister Funada, lost friends and family in the Tokyo firebombing, and it was he who placed the award around Ramey's neck. Kuter was shocked at the amount of "respect and affection" the people seemed to have for Ramey. Such cognitive dissonance was understandable. Here were, on the one side, the perpetrators of the Rape of Nanking and the Bataan Death March and, on the other, those who firebombed and dropped atomic weapons. Kuter discovered that the Japanese were highly objective people. For every atrocity committed by them, they could probably point to one committed by their former enemies. His time in Japan changed Larry Kuter: "I entered a Japanophobe and, I think, I emerged a Japanophile. That is a little too strong in both cases, but my attitude changed radically."[8]

Kuter continued his proclivity for long letter writing throughout his tenure as first FEAF and then PACAF commander. By this point in his career, it had at least occurred to both him and Ethel that someone, one day, might want to write about his actions during the war or his career overall or that he himself might pen another book. He had even started labeling his letters and musings "For Inclusion in My Source Material File." While some of his writings illuminate his job or his thoughts on issues he was dealing with, some proved patently long-winded. During one short leave period of four days, he wrote sixty pages recording what he and Ethel did on vacation. Another letter home came in at twenty single-spaced typed pages recounting his first few weeks as FEAF commander, the most interesting passage involving flying around Angkor Wat at low altitude.[9]

Kuter was not always so overly pedantic. He was meticulous about recording his meetings with the various heads of state of the countries in which FEAF had bases located. This included both South Korean president Syngman Rhee and Republic of China president Chiang Kai-Shek. Other notable leaders included Ramon Magsaysay of the Philippines and Ngo Dinh Diem of South Vietnam. These meetings began shortly after Kuter took command of FEAF. He kept copious notes on each of the world leaders he met. His position as FEAF and later PACAF commander proved to be equal parts military officer and diplomatic counselor. Foreign leaders, some of them former military commanders themselves, often found it easier to discuss matters with American military leaders than with the officials provided by the State Department, the same lesson Kuter learned when dealing with ibn Saud while he commanded the Military Air Transport Service.

Kuter met Syngman Rhee on 12 July 1955 when the Korean conflict was still fresh in the minds of its participants. Rhee was particularly concerned with the level of support he received from the United States. He was also upset about statements by the American secretary of state, John Foster Dulles, who told the press that he foresaw nothing in the future of North and South Korea but stalemate. Finally, the United States had also turned down South Korea's request for more arms and ammunition. According to Kuter, Rhee had been told that American military officers inside Korea already believed the "Korean Army was too big to handle." Kuter noted that this was a bad day to make his first call on the president. It did not help that Rhee's military assistant kept reaching into the breast pocket of his coat to produce newspaper clippings recalling each of these issues. As soon as Rhee changed the subject, this "eager-beaver" produced another clipping to steer the conversation back in the anti-American direction.[10]

Kuter became the recipient of Rhee's ire. Rhee indicated that he wanted the United States to leave South Korea, that the country would be better fighting and losing than remaining forever partitioned. He used Dulles's words against Kuter, saying that, since Americans saw "no way in the foreseeable future" in which the two countries could be united, there was no longer any point in having Americans in the country. He indicated to Kuter that South Korea might not win another war against the North but that it was better to die fighting now than die of starvation and strangulation over time. Kuter had no response.[11]

Chiang and Kuter had met previously, but, as commander of FEAF, he was to have much closer and more important contact with the generalissimo. On their first official meeting after he became commander of FEAF, Kuter said that Chiang recognized him from the Cairo conference of 1943. This is probably doubtful as Kuter, then just an assistant to Hap Arnold, played only a very minor role in the conference. Kuter himself recalled being simply a "back row spectator." It seemed that Chiang's primary concern in 1956 was not the fragile stalemate between his Nationalist country and Communist China but exactly how much aid the United States was giving to Japan.[12]

From a certain point of view, Chiang can be forgiven for this. He had often been on the receiving end of Japanese military strength, beginning in 1938, but he also used the US support of Japan to question whether the same elements would be given to the Chinese Nationalist forces, and, since he was questioning Kuter, he naturally focused on the Chinese Nationalist air force. He also wanted to know whether the United States was helping Japan recover and whether, if Japan was now a US ally, it would come to the aid of Chinese Nationalist forces in the future. Kuter needed to be truthful and tactful at the same time, or, as he recalled it, "honest without being blunt." He went on to tell Chiang: "I doubt very seriously that any U.S. policy maker has ever considered the extent to which the Japanese aviation industry should be engaged in support of the Chinese Nationalist Air Force. I am quite sure that our policy makers hope that China . . . will [itself] produce as much support for [its] own air forces as possible."[13]

The generalissimo was always direct with Kuter, as he was with all military officials. On more than one occasion he asked Kuter: "You are an expert on American air power and have visited some of our installations and seen some of the things that our Air Force is doing. What are we doing that we should not be doing? What are we failing to do that we should do? What should we be doing better than we are now doing? Tell me the things that you see that are wrong and weak in my Air Force." This question always occurred in the presence of the chief of Chiang's air force, General "Tiger" Wang Shu Ming, which made both air force officers extremely uncomfortable, for different reasons. Kuter again diplomatically answered that China's Nationalist air force was weak where all air forces, including that of the United States, were weak in properly educated and trained airmen at both the officer and the enlisted level. He noted that modern jet aircraft needed men with specialized training to fly and maintain them. If China was weak in this area, so was the United States, he argued. It was not an untruthful answer, but it was certainly a diplomatic one.[14]

In January 1957, Kuter visited Singapore. In the late 1950s, that city was still under British rule, although there was a growing independence movement that would soon take control of the country. At the time, however, Kuter visited the Royal Air Force (RAF) aerodrome on the island. He also visited the RAF in Kuala Lumpur, Malaysia. The trip was unremarkable except for an incident that Kuter called his "ordeal by blow gun." His hosts, Air Marshal Fressanges and Air Vice Marshal Kyle, desired to demonstrate to the PACAF commander local practices being used to put down Communist guerrillas in the local jungles. To do so, they needed to send him into the jungle at one of the RAF outposts, and there was only one way to get him there. His hosts bid him adieu and had one their pilots fly him on a small RAF Pioneer aircraft into the heart of the jungle. The plane landed at a small dirt-strip airfield guarded by Gurkhas and RAF police officers from New Zealand. Kuter and his RAF guard at the airstrip then marched into the jungle in search of a local Abo village.[15]

Kuter's RAF escort introduced him to the Abo chief and an assistant, the two about five feet tall in Kuter's estimation. It must have been a sight, a six-two Midwest American standing side by side with a local chieftain in the heart of the jungle. Both of the local men also carried seven-foot-long, polished bamboo blowguns that were taller than they were. The blowguns were extremely light and shot razor-sharp needles that were, in Kuter's estimation, about seven inches long. These the chief carried in a quiver at his side. The darts and blowguns were so well crafted that Kuter could not believe they were not made by machine. He also noticed that some of the darts had brown tips and looked as if they had been dipped in a resin. He was warned not to touch these as they were poisonous. The Abo chieftain demonstrated the procedures for loading and shooting the blowgun and then fired a dart precisely into a target piece of paper from a distance of one hundred paces. Kuter was very much impressed until the Abo chief reloaded the blow gun and made to hand it to him. The fastidious Kuter was shocked, but he was in tough position. He remembered: "Here in the Malayan jungle was a clear case of noblesse oblige. Just who was 'noblesse' was not too clear. At the moment there seemed to be no doubt at all, however, who was obliged."[16]

Kuter had no choice but to take the proffered blowgun. He also noted that it would have been poor taste indeed to produce a handkerchief to wipe of the mouthpiece. Attempting to replicate the chieftain's shot, and with all the force he could muster, he took aim at the same tree and blew into the gun; the dart landed about halfway there. His ire was now up: "This was no way for a general of the USAF to let a shooting match terminate!" Where before he was hesitant, he now asked for a reloaded blowgun and then fired again. He missed the target, but this time the dart sailed downrange, past the tree, and imbedded itself in a hill of clay. The Abo chieftain, as well as the New Zealand police officers, cheered and applauded.[17]

In retrospect, Kuter enjoyed this moment. It was certainly outside the norm for him or any other general officer in the US military, but, if he had learned anything, it was that the life of a theater commander brought with it the unexpected. In a way, these incidents were very much in line with his job. He was not just a regional air force commander. He was, in a sense, an ambassador of goodwill. Still, he looked back on the blowgun incident with mixed emotions. He later wrote: "There must have been a good reason why a tall dignified four star Air Force General, in command of forces with atomic weapons, should have been given a lesson in firing a primitive lethal weapon . . . deep in the Malayan jungle."[18]

A final leader worth mentioning is the president of the Republic of the Philippines, Ramon Magsaysay. He reminded Kuter somewhat of

Hap Arnold: "alert, energetic, and personable." Kuter also believed that the two "made quick decisions, frequently based on feeling, intuition or emotion." Magsaysay put down a group of Communist guerrillas known as the Huks. He motivated many of its former members to change allegiance by carefully choosing a group of "incorrigible leaders" and having them shot. He was also enormously popular among his people. His door was always open for ordinary citizens, to the point that he often saw more than a thousand of them in a single day. Kuter once asked him why, as president, he did not allow local party elected officials to see the people instead. Magsaysay pointed out that, first, lower-level elected officials could not be trusted and, second, the people of the Philippines needed their president to be "a man of the people." Kuter enjoyed the time he spent with Magsaysay in 1956 and recognized him to be very different kind of leader than what he was used to.[19]

On Sunday, 17 March 1957, twenty-five people boarded a C-47 belonging to the Philippine air force shortly after midnight. The most notable member of the party was President Magsaysay. The plane took off from the Cebu airport and climbed out for ten minutes, heading in the direction of the capital city. It then disappeared. At 3:00 that afternoon, Kuter received a phone call from Major General Ackerman, the commander of the 13th Air Force, saying that Magsaysay's plane was missing and that assets of the air force air rescue service were en route from Clark Air Force Base to aid in the search and, it was to be hoped, rescue.[20]

The plane was discovered early the next morning, having crashed into the side of Mount Manunggal at an altitude of thirty-five hundred feet. The C-47 either had not gained enough altitude or was subject to a violent mechanical failure causing it to lose altitude rapidly. Whatever the case, it did not clear the low mountain range, clipped trees, and crashed. Magsaysay's body was recovered and identified.[21]

Ambassador Douglas MacArthur II, the nephew and namesake of the World War II general, telephoned Kuter and told him to be prepared to travel to Manila for the funeral. The US ambassador to the Philippines had recently died, and no one with the State Department rank of ambassador was in the country, so Kuter would likely be the US representative since MacArthur himself, only recently arrived, could not attend. Kuter flew to Manila on Wednesday, 20 March, for the "necrological services" and funeral of Ramon Magsaysay. The term *necrological service* is worth explaining as it also confused Kuter. Tradition in the Philippines, Kuter noted, called for "a series of eulogies followed by one or more responses from members of the bereaved family." These came in the form or orations and "add[ed] heavily to the emotions of the bereaved." These occurred on Wednesday, followed by the state funeral on Friday.[22]

More than two hundred automobiles lined up for the procession. Kuter knew that there were more than two hundred because his vehicle was number 198, as were the vehicles both in front of and behind his. Looking to the rear, he noted that there was no way of telling how many numbers 199 and 200 there were. He was somewhat concerned. Already easily a standout in any crowd given his height, even when seated he was noticeable. Added to this were his beribbonned air force uniform, his hat, and the four stars on each shoulder; there was no way for him to blend in. He also noted that the C-47 that crashed had been given to the Philippine air force by the US Air Force. He worried how the people lining the street might react to him, the man representing the "responsible authorities who had provided the fifteen year old, two-engined C-47 in which their hero had been mangled and burned to death." His open-topped vehicle proceeded slowly enough that bystanders had the time to engage him in conversation.[23]

Kuter need not have been worried. Rather than any sign of demonstrations of hatred, threats, or violence, he found "frequent gestures for friendliness and unfailing pleasant reaction." Philippine veterans saluted his car, and a few even called out "Hi, Joe!" Some greeted him by name, shaking his hand, and more than one even said in English: "We are honored." Kuter's expectations were again proved to be mistaken: "The stature of the U.S. Air Force in a foreign country could not receive higher praise."[24]

The Taiwan Straits Crisis of 1958

Part of FEAF's and FECOM's—and later PACAF's and PACOM's—responsibility included the ability to respond rapidly to any crisis between mainland Communist China under Mao Tse-tung and the Chinese Nationalist forces of the Republic of China on Taiwan. The Chinese Civil War preceded the Second World War II and continued after it. In the post–World War II era, Chinese Nationalists under Chiang Kai-shek suffered defeat after defeat until forced in 1948 from the mainland to Taiwan and a number of smaller islands in Taiwan Strait. In 1949, Mao declared China to be the People's Republic of China, but he kept an eye toward the final defeat of Chinese Nationalist forces in exile. During the Truman administration, the United States initially refused to send an

American presence to Taiwan, but the outbreak of the Korean War and the continued spread of communism changed this. Thus, through the policy of containment and Cold War–era politics, the United States linked itself to the preservation of the Chinese Nationalists on Taiwan and in December 1954 signed a treaty of support with them.[25]

This did not necessarily deter the Chinese Communists, who throughout 1954 attempted invasions of many of the islands in the straits, including Amoy and Quemoy, both sitting directly off the coast of China. The United States responded to these actions. The commander and chief, FECOM, and the commander in chief, PACOM, were both told to be prepared to execute PACOM's Operations Plan 51-53. The command-and-control system set up to run this operation was disjointed, and it represented the kind of self-inflicted wound the US military sometimes inflicts on itself during conflicts. The US Air Force established a component air force that was subordinate to FEAF/FECOM but under the operational control of PACAF/PACOM since the operations plan belonged to the latter. This easily created a turf war between the two commanders in chief with regard to the transferring and shepherding of assets. In the end, the United States moved hundreds of assets onto Taiwan and patrolled over the islands alongside the Chinese Nationalist air force. The Chinese Communist forces were thus unable to make serious gains on the coastal islands, and tensions settled into a begrudging stalemate.[26]

Between 1954 and 1958, the United States continued to arm and train the Chinese Nationalist forces, also equipping them with modern jet aircraft. It consolidated FECOM and PACOM in 1957, as we have seen, and continued to expand its presence in the region, but it also prepared forces not currently in theater for rapid deployment should the need arise. While commander of FEAF/PACAF during this lull in hostilities, Kuter became intimately familiar with his responsibilities should a crisis arise, especially the components of Operations Plan 25-58, which applied to PACAF.

The summer of 1958 brought another crisis in the Taiwan Strait, one that looked for a while as if the United States would be pulled into a shooting war with China. The Chinese Communist air force stationed MiG aircraft along the coastal bases at Chenghai and Liencheng, which were normally devoid of fighter aircraft. Intelligence reports indicated that other bases were being readied for the arrival of other aircraft. Radio Peiping began giving indications that Chinese forces had every intention of soon occupying Quemoy and Matsu, preparatory to an all-out invasion of Taiwan. However, to take the islands, the Chinese Communist forces needed the United States to believe that the Nationalists could not hold them and, as a result, force Chiang to order a withdrawal of the ninety-thousand troops stationed there.[27]

On 21 August, the Soviet Union announced that it backed Communist China and planned to provide "the necessary moral and material aid in the just struggle for the liberation of Taiwan." The Soviet mouthpiece *Pravda* proclaimed: "He who threatens China . . . must not forget that he is threatening the Soviet people also, since the Soviet people are linked to China by unbreakable ties. Any aggression by the United States in the Far East will unavoidably bring about an exacerbation of the whole international situation and lead to spreading the war." If the Chinese or their Soviet allies believed that the United States would not stand with Taiwan in defense of the islands, they were sorely mistaken.[28]

The United States recognized that the 1958 crisis posed the very real possibility of all-out war between Taiwan, the United States, and China and prepared for it as such. Operations Plan 25-58 was reviewed and put into effect. Kuter, as head of PACAF, distributed the plan to subordinate units on 7 August 1958. The plan involved a classic three-phased operation: conduct patrol and reconnaissance, defeat the attacking force, and conduct air operations to destroy the Chinese Communist capability to make war. The last phase was to be conducted by the bombers of the Strategic Air Command with special payloads of nuclear weapons. Kuter's primary concern became preparation for phase 2. To bolster the forces in his region, he asked the Air Staff at the Pentagon for additional aircraft, including Tactical Air Command's Composite Air Strike Force (CASF): a squadron of F-100 *Super Sabres* and accompanying aerial tankers. Later, as the crisis unfolded, Kuter received even more CASF aircraft, including an additional squadron of F-100s, a squadron of B-57 *Canberras,* and a squadron of F-101 *Voodoos.* Finally, the air force authorized the movement of F-104 *Starfighters* from the Continental Air Defense Command to PACAF. The F-104s were disassembled and loaded on C-124 *Globemasters* and flown from California's Hamilton Air Force Base to Taiwan. Kuter wanted the F-104s not only for their capabilities but also for "psychological reasons." It took twenty-four C-124s and four C-97s to complete the transfer. This was a major move and proved just how seriously the United States took the probability of armed action in defense of Taiwan. The only request of Kuter's that was denied was having the Strategic Air Command B-36s placed on alert. This would not have hindered the possibility of nuclear operations, however, since B-47s based on Guam and armed with Mark 6 bombs were already on alert.[29]

Should war break out, Kuter prepared to use atomic weapons, and there is no doubt that he would have done so if given the order. The atomic weapons of the 1950s still represented a viable option at the tactical level of warfare. This was long before the concept of mutually assured destruction entered the lexicon, and Kuter, along with most other air force generals, still saw atomic bombs as weapons to be used, not feared. As a matter of fact, Kuter was more concerned about the effects on his aircrews if he did not use nuclear weapons. He recognized that nonnuclear operations required a higher sortie count. A later history written by the Air Force Historical Division stated: "[Kuter] believed insufficient effort had been made to convince the National Security Council that the most effective way to· deal with the enemy's numerical superiority was to use nuclear weapons."[30]

Kuter was even disappointed in the reaction the military got in advocating the use of nuclear weapons. He felt that the idea of "limited response" was a bad one and that "the United States should either be ready to use its most effective weapons—in his opinion—nuclear weapons—or stay out of the conflict." He also "complained that the military had failed to convince civilian authorities that American forces had to be free to use nuclear bombs at the outset of any conflict."[31]

In total, PACAF had more than 100 fighters of different varieties and 183 atomic-equipped fighters and bombers ready to respond. These figures did not include transports, aerial refuelers, and reconnaissance forces. Outside PACAF, the United States funneled other military assets from the other services into the region, including the aircraft carriers *Essex* and *Midway* from the US Navy's Seventh Fleet. Marine Aircraft Group 11 landed in Taiwan and prepared for defensive air operations. Throughout August and into early September, the United States moved men, materiel, and command-and-control elements to Taiwan and surrounding bases in the Pacific area. The presence of the Seventh Fleet assets in the region certainly gave the Chinese and the Soviets pause and acted to block possible Chinese movement against Taiwan. It became increasingly more likely that an errant shell or missile might kill an American service member. Kuter and his army and navy counterparts also pushed their operational responsibilities down to a task force commander on Taiwan, an indication the United States was postured for response to Chinese aggression and prepared to defend the island. The United States attempted to make it as clear as possible to the Chinese Communists and the Soviet Union that it was prepared to defend Taiwan from Communist aggression.[32]

Throughout all the preparation for the defense of Taiwan, the Chinese Nationalist air force continued to tussle and dogfight with the Communists' MiGs while the islands in the strait came under continuous shelling from the Chinese mainland. The Nationalist air force returned to its bases with amazing claims of downing Chinese Communist pilots over the strait. Kuter initially did not believe it:

> I told the "Tiger," General Wang Shuming, that I had watched exaggerated claims, too, in the United Kingdom. He insisted that I look at hours of combat fighter gun-camera film. I believe they were all verified. Of course, amazing things happened that you would see in the gun cameras. You would see Chinese Communist with their flaps down, pilots flying MiGs with their wheels down, sometimes. Whenever the first rounds were fired, they always made a gradual turn to the right, always. "Tiger" Wang's fighter boys would just blow them up there, right there, time and time after time. A couple of them were shot down and picked up on Taipei or Matsu, wearing leather helmets in jet aircraft, looking like Charles Lindbergh. You couldn't explain some of these things; they were just phenomenally bad on the Communist side and amazingly good on the Chinese side.[33]

The air-to-air engagements over the strait proved to be as amazing as the Nationalist pilots claimed. The rules of engagement agreed to between Chinese Nationalists and the United States called for the Nationalist pilots to engage in combat only in self-defense while on defensive patrol. US officers and officials worried whether they could be restrained from chasing or engaging Communist forces if sighted. Still, even with these strict rules of engagement in place, the Nationalist pilots found opportunities for aerial combat.[34]

On 8 September, twelve Nationalist F-86s engaged twelve MiG-17s, shooting down seven. On 24 September, three separate engagements resulted in the loss of ten MiGs, including the very first air-to-air kills using AIM-9 *Sidewinder* missiles. During the entirety of the crisis, Nationalist pilots shot down thirty-two aircraft while losing only four of their own fighters. It was a completely lopsided victory for the Nationalists and an embarrassment for the Chinese Communist forces as well as the Soviet Union. Later analysis of the air-to-air combat proved that the Communist pilots "demonstrated a lack of skill" and a demonstrable absence of that most important fighter pilot skill, aggressiveness. Meanwhile, the Nationalist forces under the tutelage of the United States "were well trained, confident, flew excellent combat formations, were eager to make 'kills,' and pressed every advantage."[35]

In addition to the air-to-air confrontations and the shelling of the islands, there was a separate battle at sea in which the Communist forces also suffered heavy losses and the Nationalists light losses. On 6 October, Chinese Communist defense minister, Marshal Peng Dehuai, ordered an end to the shelling of Quemoy and Matsu, ostensibly for humanitarian reasons. In truth, the Communists had come to the conclusion that they would not be able to take the islands without drawing the US military into the conflict. This was a war they were not prepared to fight and one that, after the losses already suffered, they did not believe they were capable of winning.

In the end, Kuter did nothing more or less than he was supposed to do as PACAF commander. He expertly moved the required resources where they needed to be, kept the PACOM commander informed as to the readiness of these assets, and, when prepared, handed them over to a task force commander for execution. The life of a four-star general was not meant to involve leading air force units into combat. It was meant to view the theater and other air force assets around the globe in a holistic manner. Kuter was a strategic thinker and planner, not a tactical or operational level practitioner. He had actually become quite good at his job. The kind of global mindedness required of him was something he had been practicing since his time on Arnold's staff. He had now worn the stars of a general officer for over sixteen years. He recalled years later that the air combat that occurred in 1958 was remarkable: "The fighting in the Taiwan Straits was a high point of my tour of duty in FEAF. . . . It is probably the greatest victory over Communism that has ever been attained by any military force and not at all well recognized."[36]

Kuter's career was not quite over. One assignment remained, the one that truly showed how far Kuter and the US Air Force had grown in a few decades. Kuter was moving, it might be said, to an even higher lane than he had ever inhabited before. Mankind, the United States, its air force, and Larry Kuter were moving beyond the bounds of earth. New technologies pushed man and machine into space, but this development brought with it the Cold War fear of attack from space. America's air force monitored those threats. Kuter's final assignment in the US Air Force was as the second commander of the North American Air Defense Command.

Commander in Chief, North American Air Defense Command

General Kuter's final assignment was as the second commander in chief of the North American Air Defense Command (NORAD) from 1 August 1959 until his retirement on 30 July 1962. He was named to the position on 6 May. He followed General Earl E. Partridge. He had previously followed Partridge into command of the Far East Air Forces. For an officer who had spent so much of his career helping develop and organize the US Air Force, it was a fitting final assignment. For an officer whose first flight was in a biplane made of wood and canvas, it was the culmination of a career and marked the ascendency of modern air power. Kuter's flying career began in the plains of Texas and ended in an operations center capable of receiving advance radar warning of threats and responding to them using advanced interceptor aircraft, should the Cold War unexpectedly turn hot. The air force he served was now capable of global response, and he was responsible for a theaterwide monitoring and response effort. The NORAD of Kuter's tenure proved to be not so different from that organization's modern incarnations. It was the front line of homeland defense, providing early warning in case of attack.[1]

General Laurence S. Kuter became the second commander in chief of NORAD on 1 August 1959. He also became commander in chief of the Continental Air Defense Command (CONAD). While CONAD was a joint organization comprising military members of all services, NORAD was a binational Canadian and American command backed by the weight of the NORAD Agreement. As PACAF commander in chief, Kuter had reported to the PACOM commander in chief. As the NORAD and CONAD commander in chief, he reported directly to the Joint Chiefs of Staff and the secretary of defense. However, since NORAD was a binational command, he also had to report to the senior leaders of Canada's military, the Canadian Chief of Staff Committee. He also had a Canadian deputy commander, Air Marshal C. Roy Slemon. As the NORAD commander in chief, Kuter was now responsible for the air defense of both the United States and Canada. Under him was a headquarters staff of roughly six hundred people from each of the American and Canadian military services. Outside the headquarters was a command that touched as many as 200,000 military personnel located in as many as seven hundred locations and included supersonic fighter interceptors, defensive surface-to-air missiles, and a system of radars that ran in depth from the Pacific Ocean to the Atlantic. This included the semiautomatic ground environment (SAGE) system, the distant early warning (DEW) line, the Mid-Canada line, and the Texas towers. The complexities of these systems require some descriptive details.[2]

In theory, NORAD operations detected any incoming aircraft first via the DEW line, a line of radars in northern Canada that stretched for twenty-four hundred miles. This included ship radars, which in conjunction with the land portion of the DEW line looked up and outward for threats. The US Navy also flew VW-2 *Warning Stars,* a variant of the EC-121 whose radars pointed down to detect any low-flying aircraft. In addition, there was also the Ballistic Missile Early Warning System in Alaska and Greenland, which provided coverage of both the Northwest and the Northeast. If an aircraft managed to avoid detection, the next line of defense was the mid-Canada line. If the radars of the DEW line or the mid-Canada line detected Soviet aircraft, defensive fighters would be launched to intercept them. Should all these procedures fail, there was a series of surface-to-air missile sites composed of US Army Nike missiles. Interestingly, Kuter recognized that this enormously complicated and far-flung system could fail, and he ended up spending time attempting to develop further missile defense systems, something he was not successful at despite appealing directly to the president.[3]

Oddly enough, Ent Air Force Base, the home to CONAD as well as NORAD, did not have any senior officer housing for Larry and Ethel. They had to procure off-base lodging. Kuter remembered that real estate agents lined up several "'beer baron palaces,' huge turn-of-the-century houses around Colorado Springs that nobody could possibly maintain" and required housing staff, which the general certainly did not have. Instead, Kuter again followed Partridge's lead. For the duration of his command at NORAD, he and Ethel resided in an apartment suite at the Broadmoor Hotel. The five-star hotel, built in 1918, sits on the lower side of Cheyenne Mountain, not far from where construction on the Cheyenne Mountain Operations Center was to begin during Kuter's tenure as commander.[4]

Although the pressures of being commander were great, the job certainly had its perks. Kuter felt that it was his responsibility to be "familiar with the advanced supersonic aircraft in the command and the problems of the pilots in handling these hot aircraft and firing their big weapons." Besides, he argued: "It's fun to fly in hot aircraft." Therefore, he scheduled himself orientation flights in the F-101B *Voodoo,* the F-102 *Delta Dagger,* and the F-106 *Delta Dart.* Of course, as the four-star commander of NORAD, his flights became elaborate events.[5]

In October 1959, Kuter traveled to Tyndall Air Force Base, outside of Panama City, Florida, for a fighter weapons meet. He was to ride in the backseat of an F-101 to observe the launch of an unarmed Genie missile. There was a significant amount of preparation and, he noticed, an unusual amount of worry occurring as the squadron prepared to take its commander past the sound barrier. Safety procedures covered which levers to pull should ejection become necessary, where to place arms and legs in case of an ejection, and procedures for landing either on land or in the Gulf of Mexico. Kuter noted that all this probably mattered little because, depending on altitude and speed, there was a good chance that either the ejection or the atmospherics would kill him anyway.[6]

The Genie missile that was to be shot was an air-to-air missile containing a nuclear warhead designed to decimate incoming Soviet bomber formations; the test missile would of course have had its nuclear material removed. Representatives from both the McDonnell Douglas Company (builder of the F-101) and the Hughes Aircraft Company (builder of the Genie missile) were on hand as Kuter strapped into the backseat. He noticed, somewhat ruefully, that, by the time his aircraft taxied, more than one hundred spectators were near the aircraft.[7]

The first phase of the flight went without a hitch, and Kuter broke the sound barrier for the first time, rocketing up to Mach 1.5. However, the second phase did not go according to plan. The Genie missile to be fired from the F-101 was designed to be attached to—and normally fired from—an F-106. The McDonnell Douglas representatives rigged an attachment to ensure that the Genie would function properly when fired from the F-101. Sadly for all involved, it did not work. When the moment came for it to drop from the F-101, fire its rocket, and streak toward the target, the rigged system failed. Kuter recalled: "Did the Genie fire its own rocket engine and go hurtling on its deadly way to obliterate its high speed target? Not our Genie! She just tumbled on down into the Gulf of Mexico with about the same effect as the practice bombs that were dropped into the Chesapeake Bay from a Keystone bomber thirty years earlier." He continued: "[The] Douglas people were unhappy about the failure. [The NORAD commander in chief] was unhappy. This made the Douglas people exceedingly unhappy."[8]

Kuter followed his F-101 flight with a ride in the Convair F-102 the next day. He again noticed ruefully that this day the massive number of McDonnell Douglas personnel had been replaced by an equal number of Convair employees. This time they shot an AIM-4 Falcon missile, and this time the firing went off without a hitch. The F-102's radar illuminated the target, and the Falcon flew straight and true to its intercept point. Had he known what was to come, Kuter probably would have stopped his experience in modern jet interceptors there. A few days later, he traveled to McGuire Air Force Base in New Jersey for a ride in the "newest and hottest of them all," the F-106.[9]

The F-106 was a Mach 2+ aircraft designed to intercept Soviet bombers as they came across the polar icecaps and into Canada. At the time of Kuter's sortie, it held a world's speed record at Mach 2.3, or 1,525 miles per hour. It was big, fast, and shaped like a sleek, flat, triangle. The F-106 flight was truly one to remember, but not in the way that Kuter had anticipated. For an officer whose first flight occurred in an Airco DH-4 with a four-hundred-horsepower engine, this was truly a special event. The F-106 was the newest and most modern jet of its day. It represented the pinnacle of all that could be achieved in interceptor development at the time. After a routine aerial interception of a B-57 *Canberra*, a light bomber aircraft that simulated a Soviet bomber on this mission, Kuter's pilot received permission from the SAGE system controller to take the general out for a high-speed flight.[10]

After maneuvering away from any possible traffic in the air, the pilot lit the afterburner, and the F-106 climbed through the speed dial up to Mach 2. Kuter noted that this was no Keystone bomber. They were at Mach 2.1 and seven miles above the Earth, and the pilot passed the controls to Kuter in the backseat. At that precise moment, as Kuter took control of the aircraft, all hell broke loose. The F-106 entered into a violent phenomenon known as *yaw buzz*. This entailed a series of "successive shattering booms at very rapid succession." The aircraft's tail was being battered forcefully back and forth, causing a yawing motion from one direction to the other. In other words, it moved left while the nose moved to the right, only to almost instantaneously move in the other direction. This occurred so rapidly that the instrument panel in front of Kuter blurred together. He thought for sure the movement was violent enough for the aircraft to disintegrate in flight, and he knew that, at this altitude and this speed, the results would not be conducive to his health. The pilot got the aircraft under control and the airspeed down to Mach 1.7, causing the yawing to stop. He called back to Kuter: "This is all right, General." Kuter replied: "You may think so."[11]

Kuter gave the following details of the cause of the incident:

> In brief, the Yaw Buzz phenomenon can occur at very high speeds when the variable ramps in the jet engine's air intake generate shock waves which impinge on other shock waves and set up a resonance among shock waves in and out of the long air ducts that run alongside the fuselage from forward air intakes to the reward jet engine. The booming is the successive impact of sonic booms only a foot or two outboard of the pilot and on either side. The pounding and yawing is the result of the great force of those rapidly alternating sonic booms. And with each boom swallowed by the engine, it is suddenly stalled.

The Convair company was well aware of yaw buzz but believed that the problem had been corrected. Luckily, the test pilot who initially encountered the yaw buzz was also Kuter's pilot that day and knew how to regain positive control of the aircraft. This flight gave Kuter the distinction of being the sixty-eighth American to go twice the speed of sound and the oldest person to experience the yaw buzz phenomenon.[12]

Developments in Aerospace Defense

Long gone were the days of propeller-driven bombers and piston-engine fighters operating from austere locations in North Africa, the Mediterranean, and Pacific islands. Kuter's NORAD monitored threats and prepared to respond to them with modern, technologically advanced aircraft. Those threats now came in the form not only of bombers but also of ballistic-missile attack. Developments in Soviet bombers and air-to-surface missiles necessitated a newer, faster, longer-range interceptor. As the speed of Soviets' bombers increased and the distance their air-to-surface missiles could travel also increased, the interception of the enemy became that much more complex. As speed and range increase, time of response inevitably decreases.[13]

The long-range interceptor program was the next step in the century series of US Air Force fighter-interceptor aircraft. This developed into the

XF-108 *Rapier.* Kuter considered this to be the "first real breakthrough in solving the problem of long range interceptions of enemy aircraft." The XF-108, as opposed to the other century series interceptors, was designed from the beginning to have two of everything: two engines, two men, and two or more air-to-air missiles (either conventional or nuclear). It never flew. Shrinking budgets caused the program's cancellation in September 1959. This deterred neither Kuter at NORAD nor the chairman of the Joint Chiefs, Air Force general Nathan Twining, who continued to place the now-canceled program into requirements documents. In November, Kuter also put the XF-108 into objective plans detailing the force NORAD wanted to have in the future.[14]

In 1960, Kuter testified before a Senate subcommittee on military construction. He had previously mentioned not wanting to take either the chief or the vice chief job to avoid testifying, but as a commander in chief he had no choice in the matter. Kuter explained to the subcommittee that NORAD had agreed to decrease the numbers of interceptors already in the inventory, including F-101s, F-102s, and F-106s, to clear space and funds for the required F-108. He also recommended to the air force chief of staff, General Thomas White, that he do everything in his power to get the program back on track. White agreed, mainly because he was now caught between Kuter pushing up from NORAD and Twining pushing down from the Joint Chiefs office. However, aircraft advancements were moving faster than the air force's acquisitions system. Kuter noted: "Since the last [objective plan] was published we have positive evidence of Soviet development and test of a supersonic bomber." The XF-108 was now not high enough or fast enough to intercept the Soviet threat. As Kuter continued on at NORAD, he and the air force moved forward with two separate interceptors: the improved manned interceptor and the advanced manned interceptor. By 1960, the XF-108 program ceased to be mentioned. The development of Soviet bombing doctrine and Soviet "Dash" bombers, equivalent to the air force's B-58 *Hustler* and the technological advancement of these bombers also stalled the advancement of further interceptors. The air force could not keep up with faster interceptors and moved to focusing on survivability of sites for those Soviet aircraft and bombs that slipped through the net in the opening act of World War III.[15]

Kuter, long the proponent of Air University developing doctrine for the US Air Force, sang a different tune when it came to development of joint doctrine. He now wanted the requirement for written doctrine to be moved from a service function to the Joint Chiefs: "It seemed apparent, General Kuter said, that, at least in his command, development of combat doctrine for the accomplishment of a military function should rest with the organization charged with that function. CINCONAD was charged with the responsibility for unified air defense of the U.S., but the development of doctrine for unified air defense was not his responsibility." The responsibility for doctrine development remained at the service level, meaning for the air force Air University. Since the air force could not get another advanced interceptor and Kuter could not affect doctrine, both organizations tunneled into the ground, in one case, quite literally.[16]

The Cheyenne Mountain Operations Center

As threats and technologies advanced, NORAD slowly transitioned from response to survivability. Kuter said: "We have developed the philosophy that . . . communications must be equally as hard as the environment that it serves." To that end, the Joint Chiefs and the air force looked for ways to strengthen NORAD against attack. The decision to place a new combat operations center inside Cheyenne Mountain was made in March 1959, before Kuter became commander, but he was instrumental in the development of the project.[17]

Kuter oversaw the development and initial building of what was probably the most visible symbol of America's Cold War preparations: the Cheyenne Mountain Operations Center. Even in the twenty-first century, whenever NORAD is mentioned, Cheyenne Mountain is usually the first thing to come to mind. So synonymous did the two become that, in the 1983 film *Wargames, NORAD* was used interchangeably with *operations center*. The operations center, the mountain surrounding it, and the organization NORAD blurred into a single entity. When Kuter took over command of NORAD, he also took over oversight of the Cheyenne Mountain project. He was asked to keep the program on time and under budget, two things that had not yet been accomplished.[18]

An official groundbreaking ceremony was held at the construction site on Friday, 16 June 1961. General Lee, Air Defense Command commander, and General Kuter, both wearing their respective commands' decorated hard hats, simultaneously set off the symbolic dynamite charges as General Lemnitzer of the Joint Chiefs looked on. The cost of the combat operations center, including all construction and equipment, was then estimated to be $66 million. Excavation began on 19 June 1961, and it took just over a year to hollow out the 9,565-foot mountain, but Kuter was not pleased with the initial design and asked for a "larger hole."[19]

By the middle of 1962, excavation was nearing completion. All that remained was debris cleanup, the installation of more wire mesh, and some minor tunneling. Following this, construction would begin on the internal buildings and supporting functions, including the reservoirs and power generators and, of course, the two massive twenty-five-ton blast doors that could seal the facility off from the outside world. All this would be done after Kuter's retirement, however.[20]

Final Act of Service

General Laurence Kuter believed strongly in his right to present his opinions to his superiors, all the way up to the president of the United States. While not getting any traction on his missile defense ideas, he requested permission to share his views with President Kennedy. He believed that he had failed to convince the secretary of defense and the chairman of the Joint Chiefs of his position and wanted to provide his perspective to the president. It represented a perfect example of the civilian-military relationship.

To ensure that he was not stepping out of line Kuter requested that either Secretary of Defense Robert McNamara or Chairmen of the Joint Chiefs General Lyman Lemnitzer be present as well. On 8 February 1962, he briefed President Kennedy and Vice President Johnson on the adequacy of continental defense. Kennedy sat in his favorite rocking chair, while Johnson and Kuter sat across from each other on the couches in the center of the room. Kuter advocated extending the existing warning systems to cover approaches by missiles from any direction. Of the utmost importance, however, he urged, was the installation of the Nike-Zeus ABM system, at least around Washington and major ballistic missile and bomber bases. He closed his discussion by telling Kennedy: "As your field commander charged with the responsibility for the aerospace defense of North America, I most strongly recommend that the growing gap between our defenses and the Soviet offensive capability be closed. To close it our missile warning system must be extended to cover approaches by missiles from any direction."[21]

The meeting lasted an hour, and Kuter concluded that the president "had heard [him] out." The president thanked him and showed him out of the office with the chairman. Kuter expressed regret that he did not seem to have made much of an impact. The meeting did not sway anyone's position and did not result in any major developments in policy, but that was not Kuter's goal, and he did not pursue the matter further. In an article years later, he said: "Even with sincere respect for the judgement of his immediate superiors and with loyalty to them, a commander's sense of duty and obligation to his organization and its mission may cause him to request a hearing from the highest authority. However, if rejected by the country's final governmental authority, he has fully met his duty obligation and officially his case is closed." It was enough for him to have briefed the president and presented his position.[22]

On 30 July 1962, Larry Kuter retired. The day after, the entire DEW line from Greenland to the Aleutians was completed as the final four sites of the Greenland extension (DEW East) became operational. During Kuter's time at NORAD, the Cheyenne Mountain Operations Center was begun and excavation completed and the North American defense apparatus in the form of the DEW and Mid-Canada lines brought into full operational capability.[23]

On his retirement, Kuter had spent thirty-five years in uniform: first in the US Army, then the US Army Air Corps, then the US Army Air Forces, and finally the US Air Force. He started out as a field artillery officer only to leave that branch behind, but not for the promise that the air corps held for his career. His first fifteen years of service saw him rise slowly from second lieutenant to lieutenant colonel. He was a general officer for the remainder of his twenty more years of service. This placed him in that small cadre of air force pioneers of the Second World War generation who wore general's stars the majority of their careers. This included his contemporaries Curtis LeMay, Lauris Norstad, and Hoyt Vandenberg. Each of these men played a unique and noteworthy role in the development of air power and the air force.

Kuter said of retiring from the air force: "I would have loved to stay in. Without any question, every day that I ever had in the Air Force was a day that, if I had been a rich man, I would have paid a lot to be able to do those things. I didn't want to leave at all." There was nothing left for him to do, however, no position save chief or vice chief.[24]

Retirement

After leaving the air force, Larry and Ethel moved into an apartment in New York City, and Larry went to work at Pan Am World Airways as a vice president. He stayed in this position from 1962 to 1970, during which time his biggest contribution was aiding in the development of the 747. Several airlines had unsuccessfully attempted to recruit him in the aftermath of World War II, but in mandatory retirement he felt that he was too young to hang up working entirely. He also continued his proclivity for writing and in 1973 published a second book, *The Great Gamble,* about the development of the 747. Larry and Ethel's annual Christmas letters, preserved in some of the thirty-five scrapbooks that Ethel kept of their adventures, showed that they traveled extensively as a result of Larry's work at Pan Am. In 1963, they visited the Far East and Europe. The next year found them in Hawaii, Afghanistan, and Alaska but also spending time with their grandchildren, Larry, Robin, and Don, and exploring New York City. Also, Larry's mother passed away in 1964 at age eighty-two. The world traveling continued throughout the mid- to late 1960s and Larry's time at Pan Am. There is a picture from Christmas 1968 with Larry sitting on the couch and two of his grandchildren on the floor watching television. The photograph is labeled "Astronauts send greetings from the moon." At that moment, Frank Borman, Bill Anders, and Jim Lovell were in Apollo 8 orbiting the moon.[25]

Retirement did not come without its commitments, however. Kuter's analytic skills—always in demand throughout his career—were put to use again. In the late 1960s, he was called to serve, along with General Mark Clark, Admiral David McDonald, and George Ball, on the Pueblo Committee. In 1968, the USS *Pueblo,* an intelligence-gathering vessel for the US Navy, was captured and boarded by North Korean troops who claimed that the vessel was in North Korean waters. This committee was not established to place blame or to "fix responsibility for the incident," only to "derive lessons from this incident that might result in more secure and effective intelligence gathering operations in the future." The committee's report was issued to President Lyndon Johnson on 7 February 7 1968 and Kuter returned to work at Pan Am. Although Kuter knew President Johnson from his time as NORAD commander, this committee work now meant that he had worked directly for or with every president since Franklin Roosevelt.[26]

Final retirement from Pan Am came in 1970. Larry and Ethel Kuter now filled their days with more traveling. They left New York City, and, after plans to move into a new apartment in Colorado Springs fell through, they moved to Naples, Florida. Although their love for traveling continued to take them to new locations, they were finally settled in the last home they would have together. There they resided for the next decade. They both earned basic seamanship certificates from the Coast Guard Auxiliary. Larry and Ethel Kuter also played golf—a lot of it.

Larry took to the golf course whenever he had the opportunity, and his travels during the course of his years with Pan Am did not change this. He played in the Far East, in Europe, and in Kabul, Afghanistan. He played with Arnold Palmer, and he wrote articles for golfing magazines.[27]

The scrapbooks that Ethel produced throughout her and Larry's life together also show one other aspect of Larry Kuter previously not mentioned. He was rarely without a cigarette in his hand. He never mentions when he first started smoking, but certainly from World War II forward he was always smoking. This was completely normal for the time. In fact, it would have been more unusual had he not smoked, but even into his later years he always had a cigarette in his hand, even in casual photographs, at least when he was not holding a golf club. As a result, he developed emphysema.

Conclusion

The Kuters collectively wrote hundreds of letters during their life together. Beyond their letters to each other, they routinely wrote long missives to their families keeping them appraised of current goings-on. These letters began during Larry's time in the Presidio and ran through his time as commander of NORAD and beyond. Beyond the letters, there were the scrapbooks, photographs, and numerous other materials that Ethel and Larry kept before donating the entirety of the collection to the Special Collections Branch of the US Air Force Academy library. Amassed together, the collection constitutes an almost daily entry of their activities from high school through retirement.

Ethel Kuter's diary entries from 1979 show that Larry's strength was fading and that the emphysema was slowly killing him. Together they worked on his autobiography, struggling to get it into a publishable form. A diary entry from 2 October indicated: "Type North Africa 5 pages." The next day she noted, "Typed all day," adding: "There have been so many magic moments in my life with Larry." She recorded that 8 October was a "low day" and that Larry had become "so frail." A week later he told her: "You think in terms of years—I think in terms of weeks." The next day, 14 October, he collapsed. This required a wheelchair to be delivered the next day and he was rarely out of it in the coming weeks. Ethel knew the end was approaching but did not want to frighten the family. Still, she recognized that Larry was now a "very sick man." A month later saw him rarely leave his bed and sleeping a great deal. Ethel continued to type the manuscript.[1]

On 18 November, Ethel finished typing the draft chapter on Larry's experiences in North Africa during the Second World War. Larry said: "I am glad to have that in writing. The concept of Tactical Air Force is historically important. For the U.S. it was born and it grew in [the Northwest African Tactical Air Force]. I take some pride in its plan and in its consummation." This was the last section they were able to complete.[2]

Larry's health continued to deteriorate in the next few weeks, and Ethel was never far from his side. She continued to type, but it became obvious that they wouldn't finish World War II, much less the rest of his career. Still, they enjoyed this time together, reliving his experiences and their lives together. On the evening of 29 November, Ethel left Larry and went to lie down in another room. Laurence Kuter died at 2:30 A.M. on 30 November 1979.[3]

Kuter was buried at the US Air Force Academy in Colorado Springs, Colorado, alongside other air power luminaries with whom he served long before the academy was ever created: Haywood Hansell, Curtis LeMay, and Carl Spaatz. Although he was instrumental in the creation of the academy, he was actually opposed to it being located in Colorado Springs. He felt that having the it in the center of the country placed it too far from most of the population and too far from major universities, including the other service academies. As he remembered: "I was not a bit happy with the selection of Colorado Springs." So bitter was he about the location and the high altitude that, after a visit to the academy in 1962, he vowed that his next would be "one where the oxygen won't bother me": "I will be going out in a small urn."[4]

Others were not so glib about his death. The *New York Times* called him "an architect of air power." This epithet was especially fitting since his daughter, Roxanne Kuter Williamson, earned her doctorate in architecture. The chief of staff of the air force, General Lew Allen, said: "Even if his career had ended in 1941, he would have earned a lasting place in the Air Force Hall of Fame. But his accomplishments to that point added to those of the next twenty years establish Kuter as one of the shining lights of the Air Force." Kuter's funeral was held at noon on 14 December 1979 in the chapel of the US Air Force Academy.[5]

His lifelong friend Possum Hansell wrote to Ethel shortly after Larry's death. Ethel invited Hansell to be one of Larry's eulogists, but he was unable to make the trip to Colorado. Hansell wrote:

> After I talked with you on the telephone I rummaged around among my files and found a number of pictures that took me back to old times—the old times that we all experienced together. They were pictures of Larry and me and our associates at Langley and Maxwell and Washington and Westover and at Brampton Grange in England. There is a memorable snapshot taken at Brampton Grange . . . of Larry and me at the time when I took over the 1st Bomb Wing from him. . . . [I]t shows us full of good spirits and confidence and the ebullience of youth.[6]

He remembered that Larry "recognized and relished the absurd and ridiculous and expressed his appreciation in sardonic but seldom acerbic quips," and he apologized for being unable to travel (he was, after all, seventy-six). He wrote to her that he was "deeply touched" and honored at the action. He finished by writing that, had he given the eulogy, it would have ended as follows:

> He was truly a man for all seasons. In the springtime of his youth he was a bomber pilot in the formative adolescence of our air power. In the summer of his early maturity he was a student of his profession and a teacher of evolving principles. In the autumn of his maturity he was a commander and a planner of grand designs, and a strategist of air warfare. And in the winter of his later life, he was an educator, a commander of vast forces for the defense of his country, and a sage counselor and leader in the military and civilian transportation. Through it all he seasoned every day with a leavening of humor that kept the stream of experience in balanced perspective.[7]

Kuter was nothing if not a man of his times. He was opposed to women being admitted to the academy and felt that the Reserve Officer Training Corps at colleges and universities around the country could provide female officers with the necessary education. Still, in the end he was very satisfied with the institution that the academy became: "I am delighted with it—just delighted with it. I wouldn't do a thing to change it. Everything about it. I'd love to have my grandsons there, and they couldn't be less interested."[8]

In the end, Kuter joined hundreds of other airmen buried on the tranquil hillside cemetery grounds. Much like the low-key academy graves, Kuter's notice among the pioneers of the history of air power has been somewhat muted, yet very few other officers in the nascent air force had such a tremendous influence on its organizational development; perhaps only Arnold himself had more of an impact. Few air force officers saw as many theaters of operation as Kuter did, and, although his combat contributions were less notable than were those of other commanders in the 8th Air Force, few other officers were as highly sought after as he was. He was everywhere the air force was, and, as a result, his fingerprints can be found throughout air force operations in the Second World War.

After his death, Ethel struggled on with collecting and archiving the material about their lives together. In 1980, she wrote a letter to a friend in which she said: "[Larry] had done a great deal of writing of articles while we were in Naples after his retirement from Pan Am. . . . Unfortunately, he only got as far as 1943. . . . I would like to go on with his story." She never finished her story either, but what remains in her papers is a rich history told from both perspectives.[9]

After all this, why write a biography of Laurence Kuter? Any number of other airmen are certainly due their own treatment at this point, and, in the last fifteen to twenty years, air power—and, more myopically, air force—historians have moved beyond the focus on Billy Mitchell and Hap Arnold. Fine work on George Kenney, Claire Chennault, and Carl Spaatz has been produced, but still worthy of investigation are Joe McNarney, Lauris Norstad, Stratemeyer, Twining, and especially Curtis LeMay. Since I work at the North American Aerospace Defense Command (NORAD), Laurence Kuter seemed like a logical "person of exceptional performance" (as the Air Force Historical Research Center labels them) to explore, not to mention the mountain of archival sources he left behind.[10]

In memory it was said: "The name Kuter never became a household term instantly recognizable by the man in the street." Even the pronunciation of the name itself is still a point of contention. Still: "His career was in fact distinguished and his role in shaping the Air Force was worthy of careful investigation." So why a biography of General Laurence S. Kuter? The historiography needs one, and the air force and historians of aerial warfare should demand one.[11]

Kuter's impact is probably understated inside the air force. Streets bear his name, along with those of George, Hansell, Walker, and MacNarney, although it is doubtful that very many pause to think about such things. A portrait of Kuter hangs inside the Air University Library alongside those of the other Air University commanders. His picture still hangs in the NORAD headquarters building. That particular wall of photographs composed of NORAD and US Northern Command commanders now has twenty-three different portraits. Kuter's is at the top, just to the right of Partridge's. Maybe this is the reason Kuter has often been the focus of so little attention. He was always the deputy or the second to arrive somewhere, always instrumental in organizing and equipping but never gaining the hero's limelight. Architects seldom get the same notoriety as builders.

There are other subtle reminders of Larry Kuter's impact on the air force, two of them at the US Air Force Academy. First, the winner of the annual US Air Force Academy versus University of Hawaii football game receives a trophy named in his honor: the Laurence S. Kuter trophy. As of 2016, the teams had met twenty times, with air force holding the winning record of thirteen wins, six losses, and one draw. Ethel remained invested in presenting the trophy well into the 1980s. She was also a frequent attendant at other events at the academy, including graduations. Although Larry Kuter was a West Point man who had his differences with the air force academy, Ethel, in her own way, adopted the school. To some extent, she carried the torch for her husband's professional interests after his passing. In 1980, she donated a series of ornately carved hunting guns to the academy's gun club.[12]

Then there is the story of the ancient Japanese lantern gifted to the Kuters when they left Japan in 1956. The lantern traveled with them to Hawaii and sat in their backyard there, but, on moving to Colorado Springs, they had no place to put it since they were living in the Broadmoor Hotel. Deciding that the lantern needed to be displayed somewhere, they came to an agreement with a local family that it could sit in their Japanese garden until the Kuters could reclaim it. In retirement, the Kuters moved into a condominium in Florida, and the lantern remained the possession of the friends, although the nature of the relationship changed shortly. In 1972, Kuter attempted to have the lantern transferred to the grounds of the air force academy. This was not accomplished. Whether through unwillingness or misunderstanding, it remained in the possession of the family in Colorado Springs. After Larry Kuter died, the lantern was again the cause of dispute when the family possessing it refused to allow it to be moved and made attempts to lock it into their personal estate, claiming that it was a gift from the Kuters. All records indicate this was patently untrue. Ethel, ever the protector of Larry's reputation and memory, refused to allow this to happen, and, through a series of maneuvers, she finally secured the lantern's removal. Today, the stone lantern, estimated to be more than seven hundred years old and a survivor of the firebombing of Tokyo, finally rests in the backyard of the Carlton House, the home of the superintendent of the air force academy. Much like the contributions of Kuter himself, the lantern stands as an understated representation of the man. Less than five miles away from its final resting place, Larry and Ethel Kuter are buried at the air force academy cemetery.[13]

After his death, *Air Force Magazine* profiled General Kuter in two issues. Written by Haywood Hansell, the profile was Kuter's friend's chance to publicly eulogize the man whose funeral he had not been able to attend. Hansell summed up in a few sentences what this book has taken so many pages to say: "In the space of thirty-five years between his graduation as a second lieutenant pilot in the Army Air Corps and his retirement as a four-star general in the US Air Force, Larry contributed to the development and advancement of American airpower at every step up the ladder. Larry Kuter's contributions to airpower are too numerous to name."[14]

This would be a fitting enough tribute, and his contributions might be "too numerous to name," but that should not stop one from trying, and Haywood Hansell did just that, calling his friend "strategist, tactician, planner, educator, military statesman, and commander of strategic, tactical, airlift, and air defense forces": "He played a major part in the development of World War II airpower and in the [air force's] continued evolution during the post war years." Larry Kuter was instrumental in the creation of the US Air Force. If Hap Arnold was its father, then Larry Kuter was its architect.[15]

Acknowledgments

This book began as a minor research paper while I was attending the Air Command and Staff College (ACSC), and it blossomed and took off from there. Once I completed the paper, I knew that I had to continue, expand, and edit and alter it into a workable manuscript. What started out as a minor project for work quickly evolved into a personal attempt to write another book and to fill in some holes in what I found existed in the history of the US Air Force.

I owe my attendance at the in-residence program at ACSC, and thus the genesis of this work, to the director of the Air Force History and Museum Program, Mr. Walt Grudzinskas. At ACSC, I would like to thank the faculty members and colleagues Dr. Paul Springer and Dr. John Terino for their help and support in getting the initial paper off the ground.

Across the street from ACSC sits the Air Force Historical Research Agency, where the great team under Dr. Charlie O'Connell helped with primary source location when dealing with both the original documents and those materials that have been preserved electronically. These stellar members included Sam Shearin, Leander Morris, Tammy Horton, and Maranda Gilmore.

Dr. Christopher Rein of the US Army's Combat Studies Institute and Dr. Trevor Albertson of ACSC both assisted my work by suggesting or forwarding other primary sources on Kuter that they discovered while working on their own projects. Dr. Rein and Dr. Robert S. Ehlers Jr. both read this work in its entirety and provided corrections that improved the quality of the final product. For their dedication and their contributions, I am grateful to both of them.

The primary repository for materials on General Laurence S. Kuter is the Special Collections Branch at the US Air Force Academy library. I would never have been able to do this work without the help of the director, Dr. Mary Ruwell, and her deputy, John Beardsley, who not only allowed me to pour through the collections but were also willing to go through the trouble of getting this researcher into the cadet area, which I can only assume was as difficult as traveling between West and East Berlin used to be.

As I continued down the path of writing a Kuter biography, I found myself reaching out to locate artifacts. In this endeavor, I would like to thank Meredith Harlow, a museum specialist at Headquarters, US Air Force Academy, who helped with information on the Japanese stone lantern, and Tiffany Arnold, assistant curator at the Midway Museum in Rockford, Illinois, who helped locate the medals and memorabilia now stored in the Midway's archives. I also owe a debt to the US Air Force Academy Athletic Department, particularly Jim Trego, the senior associate athletic director, and Colonel Tony McKenzie for help obtaining a picture of the General Laurence S. Kuter Trophy, which I had hoped would remain in the possession of the US Air Force Academy for many years to come. Unfortunately, on 22 October 2016, the University of Hawaii "Bows" narrowly defeated the air force academy 34–27 in double overtime, sending the trophy back to the University of Hawaii. In Hawaii's athletic department, I wish to thank Derek Inouchi for his assistance in locating additional photos of the trophy for use in this book.

Other air force history offices were generous enough to electronically send their sources to me, including the Air Mobility Command history office and their command historian Mr. Ellery D. Wallwork as well as the staff historian Mr. Jeffery S. Michalke.

Of particular importance to this endeavor was the command historian at the North American Aerospace Defense Command (NORAD) and US Northern Command history office, Dr. Lance Blyth, who not only helped in locating and going through historical documents relating to Kuter's tenure as NORAD commander in chief but also patiently listened to me drone on about Larry Kuter in general. As this is the second such manuscript he has been involved with, I owe him doubly.

I want to send a very special thanks to the entire team at the University Press of Kentucky, including the director, Leila Salisbury, *my* editor, Allison Webster, the marketing team of Jacqueline Wilson, Amy Harris, Fred McCormick, and Cameron Ludwick, my copyeditor, Joseph Brown, and Sarah Olson and Melissa Hammer. It was such a pleasure to work with this great press a second time.

Finally, to my family: Heather, Savannah, and Aspen, who were forced to do without me for the ten months I attended training. Your sacrifices make what I do possible. I hope this book is a demonstration that I used my free time wisely.

Notes

Preface

1. Lloyd E. Ambrosius, ed., *Writing Biography: Historians and Their Craft* (Lincoln: University of Nebraska Press, 2004), jacket blurb.

Introduction

1. Mary Dixie Dysart, *The Archives at the Air Force Historical Research Agency* (Maxwell Air Force Base, AL: Air Force Historical Research Agency, 2012); Brigadier General Laurence S. Kuter, Deputy Chief of the Air Staff, Army Air Force Historical Program, 19 July 1942, quoted in Lieutenant Colonel Clanton W. Williams, Acting Chief, Historical Division, AC/AS, Intelligence, "Army Air Force Historical Program," n.d., IRIS 116419, Air Force Historical Research Agency (AFHRA), Maxwell Air Force Base, AL; Wesley Craven and James Lea Cate, eds., *The Army Air Forces in World War II*, 7 vols. (Washington, DC: Office of Air Force History, 1983), 3:iii.

2. "General Laurence S. Kuter," US Air Force Biographies, http://www. af.mil/AboutUs/Biographies/Display/tabid/225/Article/106523/general-laurence-s-kuter.aspx; James Parton, *"Air Force Spoken Here": General Ira Eaker and the Command of the Air* (Maxwell Air Force Base, AL: Air University Press, 2000), 214; Daniel R. Mortensen, "The Legend of Laurence Kuter: Agent for Airpower Doctrine," in *Airpower and Ground Armies: Essays on the Evolution of Anglo-American Air Doctrine, 1940–43*, ed. Daniel R. Mortensen (Maxwell Air Force Base, AL: Air University Press, 1998), 64–99, 69.

3. Mortensen, "The Legend of Laurence Kuter," 71; Phillip S. Meilinger, *Airmen and Air Theory: A Review of the Sources* (Maxwell Air Force Base, AL: Air University Press, 2001), 34–35, 91; "Laurence S. Kuter 1927," US Military Academy Association of Graduates Memorial Page, http://apps.westpointaog. org/Memorials/Article/8066.

4. "Laurence S. Kuter 1927," US Military Academy Association of Graduates Memorial Page.

5. Laurence S. Kuter, *Airman at Yalta* (New York: Duell, Sloan, & Pearce, 1955), and *The Great Gamble: The Boeing 747: The Boeing–Pan Am Project to Develop, Produce, and Introduce the 747* (Tuscaloosa: University of Alabama Press, 1973); "Growth of Air Power," by Laurence S. Kuter, n.d., 1, 168.7012-28, AFHRA.

Kuter spent the last several months of his life working on his autobiography, which he titled "Growth of Air Power." When he died in November 1979, he had brought the narrative up only through his time in North Africa. The unfinished manuscript covers his early life and military career through 1943. Years later, Ethel Kuter's own unpublished biographies filled in some of the gaps that remain. Kuter also spent a lot of times over the rest of his career writing things down in stories and letters for inclusion in a book, leaving a rich written record even though he kept no formal diary.

1. Beginnings, West Point, and Early Assignments

1. "Growth of Air Power," n.d., 1, 168.7012-28, Air Force Historical Research Agency (AFHRA), Maxwell Air Force Base, AL.

2. Laurence Kuter Oral History, interview conducted by Hugh N. Ahmann and Tom Sturm, 2 vols., 30 September–3 October 1974, vol. 1, p. 19, K239.0512-810, L. S. Kuter Papers, AFHRA; "Along with Larry," by Ethel Kuter, n.d., MS-18, Addendum-1, folder 2, box 12, Special Collections, McDermott Library, US Air Force Academy (USAFA).

Ethel Kuter stated in "Along with Larry" that it was never meant to be published, but that it was not meant to be kept secret either, and that it was included in her papers as a reference to the relationship between her and Larry. It is a combination of her thoughts and remembrances as well as segments from letters and diaries written by her.

The earlier parts of the manuscript were laid out by chapter and included page numbers. Toward the end, however, Ethel's papers became intertwined with Larry's and no longer maintained a coherent structure. I have used the title "Along with Larry" with page numbers where it is clear that Ethel was the author and used the section title in place of page numbers when it seems clear that the material in question is Larry's remembrances. Ethel's attempt to carry on Larry's story goes up only to 1946. Despite this, both she and Larry left a rich record of stories and letters not officially part of either manuscript detailing the rest of his military career.

3. "Growth of Air Power," 8.

4. "Along with Larry," 10, 17–18; "Growth of Air Power," 13.

5. "Along with Larry," 26.

6. "Persons of Exceptional Performance Records for General Laurence S. Kuter" (hereafter "PEP Records"), n.d., folder 1, 141.290-48, AFHRA.

7. "Growth of Air Power," 17; "PEP Records," folder 4. There is some discrepancy about who actually appointed Kuter. Kuter remembered that it was a Senator Medill McCormick, but the paper record in his official file has four separate letters: two indicating that Kuter was initially appointed as an alternate by the Honorable Charles E. Fuller, House of Representatives, and two from the office of Senator William B. McKinley appointing Kuter as a primary after two

other candidates failed to meet the requirements. It seems likely that Kuter was initially appointed as an alternate but that Captain Fisher continued his pursuit of a primary appointment for Kuter with Senator McKinley. In later years, Kuter probably incorrectly identified Medill McCormick as his sponsor. Either way, there is no doubt that he was accepted to West Point through the solid efforts of Captain Fisher.

8. Laurence Kuter Oral History, vol. 1, p. 14; "Growth of Air Power," 13–15, 18.

9. "Along with Larry," 29.

10. "Growth of Air Power," 22.

11. Laurence Kuter Oral History, vol. 1, pp. 12, 20.

12. "Along with Larry," 33. Each of the letters is preserved today in the Special Collections branch of the Air Force Academy Library (boxes 1–3, MS-18, Addendum 1, USAFA). The letters include not only Ethel's and Laurence's to each other but also his letters to his parents, friends, and other relatives.

13. Typed letter transcripts dated summer 1923, box 10, MS-18, Addendum 1.

14. Laurence Kuter Oral History, vol. 1, pp. 20–21.

15. Letter to Ethel, 17 April 1926, in "Along with Larry," 56.

16. "Growth of Air Power," 27; "PEP Records," folder 1.

17. Untitled document, folder 4, box 10, MS-18, Addendum 1.

18. Ibid.

19. "Growth of Air Power," 28; letter to Ethel, 19 February 1927, in "Along with Larry," 68.

20. "Growth of Air Power," 30.

21. Letter 510, box 3, MS-18, Addendum 1; "Along with Larry," 77.

22. Scrapbooks, vol. 1, June 1927–December 1933, MS- 18, Kuter Papers; "Along with Larry," 78.

23. Laurence Kuter Oral History, vol. 2, p. 6, and vol. 1, p. 35. Kuter and his wife were actually staying at the home of another officer who was away while their residence was being refurbished and freshly painted. This also explains why Kuter did not have a key to his own home when he found himself locked out that evening (see below).

24. Laurence Kuter Oral History, vol. 1, p. 41; "PEP Records," folder 4; "Along with Larry," 85.

25. Laurence Kuter Oral History, vol. 2, p. 6; Scrapbooks, vol. 1, June 1927–December 1933.

26. Laurence Kuter Oral History, vol. 2, p. 6; Scrapbooks, vol. 1, June 1927–December 1933; "Along with Larry," 88.

27. "Along with Larry," 90, 93.

28. Laurence Kuter Oral History, vol. 2, p. 7; "Along with Larry," 94–95.

29. "Growth of Air Power," 54.

30. "Along with Larry," 99–100.

31. Laurence Kuter Oral History, vol. 2, pp. 5, 9–10; "PEP Records," folder 4; Rebecca H. Cameron, *Training to Fly: Military Flight Training, 1907–1945* (Washington, DC: Air Force History and Museums Program, 1999), 224.

32. "Growth of Air Power," 59.

33. Ibid., 61.

34. Ibid., 62.

35. Ibid., 65.

36. Ibid., 66–67.

37. Ibid., 69; "PEP Records," folder 4.

38. "America's First Team."

39. "Growth of Air Power," 73.

40. Untitled document, folder 2, box 12, MS-18, Addendum 1; Haywood S. Hansell Jr., "General Laurence S. Kuter, 1905–1979," *Aerospace Historian,* June 1980, 91–94.

41. The commander of the unit on Kuter's arrival was in Walter Reed for psychiatric conditions, and Kuter never had contact with him. "Growth of Air Power," 76, 80.

42. Plum Tree Island is now a national wildlife refuge. Almost the entire island remains off-limits owing to an incalculable amount of unexploded ordinance dropped on it in the 1920s and 1930s. "Plum Tree Island," US Fish and Wildlife Service, http://www.fws.gov/refuge/plum_tree_island; "America's First Team."

43. Laurence Kuter Oral History, vol. 2, pp. 84–85; Martha Byrd, *Chennault: Giving Wings to the Tiger* (Tuscaloosa: University of Alabama Press, 1987), 41–42.

44. Laurence Kuter Oral History, vol. 2, pp. 87–90.

45. "Growth of Air Power," 85–86; "PEP Records," folder 4.

46. "Growth of Air Power," 88.

47. Henry H. Arnold, *Global Mission* (New York: Harper & Bros., 1949), 142–44.

48. "Growth of Air Power," 92.

49. Ibid., 92.

50. Ibid., 93.

51. Ibid., 93–94.

52. Arnold, *Global Mission,* 145.

53. "Growth of Air Power," 95–96.

54. "Serious Crashes" and "Summary of Accidents," 17 April 1934, 248.211-69, EZAACMO, AFHRA.

55. "Growth of Air Power," 97.

56. "Eastern Zone Army Air Corps Mail Operations," February 10–May 25, 1934, 8, 248.211-69, AFHRA.

2. The Air Corps Tactical School

1. Phillip S. Meilinger, *Bomber: The Formation and Early Years of Strategic Air Command* (Maxwell Air Force Base, AL: Air University Press, 2012), 15;

LeMay quoted in Conrad C. Crane, *Bombs, Cities, and Civilians: American Airpower Strategy in World War II* (Lawrence: University Press of Kansas, 1993), 11.

2. ACTS was also known in several different iterations as the Air Service Field Officers School and the Air Service Tactical School. For simplicity's sake, I have used Air Corps Tactical School throughout. See Alan Stephens, ed., *The War in the Air, 1914–1994* (Maxwell Air Force Base, AL: Air University Press, 2001), 38; and Maurer Maurer, *Aviation in the U.S. Army, 1919–1939* (Washington, DC: Office of Air Force History, 1987), 65.

3. Kuter quoted in Thomas E. Griffith Jr., *MacArthur's Airman: George C. Kenney and the War in the Southwest Pacific* (Lawrence: University Press of Kansas, 1998), 24; Laurence Kuter Oral History, vol. 1, p. 165; Robert T. Finney, *History of the Air Corps Tactical School, 1920–1940* (1955; Maxwell Air Force Base, AL: Air University Press, 1998), 115–41; Charles Griffith, *The Quest: Haywood Hansell and American Strategic Bombing in World War II* (Maxwell Air Force Base, AL: Air University Press, 1999), 45.

4. Stephens, ed., *The War in the Air*, 38; Keith Middlemas and Anthony John Lane Barnes, *Baldwin: A Biography* (London: Macmillan, 1970), 735. At the time, Lord Stanley Baldwin was lord president of the Council.

5. Laurence Kuter Oral History, vol. 1, p. 118. There is still debate about how familiar Kuter, or the rest of the ACTS faculty, was with Giulio Douhet's *The Command of the Air* (1921). There exists evidence that there was a copy at ACTS as early as 1923 (while the school was at Langley Field). However, by 1933, the book was certainly at Maxwell Field, but just who might have been reading it remains unclear. Kuter does not specifically mention Douhet in any of his bombardment lectures. See Crane. *Bombs, Cites, and Civilians*, 17–18.

6. "Growth of Air Power," 106.

7. Ibid., 113; "PEP Records," folder 4.

8. "Growth of Air Power," 115–16.

9. Ibid., 117.

10. Arthur Conan Doyle, A Scandal in Bohemia (New York: Barnes and Noble Classics, 1891), 4. (Instead of: 10. Arthur Conan Doyle, A Scandal in Bohemia (City: Publisher, 1891), 4.

11. "Along with Larry," 129. Some of these duplex houses still stood in 2016, and the ACTS headquarters building is now the headquarters building for Air University, which would eventually be another stop in Kuter's career when he commanded the organization in the 1950s. Finney, *History of the Air Corps Tactical School*, 124–25.

12. "Along with Larry," 130. Many of the buildings and streets on Maxwell Air Force Base today are named after early ACTS members; the Air University library is named after Fairchild.

13. Jeffrey C. Benton, *They Served Here: Thirty-Three Maxwell Men* (Maxwell Air Force Base, AL: Air University Press, 1999), 35; Finney, *History of the Air Corps Tactical School*, 40, 124; Scrapbooks, vol. 2, pt. 1, January 1934–

December 1937; National Park Service, "National Register of Historic Places—Nomination Form for Maxwell Air Force Base Senior Officer's Quarters Historic District," http://pdfhost.focus.nps.gov/docs/nrhp/text/87002177.pdf.

14. Scrapbooks, vol. 2, pt. 1, January 1934–December 1937.

15. Crane, *Bombs, Cities, and Civilians,* 19.

16. Finney, *History of the Air Corps Tactical School,* 124; Byrd, *Chennault,* 31, 40, 61–62; Laurence Kuter Oral History, vol. 1, pp. 112, 114.

17. Byrd, *Chennault,* 63–64.

18. Laurence Kuter Oral History, vol. 1, pp. 112, 114.

19. Meilinger, *Bomber,* 19; Haywood S. Hansell (MS-6), Speech to Air War College, "The Development of the United States Concept of Bombardment Operations," 16 February 1951, Special Collections Branch, USAFA.

20. Michael S. Sherry, *The Rise of American Air Power: The Creation of Armageddon* (New Haven, CT: Yale University Press, 1987), 88–89.

21. "Along with Larry," 136, 152.

22. "Extracts from the Course of Major Orthlieb, 1920–1921," n.d., 168.7012-15, Kuter Papers; "The Bombardment of Railway Stations and Railroads," n.d., 168.7012-17, Kuter Papers; "Future Policy in the Air," n.d., 168.7012-19, Kuter Papers.

23. "Lecture: The Power and Effect of the Demolition Bomb," 27 January 1938, 168.7012-23, Kuter Papers.

24. ACTS "Bombardment Course" Lesson Plan, folder 1, box 1, ser. 2, MS-18, Special Collections, USAFA.

25. Scrapbooks, vol. 2, pt. 2, January 1938–April 1939.

26. ACTS "American Air Power School Theories vs. World War Facts" Lesson Plan, folder 2, box 1, ser. 2, MS-18.

27. ACTS "Naval Operations" Lesson Plan, folder 3, box 1, ser. 2, MS-18.

28. Ibid.

29. Kuter quoted in Robert Frank Futrell, *Ideas, Concepts, Doctrine: Basic Thinking in the United States Air Force, 1907–1960* (1971; Maxwell Air Force Base, AL: Air University Press, 1989), 88.

30. Laurence Kuter Oral History, vol. 2, p. 13.

31. Ibid., vol. 1, pp. 517–19; "Along with Larry," 153–54.

32. Memo for the editor of *The Coast Artillery Journal,* 12 May 1938, 168.7012-11, Kuter Papers; letter from ACTS commandant to *The Coast Artillery Journal,* 9 April 1939, 168.7012-11, Kuter Papers; drafts and copies of articles written by Kuter, 168.7012-11, Kuter Papers.

33. Articles correspondence for *The Coast Artillery Journal,* 10 February 1938, 168.7012-11, Kuter Papers; Geoffrey Perret, *Winged Victory: The Army Air Forces in World War II* (New York: Random House, 1993), 330–31.

34. ACTS letter and briefing sent to chief of the Air Corps, 30 December 1938, 168.7012-23, Kuter Papers.

35. Ibid.

36. Ibid.

37. "Organization of the Top Echelons during World War II," speech given to Air War College, 28 February 1949, MS-18; Scrapbooks, vol. 3, pt. 1, May 1939–February 1942; "Along with Larry," 154.

38. "Along with Larry," 161.

3. The Coming War

1. "Growth of Air Power," 140; Scrapbooks, vol. 3, pt. 1, May 1939–February 1942.

2. "Organization of the Top Echelons during World War II"; James C. Gaston, *Planning the American Air War: Four Men and Nine Days in 1941* (Washington, DC: National Defense University Press, 1982), 39; Laurence Kuter Oral History, vol. 2, p. 19.

3. "Growth of Air Power," 142.

4. Laurence Kuter Oral History, vol. 1, p. 196. Currently, the General Staff is known as the Joint Staff and works under the chairman of the Joint Chiefs.

5. Sherry, *The Rise of American Air Power*, 88.

6. Crane, *Bombs, Cities, and Civilians*, 19, 25. The US Army Air Corps was reorganized in July 1941 into the US Army Air Forces.

7. Haywood S. Hansell Jr., *The Air Plan the Defeated Hitler* (Atlanta: Higgins-McArthur/Longino & Porter, 1972), 70.

8. Ibid.

9. David E. Johnson, *Fast Tanks and Heavy Bombers: Innovation in the U.S. Army, 1917–1945* (Ithaca, NY: Cornell University Press 1998), 169; Donald L. Miller, *Masters of the Air: America's Bomber Boys Who Fought the Air War against Nazi Germany* (New York: Simon & Schuster, 2006), 46; "Organization of the Top Echelons during World War II"; Kuter, *Airman at Yalta*, 23.

10. Haywood S. Hansell Jr., "Gen. Laurence S. Kuter," *Air Force Magazine*, June 1980, 95–96, and *The Strategic Air War against Germany and Japan: A Memoir* (Washington, DC: Office of Air Force History, 1986), 31; Griffith, *The Quest*, 67.

11. Kuter, *Airman at Yalta*, 23; Martha Byrd, *Kenneth N. Walker: Airpower's Untempered Crusader* (Maxwell Air Force Base, AL: Air University Press, 1997), xii.

12. "Growth of Air Power," 159.

13. Hansell, *The Air Plan That Defeated Hitler*, 90–93. There remains some confusion over who received the AWPD-1 brief and when they received it. In Hansell's account, the brief that went to the chief of the air corps was with George Brett. Kuter remembered it going to Barton Yount. Yount was not in Washington at this time, and Brett was still acting chief. Hap Arnold was now assistant chief of staff of the army for the army air forces, and Brett's position had become redundant, but probably Brett received the brief first, and Arnold received it when Marshall did.

14. Hansell, *The Air Plan That Defeated Hitler,* 94; "Growth of Air Power," 160.

15. "Growth of Air Power," 160.

16. Arnold, *Global Mission,* 245; Hansell, *The Air Plan That Defeated Hitler,* 88.

17. Laurence Kuter Oral History, vol. 1, p. 115; "Growth of Air Power," 141; Hansell, *The Air Plan That Defeated Hitler,* 96.

18. Folder 6, box 7, MS-18, Addendum 1.

19. Kuter notes that, prior to the outbreak of hostilities and the United States declaring war, it was not unusual for officers to work in their civilian clothes and wear uniforms only when required, e.g., for an official briefing. Sometimes that was as infrequently as one day a month and only then simply to ensure that the officer in question owned at least one serviceable uniform. "Growth of Air Power," 165.

20. Ibid., 167.

21. "Memorandum for the Chief of Staff," 13 January 1942, 168.7012-1, AFHRA.

22. Ibid.

23. "Organization of the Top Echelons during World War II"; Charles D. Bright, ed., *Historical Dictionary of the U.S. Air Force* (New York: Greenwood, 1992), 332; folder 6, MS-18.

24. Gaston, *Planning the American Air War,* 37; "Growth of Air Power," 169.

25. Gaston, *Planning the American Air War,* 39; "Growth of Air Power," 170.

26. "Growth of Air Power," 173.

27. Futrell, *Ideas, Concepts, Doctrine . . . 1907–1960,* 129.

28. "Growth of Air Power," 180.

29. Ibid., 181; "Organization of the Army Air Forces as of 24 March 1942," folder 7, box 1, MS-18.

30. Laurence S. Kuter, "The General vs. the Establishment: General H. H. Arnold and the Air Staff," *Aerospace Historian,* December 1974, 185–89.

31. "Arnold's Staff Notes, HQ-AAF, Interview with Major General Lyman Whitten," 9 December 1970, 1102994, AFHRA; Kuter, "The General vs. the Establishment," 188; "Organization of the Army Air Forces"; Murray Green interview with Kuter, 17 April 1970, MS-33, USAFA.

32. "Growth of Air Power," 194; Kuter, "The General vs. the Establishment," 185.

33. "Growth of Air Power," 181–82.

34. Ibid., 181.

35. Ibid., 187.

36. Ernest J. King and Walter Muir Whitehill, *Fleet Admiral King: A Naval Record* (New York: Da Capo, 1976), 454.

37. "Memorandum for Kuter: Inspection of the Pacific Area," 14 September 1942, K702.152, AFHRA.

38. Ibid.

39. Ibid.

40. Ibid.

41. Robert S. Ehlers Jr., *The Mediterranean Air War: Airpower and Allied Victory in World War II* (Lawrence: University Press of Kansas, 2015), 43–45, 224–26.

42. Jeffery S. Underwood, *The Wings of Democracy: The Influence of Air Power on the Roosevelt Administration, 1933–1941* (College Station: Texas A&M University Press, 1991), 183.

43. "Memorandum for Kuter: Inspection of the Pacific Area."

44. "Growth of Air Power," 181.

45. Ibid., 208.

4. The European Theater of Operations

1. "Growth of Air Power," 210; "General Laurence S. Kuter," US Air Force Biographies.

2. "Growth of Air Power," 239; "PEP Records," folder 1.

3. "Growth of Air Power," 246.

4. Ibid., 242.

5. Miller, *Masters of the Air,* 148; Laurence Kuter Oral History, vol. 1, pp. 200, 275.

6. "Growth of Air Power," 244.

7. Folder 3, box 9, MS-18, Addendum 1.

8. Laurence Kuter Oral History, vol. 1, p. 115; James H. Doolittle, *I Could Never Be So Lucky Again* (Atglen, PA: Schiffer, 1995), 337–38.

9. Kuter, *Airman at Yalta,* 27; Laurence Kuter Oral History, vol. 1, p. 274.

10. Miller, *Masters of the Air,* 148.

11. "Growth of Air Power," 251.

12. Ibid., 251.

13. Laurence Kuter Oral History, vol. 1, pp. 137, 267–68; Richard H. Kohn and Joseph P. Harahan, eds., *Strategic Air Warfare: An Interview with Generals Curtis E. LeMay, Leon W. Johnson, David A. Burchinal, and Jack J. Catton* (Washington, DC: Office of Air Force History, 1988), 27; Curtis E. LeMay Oral History, 15 June 1984, p. 47, K239.0512-2115, AFHRA; Craven and Cate, eds., *The Army Air Forces in World War II,* 2:264–67.

14. "Growth of Air Power," 251.

15. Byrd, *Kenneth N. Walker,* 115; Parton, *"Air Force Spoken Here."*

16. Parton, *"Air Force Spoken Here,"* 211–12.

17. Ibid.; Laurence Kuter Oral History, vol. 1, p. 267; Paul Kennedy, *Engineers of Victory: The Problem Solvers Who Turned the Tide in the Second World War* (New York: Random House, 2013), 113–14.

18. "PEP Records," folder 1; Parton, *"Air Force Spoken Here,"* 211–12.

19. "Growth of Air Power," 263.

20. Ibid., 261; I. C. Eaker Oral History, 10–12 February 1975, pp. 171–72, K239.0512-829 C.1171-72, AFHRA.

21. Mortensen, "The Legend of Laurence Kuter," 67; Laurence Kuter Oral History, vol. 1, pp. 280–81.

5. North Africa

1. General Order no. 1, 18 February 1943, "Mediterranean Allied Tactical Air Forces Files, Air Aspect General Orders," MICFILM roll 24998, AFHRA; Kit C. Carter and Robert Mueller, *Combat Chronology: 1941–1945* (Washington, DC: Center for Air Force History, 1991).

2. Memorandum from Spaatz to his air forces, 16 April 1943, "Mediterranean Allied Tactical Air Forces Files, Air Aspect General Orders."

3. Vincent Orange, *Coningham: A Biography of Air Marshal Sir Arthur Coningham* (London: Methuen, 1990), 130–31; "Growth of Air Power," 266.

4. Letter from Sorenson to Kuter, 3 January 1943, 583, MICHFILM Reel 34142, Haywood S. Hansell Collection, AFHRA.

5. Ibid.

6. Letter from Kuter to Hansell, 23 January 1943, 589, MICHFILM Reel 34142; letter from Hansell to Kuter, 11 February 1943, 590, MICHFILM Reel 34142. There is some debate among historians as to whether Kuter sent Hansell a crate of oranges or, seeing as he was in North Africa at the time, a crate of tangerines. Kuter referred to "citrus fruit," while Hansell indicated that the crate contained oranges.

7. Letter from Hansell to Sorensen, 11 February 1943, 592, MICHFILM Reel 34142.

8. Orange, *Coningham,* 136.

9. Ibid., 146; "Growth of Air Power," 284.

10. "Growth of Air Power," 285.

11. Ibid., 286.

12. Ibid., 287.

13. Orange, *Coningham,* 148.

14. Memorandum 7, Kuter to 3rd Service Area Command, 12th Air Support Command, 4 March 1943, "Mediterranean Allied Tactical Air Forces Files, Correspondence, General Kuter's," MICFILM Roll 24998.

15. Memorandum 9, Kuter to Spaatz, 5 April 1943, "Mediterranean Allied Tactical Air Forces Files, Correspondence, General Kuter's."

16. Memorandum 3, Coningham to 2nd Air Support Command et al.,17 April 1943, "Mediterranean Allied Tactical Air Forces Files, Correspondence, General Kuter's."

17. Ibid.

18. Manuscript, 210, MICHFILM Reel 34142.

19. Montgomery quoted in ibid., 211.

20. "Growth of Air Power," 283.

21. Kuter Speech to Squadron Officer School, 9 November 1954, M-U 38043 K97a, Fairchild Documents, Muir S. Fairchild Research Information Center (MSFRIC).

22. Christopher M. Rein, *The North African Air Campaign: U.S. Army Forces from El Alamein to Salerno* (Lawrence: University Press of Kansas, 2012), 126–27; Ehlers, *The Mediterranean Air War,* 261; "Growth of Air Power," 287 ("worked over"); Douglas Porch, *The Path to Victory: The Mediterranean Theater in World War II* (New York: Farrar, Straus, Giroux, 2004), 407.

23. "Growth of Air Power," 288.

24. Ibid., 290; Rein, *The North African Air Campaign,* 128.

25. Rein, *The North African Air Campaign,* 128; Ehlers, *The Mediterranean Air War,* 285.

26. "Growth of Air Power," 291.

27. Ibid., 292.

28. Doolittle, *I Could Never Be So Lucky Again,* 344.

29. Folder "Eyes Only," 15 February–30 April 1943 (3), box 13, Walter Bedell Smith Papers, Dwight David Eisenhower Presidential Library; "Growth of Air Power," 294.

30. "Growth of Air Power," 293–94.

31. "Organization of American Air Forces," folder 6, box 2, MS-18.

32. Ibid.

33. Ehlers, *The Mediterranean Air War,* 257.

34. "PEP Records," folder 1.

6. Back to Washington and Hap's Stand-In

1. *Command and Employment of Air Power,* Field Manual 100-20 (Washington, DC: US War Department, 21 July 1943).

2. Green interview with Kuter; Johnson, *Fast Tanks and Heavy Bombers,* 213.

3. Griffith, *MacArthur's Airman.*

4. Memo from Arnold to Kuter regarding General Kenney Report, 29 June 1943, folder 1, 168.7012-1, Kuter Papers.

5. Byrd, *Kenneth N. Walker,* 118–20.

6. Response letter from Kuter to Arnold for signature, 1 July 1943, folder 1, 168.7012-1, Kuter Papers.

7. Ibid.

8. Ibid.

9. "Growth of Air Power," 208; Laurence Kuter Oral History, vol. 1, p. 244.

10. Richard H. Kohn and Joseph P. Harahan, eds., *Air Superiority in World*

War II and Korea: An Interview with Gen. James Ferguson, Gen. Robert M. Lee, Gen. William Momyer and Lt. Gen. Elwood R. Quesada (Washington, DC: Office of Air Force History, 1983), 36.

11. David R. Mets, "A Glider in the Propwash of the Royal Air Force," in Mortensen, ed., *Airpower and Ground Armies,* 30–63, 34.

12. *Command and Employment of Air Power.*

13. Ibid.

14. Memo to chief of Air Staff, 10 August 1943, and memo to Arnold, 9 August 1943, folder 1, 168.7012-1, Kuter Papers. The B-35 was a "flying wing" bomber built by John Northrup that first flew in 1946.

15. Memo to Arnold, 9 August 1943, folder 1, 168.7012-1, Kuter Papers.

16. Memo to General Arnold on German Air Force, 6 August 1943, folder 1, 168.7012-1, Kuter Papers.

17. Letter from Kuter to Green, 24 October 1971, MS-33.

18. Phillip S. Meilinger, "Alexander P. de Seversky and American Airpower," in *The Paths of Heaven: The Evolution of Airpower Theory,* ed. Phillip S. Meilinger (Maxwell Air Force Base, AL: Air University Press, 1997), 239–78, 241. For simplicity, I have used Seversky throughout.

19. Meilinger, "Alexander P. de Seversky and American Airpower," 242.

20. Perret, *Winged Victory,* 105.

21 Ibid.

22. Meilinger, "Alexander P. de Seversky and American Airpower," 246.

23. Futrell, *Ideas, Concepts, Doctrine . . . 1907–1960,* 438; William Mitchell, *Winged Defense: The Development and Possibilities of Air Power—Economic and Military* (New York: Dover, 2006), xii; Meilinger, "Alexander P. de Seversky and American Airpower," 256.

24. Alexander P. De Seversky, *Victory through Air Power* (New York: Simon & Schuster, 1942), 254.

25. Charles Beard quote from De Seversky, *Victory through Air Power,* dustjacket.

26. Russell E. Lee, "Impact of *Victory through Air Power*: Pt. 1, The Army Air Force's Reaction," *Air Power History,* Summer 1993, 3–13, James K. Libbey, *Alexander P. de Seversky and the Quest for Air Power* (Washington, DC: Potomac, 2013), 202.

27. Lee, "Impact of *Victory through Air Power.*"

28. Ibid.

29. Letter from Harold George to Murray Green, 19 September 1971, MS-33; Libbey, *Alexander P. de Seversky,* 198.

30. Letter from Harold George to Murray Green, 19 September 1971, MS-33; Murray Green interview with Kuter notes, MS-33; Green interview with Kuter, MS-33.

31. Letter from Harold George to Murray Green, 19 September 1971, MS-33; interview with Alexander de Seversky 16 April 1970, MS-33; note from Kuter to Green on Seversky's account of the incident, n.d., MS-33.

32. Letter from Harold George to Murray Green, 19 September 1971, MS-33; Libbey, *Alexander P. de Seversky*, 200.

33. Lee, "Impact of *Victory through Air Power*."

34. Richard Shale, *Donald Duck Joins Up* (Ann Arbor, MI: UMI Research Press, 1982), 68; Leonard Maltin, *The Disney Films* (New York: Crown, 1973), 61.

35. James Agee, *Agee on Film* (New York: Modern Library, 1958), 25.

36. "The Screen; The Globe Presents 'Victory through Air Power,' a Disney Illustration of Major de Seversky's Book," *New York Times*, 19 July 1943.

37. Folder 9, box 2, MS-18.

38. Libbey, *Alexander P. de Seversky*, 209.

39. Lee, "Impact of *Victory through Air Power*."

40. Libbey, *Alexander P. de Seversky*, 207; proposed draft of reply to Mr. Seversky, 6 August 1943, folder 1, 168.7012-1, Kuter Papers; memo to Arnold, 3 August 1943, folder 1, 168.7012-1, Kuter Papers; Green notes, "Plan to Make Seversky Put Up or Shut Up," MS-33.

41. Memo to Major Wildman on forthcoming B-29 test, 15 September 1943, folder 1, 168.7012-1, Kuter Papers.

42. Memo to General Grant, 15 September 1943, folder 1, 168.7012-1, Kuter Papers.

43. Arnold, *Global Mission*, 454–55; Laurence Kuter Oral History, vol. 1, p. 402.

44. Laurence Kuter Oral History, vol. 1, p. 402.

45. "Cairo Conference, Larry's Notes," folder 4, box 4, MS-18, Addendum 1.

46. "Air Operations in Western Europe in 1944," 4 February 1944, 168.04-27, 1943, AFHRA.

47. Ibid.

48. Ibid.

49. Laurence Kuter Oral History, vol. 1, pp. 290, 381.

50. "Notes on Kuter's Trip around the World," folder 5, box 4, MS-18, Addendum 1; Laurence Kuter Oral History, vol. 1, p. 405.

51. "Notes on Kuter's Trip around the World."

52. Interview with Kuter, 16 July 1969, MS-33; Griffith, *MacArthur's Airman*, 181; George C. Kenney, *General Kenney Reports: A Personal History of the Pacific War* (Washington, DC: Air Force History and Museum Program, 1997), 378.

53. "Notes on Kuter's Trip around the World."

54. "Notes on Kuter's Trip around the World." The excerpt from Ethel's notes should be with her manuscript, which it is not. In fact, the entirety of 1944 is missing from the "Along with Larry" manuscript and scattered throughout the addendum to the Kuter series.

55. "Notes on Trip to England, France and Italy, May 28th to June 21st 1944," folder 2, box 1, MS-18, Addendum 2, ASAFA; "Notes on Kuter's Trip around the World."

56. Gen. Laurence S. Kuter, "D-Day: June 6, 1944," *Air Force Magazine,* June 1979, 000, reprinted June 1984. The printed story of Kuter's experiences on D-Day was taken from the same notes he took during and after the trip.

57. "Notes on Trip to England, France and Italy"; Kuter, "D-Day."

58. "Notes on Trip to England, France and Italy."

59. Ibid.; Kuter, "D-Day."

60. Kuter, "D-Day"; Miller, *Masters of the Air,* 7.

61. "Notes on Trip to England, France and Italy."

62. Ibid.

63. Ibid.

64. Kuter, "D-Day."

65. "Notes on Trip to England, France and Italy"; Thomas A. Hughes, *Over Lord: General Pete Quesada and the Triumph of Tactical Air Power in World War II* (New York: Free Press, 1995), 7–9.

66. "Notes on Trip to England, France and Italy."

67. Ehlers, *The Mediterranean Air War,* 338–39; "Notes on Trip to England, France and Italy."

68. "Notes on Trip to England, France and Italy."

69. Ibid.

70. Ibid.

71. "Notes on Kuter's Trip around the World"; "Notes on Trip to England, France and Italy."

72. "Memo for Col. Dean: Memo of Phone Conv. w/ Gen. McFarland," 12 October 1944, folder 1, 168.7012-1, Kuter Papers.

73. "Memorandum for Major General L. S. Kuter," 22 October 1944, and "Memorandum from Kuter to Undersecretary of War," 1 November 1944, 168.7012-24, Kuter Papers.

74. R. Cargill Hall, ed., *Case Studies in Strategic Bombardment* (Washington DC: Air Force History and Museums Program, 1998), 344–45; *United States Strategic Bombing Surveys* (Maxwell Air Force Base, AL: Air University Press, 1987), 73, 92–93; Kenneth P. Werrell, *Blankets of Fire: U.S. Bombers over Japan during World War II* (Washington, DC: Smithsonian Institution Press, 1996), 231; Herman S. Wolk, *Cataclysm: General Hap Arnold and the Defeat of Japan* (Denton: University of North Texas Press, 2010), 180.

75. Arnold quoted in Dik Allen Daso, *Hap Arnold and the Evolution of American Airpower* (Washington, DC: Smithsonian Institution Press, 2001), 203.

76. Kuter, *Airman at Yalta,* 176; unsent letter from Ethel Kuter to Larry's parents, February 1945, folder 7, box 10, MS-18.

77. "Winston Churchill: Politician around the Clock," folder 19, box 8, MS-18, Addendum 1.

78. Kuter, *Airman at Yalta,* 13, 19.

79. Ibid., 134.

80. Ibid., 150; Craven and Cate, eds., *The Army Air Forces in World War II,* 3:xiv.

81. Kuter, *Airman at Yalta,* 152; Craven and Cate, eds., *The Army Air Forces in World War II,* 3:749–50.

82. Kuter, *Airman at Yalta,* 160.

83. Ibid., 166.

84. Letter from Arnold to Kuter, 20 February 1945, "PEP Records," folder 1; Arnold, *Global Mission,* 537.

85. "Along with Larry," 1.

86. Unsent letter, February 1945, folder 7, box 10, MS-18, Addendum 1.

87. "Along with Larry," "January to May 1945."

88. Meilinger, *Bomber,* 65.

89. "Along with Larry," "January to May 1945"; "Larry in the Pacific: May to July 1945," folder 2, box 12, MS-18, Addendum 1; Laurence Kuter Oral History, vol. 1, p. 410. Curtis LeMay also suffered from Bell's palsy, but he had a significantly worse case than Kuter did, and to hide the affliction he almost always had a cigar in his mouth.

7. The Pacific, War's End, and Air Transport Command

1. "PEP Records," folder 4; Laurence Kuter Oral History, vol. 1, pp. 416–17.

2. "Larry in the Pacific"; Laurence Kuter Oral History, vol. 1, pp. 415–16.

3. Wolk, *Cataclysm,* 120.

4. "Larry in the Pacific."

5. Stratemeyer Diary, 26 May–31 December 1945, 34, MS-28, George Stratemeyer Collection, USAFA.

6. Ibid., 36.

7. "Larry in the Pacific."

8. Ibid.

9. Untitled document, July–September 1945, folder 6, box 4, MS-18, Addendum 1.

10. "Larry in the Pacific."

11. Kenney, *General Kenney Reports,* 378.

12. Kenney quoted in Griffith, *MacArthur's Airman,* 181, 220.

13. Untitled document, July–September 1945, folder 6, box 4, MS-18, Addendum 1; Stratemeyer Diary, 26 May–31 December 1945, 56.

14. "Larry in the Pacific."

15. Doulens quoted in ibid.

16. Ibid.

17. Untitled document, July–September 1945, folder 6, box 4, MS-18, Addendum 1.

18. "PEP Records," folder 4.

19. Ibid.

20. Ibid., folder 1.

21. "Remarks by General Laurence S. Kuter, USAF at the 42nd Annual Dinner of the Circumnavigator's Club," 18 January 1950, folder 2, box 29, MS-18.

22. "Along with Larry," "Atlantic Division, Air Transport Command September 1945 . . . September 1946."

23. "Along with Larry," "Atlantic Division, Air Transport Command September 1945 . . . September 1946."

24. Laurence Kuter Oral History, vol. 1, p. 433; "Along with Larry," "Atlantic Division, Air Transport Command September 1945 . . . September 1946."

25. "Along with Larry," "Atlantic Division, Air Transport Command September 1945 . . . September 1946."

26. Ibid.

27. "PEP Records," folders 1, 4; Laurence Kuter Oral History, vol. 1, p. 443. Kuter's personal records contain the act of the Eightieth Congress authorizing President Truman to appoint Kuter as well as Truman's letter appointing him to the rank of minister.

28. Laurence Kuter Oral History, vol. 1, p. 446.

29. Ibid.

30. "PEP Records," folder 3; Laurence Kuter Oral History, vol. 1, p. 462.

31. Laurence Kuter Oral History, vol. 2, p. 81.

32. Copy of "Truman's Secret Management of the Airlines," *Aerospace Historian,* September 1977, folder 18, MS-18, Addendum 1.

33. Laurence Kuter Oral History, vol. 2, p. 81; copy of "Truman's Secret Management of the Airlines."

34. Copy of "Truman's Secret Management of the Airlines."

35. Laurence Kuter Oral History, vol. 1, pp. 462, 468; "MATS Headquarters Letters, 1 September 1948–15 November 1951," folder 6, box 11, MS-18, Addendum 1.

36. Letter 1, "MATS Headquarters Letters."

37. "Address before the Institute of Aeronautical Sciences," 24 January 49, 168.7012-27, AFHRA.

38. William H. Tunner, *Over the Hump* (1969; Washington, DC: Air Force History and Museums Program, 1998), 160.

39. Laurence Kuter Oral History, vol. 1, p. 480.

40. Ibid.

41. Ibid., 478–79.

42. Ibid., 478, 481.

43. Daniel F. Harrington, *Berlin on the Brink: The Blockade, the Airlift, and the Early Cold War* (Lexington: University Press of Kentucky, 2012), 238–39.

44. Letters between Kuter and Tunner, 3 August 1948, folder 31, box 1, Air Mobility Command, Office of History (AMC).

45. Kuter letter to Tunner quoted in Harrington, *Berlin on the Brink,* 238. The letter can also be found in Letters between Kuter and Tunner.

46. Harrington, *Berlin on the Brink,* 248–49.

47. "Address before the Institute of Aeronautical Sciences."

48. "Abdul-Aziz ibn Saud Nuclear Bedouin," folder 9, box 6, MS-18, Addendum 1.

49. Ibid.

50. "Commanders Conference," 25–27 April 1950, National Security Archive (NSA), George Washington University (GWU).

51. "The Royal Stag," folder 13, box 5, MS-18, Addendum 1.

52. Ibid.

53. Ibid.

54. Ibid.

55. Ibid.

56. Ibid.

8. Air University

1. Letter to family "From Washington Back to Maxwell," folder 1, box 4, MS-18, Addendum 1.

2. Laurence Kuter Oral History, vol. 1, p. 522.

3. Ibid., 524, 541.

4. Ibid., 524, 538.

5. Ibid., 565.

6. "The Bear Guide," folder 12, box 5, MS-18, Addendum 1; "The Bear Facts," folder 12, box 5, MS-18, Addendum 1.

7. "The Bear Guide"; "The Bear Facts."

8. "The Bear Guide"; "The Bear Facts."

9. "The Bear Guide"; "The Bear Facts."

10"The Bear Guide"; "The Bear Facts."

11. "The Bear Guide"; "The Bear Facts."

12. "The Bear Guide"; "The Bear Facts."

13. Letter to family "From Washington Back to Maxwell."

14. Laurence Kuter Oral History, vol. 1, p. 522.

15. Letter to family "From Washington Back to Maxwell."

16. Letter to family "From Washington Back to Maxwell." Kuter's name did come up later as a possible chairman of the Joint Chiefs while he was serving as the commander of the Pacific Air Forces.

17. Laurence Kuter Oral History, vol. 1, p. 553.

18. Ibid., 562.

19. "The Stature of an Air Force Career," n.d., folder 5, box 29, MS-18.

20. At this time, SOS was nested under ACSS. In July 1959, after Kuter had left Air University, the status of ACSS was elevated to that of a college. Nevertheless, Kuter's 9 November 1954 speech refers to the school as the Air Command and Staff College.

21. Speech given by Kuter to ACSS, 17 December 1954, M-U 38043 K97a.

22. Ibid.

23. Laurence Kuter Oral History, vol. 1, p. 564.

24. Ibid., vol. 2, p. 363.

25. Ibid., vol. 1, p. 558.

26. "HQ, Air University Press Release," 14 May 1955, K239.293 Kuter, AFHRA; letter from Ethel to family, n.d., folder 1, box 2, MS-18, Addendum 2.

9. Fixing the Far East Air Forces and Creating the Pacific Air Forces

1. Letter to family, 22 January 1957, folder 1, box 2, MS-18, Addendum 2.

2. "Sayonara in Japan—Aloha in Hawaii," folder 1, box 2, MS-18, Addendum 2.

3. Edward J. Drea et al., *History of the Unified Command Plan* (Washington, DC: Joint History Office, Office of the Chairman of the Joint Chiefs of Staff, 2013), 18–19.

4. "Sayonara in Japan—Aloha in Hawaii"; Drea et al., *History of the Unified Command Plan*, 18–19.

5. "Sayonara in Japan—Aloha in Hawaii."

6. Laurence Kuter Oral History, vol. 1, p. 570; letter from Ethel to family, n.d., folder 1, box 2, MS-18, Addendum 2.

7. "Sayonara in Japan—Aloha in Hawaii"; letter from Larry Kuter to General Clark, Superintendent of the Air Force Academy, 22 August 1972, folder 2, box 5, MS-18, Addendum 1.

8. "Objectivity," folder 9, box 6, MS-18, Addendum 1; Laurence Kuter Oral History, vol. 1, p. 571.

9. "Kanko Kuter," folder 1, box 2, MS-18, Addendum 2; "Observations on Personalities and Trends in the Far East/Pacific," folder 12, box 45, MS-18; letter to Faith, 12 July 1955, folder 2, box 45, MS-18.

10. "Observations on Personalities and Trends"; "Anecdote," folder 9, box 6, MS-18, Addendum 1.

11. "Observations on Personalities and Trends."

12. "President Chiang Kai-Shek," folder 6, box 6, MS-18, Addendum 1.

13. Ibid.

14. Laurence Kuter Oral History, vol. 2, p. 133.

15. "Ordeal by Blow Gun," folder 13, box 5, MS-18, Addendum 1; letter to family, 22 January 1957, MS-18, Addendum 2. The Abo villagers whom Kuter described in his letters are most likely members of the indigenous people known today as the Batek, who still reside in the rainforests.

16. Letter to family, 22 January 1957, folder 1, box 2, MS-18, Addendum 2.

17. Ibid.

18. "Ordeal by Blow Gun."

19. "Ramon Magsaysay, President of the Republic of the Philippines," folder 9, box 6, MS-18, Addendum 1; "President Magsaysay Seizes Opportunities," folder 9, box 6, MS-18, Addendum 1.

20. "Death of a Friend," *Time,* 25 March 1957; "Magsaysay Dead with 24

in Plane," *New York Times,* 18 March 1957; "Week in Manila," folder 1, box 2, MS-18, Addendum 2.

21. "Magsaysay Dead with 24 in Plane"; "Week in Manila."

22. "Week in Manila."

23. Ibid.

24. Ibid.

25. USAF Historical Division Liaison Office, "Air Operations in the Taiwan Crisis of 1958," NSA, GWU.

26. USAF Historical Division Liaison Office, "Air Operations in the Taiwan Crisis of 1958."

27. "Taiwan Straits Crisis," folder 5, box 11, MS-18, Addendum 1; USAF Historical Division Liaison Office, "Air Operations in the Taiwan Crisis of 1958."

28. "Taiwan Straits Crisis."

29. Ibid.; USAF Historical Division Liaison Office, "Air Operations in the Taiwan Crisis of 1958," 15–23, 48.

30. USAF Historical Division Liaison Office, "Air Operations in the Taiwan Crisis of 1958," 28; Edward Kaplan, *To Kill Nations: American Strategy in the Air-Atomic Age and the Rise of Mutually Assured Destruction* (Ithaca, NY: Cornell University Press, 2015), 1–2.

31. Walter Pincus, "Eisenhower Advisers Discussed Using Nuclear Weapons in China," *Washington Post,* 30 April 2008.

32. USAF Historical Division Liaison Office, "Air Operations in the Taiwan Crisis of 1958," 23.

33. Laurence Kuter Oral History, vol. 2, p. 366.

34. USAF Historical Division Liaison Office, "Air Operations in the Taiwan Crisis of 1958," 37.

35. Ibid., 38.

36. Laurence Kuter Oral History, vol. 2, pp. 571–72.

10. Commander in Chief, North American Air Defense Command

1. "HQ, Air University Press Release." The North American Air Defense Command did not the North American Aerospace Defense Command until the early 1980s.

2. "From PACAF to NORAD," folder 2, box 2, MS-18, Addendum 2.

3. "From PACAF to NORAD"; "A Brief History of NORAD," 13 December 2013, NORAD-USNORTHCOM History Office.

4. Phone Directory, 1962, NORAD-USNORTHCOM History Office; Laurence Kuter Oral History, vol. 1, p. 583.

5. "From PACAF to NORAD."

6. Ibid.

7. Ibid.

8. Ibid.

9. Ibid.

10. Ibid.

11. Ibid.

12. Ibid.

13. "NORAD's Quest for Nike Zeus and a Long Range Interceptor," 1 July 1962, NORAD-USNORTHCOM History Office.

14. Marcelle Size Knaack, *Encyclopedia of US Air Force Aircraft and Missile Systems,* vol. 1, *Post–World War II Fighters, 1945–1973* (Washington, DC: Office of Air Force History, 1978), 331; "NORAD's Quest for Nike Zeus and a Long Range Interceptor."

15. "NORAD's Quest for Nike Zeus and a Long Range Interceptor"; "NORAD/CONAD Historical Summary," July–December 1961, 74, NORAD-USNORTHCOM History Office.

16. "NORAD/CONAD Historical Summary," July–December 1960, 48.

17. "NORAD/CONAD Historical Summary," January–June 1961, 64–65.

18. "NORAD's Underground Combat Operations Center, 1956–1966," January 1956, 15, NORAD-USNORTHCOM History Office.

19. Ibid., 21; Scrapbooks, vol. 1, January–May 1961.

20. "NORAD/CONAD Historical Summary," January–June 1962, 46; "Historical Review of North American Aerospace Defense, 1946–1970," 1 October 1970, 55.

21. Letter from Larry Kuter to Possum Hansell, 24 January 1973, folder 23, box 8, MS-18, Addendum 1; Laurence S. Kuter, "JFK and LBJ Consider Aerospace Defense," *Aerospace Historian,* March 1979, 1–4. The *Aerospace Historian* article indicates that day of the meeting was 8 February, and Kuter's letter to Hansell gives it as 11 February. I have chosen the former as the more likely.

22. Letter from Larry Kuter to Possum Hansell, 24 January 1973, folder 23, box 8, MS-18, Addendum 1; Kuter, "JFK and LBJ Consider Aerospace Defense."

23. "A Brief History of NORAD."

24. Laurence Kuter Oral History, vol. 1, p. 609.

25. Scrapbooks, vol. 35, 1963.

26. "Pueblo Committee Report to the President," 7 February 1968, NSA, GWU. This report is also available at the Library of President Lyndon Johnson.

27. Scrapbooks, vol. 35, 1963.

Conclusion

1. 1979 Diary, box 6, MS-18, Addendum 2.

2. Letter from Ethel to accompany Larry's memorialization, 8 December 1979, folder 2, box 12, MS-18, Addendum 1.

3. Ibid.

4. Laurence Kuter Oral History, vol. 1, p. 544.

5. Funeral documents (group of pages typed by Ethel), folder 10, box 12, MS-18, Addendum 1.

6. Letter from Haywood S. Hansell Jr. to Ethel Kuter, 18 December 1979, folder 3, box 9, MS-18, Addendum 1.

7. Ibid.; Hansell, "General Laurence S. Kuter: 1905–1979."

8. Laurence Kuter Oral History, vol. 1, p. 546.

9. Letter to Miss Mary Marinan, 27 October 1980, folder 1, box 8, MS-18, Addendum 1.

10. "PEP Records," folders 1–7.

11. Copy of article, folder 2, box 12, MS-18, Addendum 1; I. B. Holley Jr., "An Air Force General: Laurence Sherman Kuter," *Aerospace Historian,* June 1980, 95–97.

12. Series of clippings about Ethel's involvement at the air force academy after Larry's death and about the trophy bearing his name, folders 15, 17, box 4, MS-18, Addendum 1.

13. Letter from Larry Kuter to General Clark, Superintendent of the Air Force Academy, 22 August 1972, folder 2, box 5, MS-18, Addendum 1; letter from Ethel Kuter to undisclosed recipients, n.d., "The Japanese stone lantern from the garden of CINCFEAF in Tokyo . . . now in Colorado." While Ethel's letter is undated, it was sent after Larry's death and sometime in 1980.

14. Haywood S. Hansell Jr., "General Laurence S. Kuter, 1905–1979," *Air Force Magazine,* June 1980, 91–94.

15. Letter from Ethel to accompany Larry's memorialization, n.d., folder 2, box 12, MS-18, Addendum 1.

Bibliography

Collections

Special Collections, McDermott Library, US Air Force Academy (USAFA)

Four principal sets of special collections were used from the air force academy library: the Laurence S. Kuter, Haywood Hansell, George Stratemeyer, and Murray Green Papers. The USAFA Special Collections also held copies of the National Archives and Records Administration H. H. Arnold Papers.

MS-18; MS-18 Addendum 1; MS-18 Addendum 2. The Laurence S. Kuter collection of correspondence, speeches and addresses, printed matter, manuscripts, portraits, diaries, biographies, and fifty-one bound scrapbooks (47 cm by 43 cm) containing photos, news clippings, correspondence, and memorabilia from Kuter's military career and personal life from 1927 to 1963. Significant correspondence relates to Kuter's involvement in the development of air doctrine and air power during World War II and his role as the army air forces representative to the Yalta Conference in 1945. A copy of Kuter's *Airman at Yalta,* which describes his experiences before and after the conference, is included in the collection. Items posted online represent just a small fraction of the Special Collections holdings. The scrapbooks are especially interesting for the sheer volume of what the Kuter family carefully preserved, including everything from Kuter and his wife's wedding certificate, to their daughter Roxanne's report cards, to Kuter's first gray hair (tied to a string, wrapped in tissue, and ensconced in an envelope).

MS-6. A collection of materials from the beginning of Haywood Hansell's military career in 1933 through his retirement years and up to his death in 1988. A large portion of the items pertain to his role as an instructor and lecturer at the Air Corps Tactical School at Maxwell Field, Alabama, during the 1930s. There are also personal notebooks that include letters, photographs, and clippings describing highlights of Hansell's career. The collection also includes a preliminary manuscript entitled "American Air Power in World War II."

MS-28. A collection of original papers written and gathered by General George E. Stratemeyer during his service as commander of the India-Burma Sector of the China-Burma-India Theater of Operations during World War II. Included is Stratemeyer's World War II diary, official correspondence that he maintained during the China-Burma-India campaign, personal correspondence with his wife, scrapbooks relating to the China-Burma-India campaign, printed materials, and photographs of Stratemeyer's "Flying Circus."

MS-33. The air force historian Murray Green spent four decades researching a definitive biography of Henry H. Arnold. Although he never finished, he left behind a collection of interviews with major participants, including Harold George, Larry Kuter, and Alexander de Seversky.

Air Force Historical Research Agency

The Air Force Historical Research Agency collection is categorized by the date an item is archived and not necessarily thematically or chronologically. Therefore, to locate files on a particular person of interest, it becomes necessary to know where that person served at a particular time in history. This presented significant challenges for locating General Kuter's records as he traveled so many places, particularly during the Second World War, and was sometimes in a particular location for only a very short period of time. However, the most salient records for the career of General Kuter include the following:

Laurence Kuter Oral History, 30 September–3 October 1974, K239.0512-810, vols. 1 and 2;
Personnel of Exceptional Performance Records, Kuter, L. S., 141.290-48, folders 1–6;
K239.293 Kuter;
Oral history interviews with Ira C. Eaker, Carl A. Spaatz, Curtis E. LeMay, and Leon W. Johnson.

Eisenhower Presidential Library

Walter Bedell Smith, box 13, folder "Eyes Only," 15 February–30 April 1943.

Muir S. Fairchild Research and Information Center

Fairchild Documents, M-U 38043, K97a, speeches given by Lieutenant General Kuter to the Squadron Officer School and Air Command and Staff College on 9 November and 17 December 1954, respectively.

US Northern Command, Office of History

The Office of History at the US Northern Command (USNORTHCOM) and the North American Aerospace Defense Command (NORAD) is principally responsible for developing plans and policies and writing the command's histories. The historians in this office respond to high-level historical research requests and conduct scholarly research on issues related to the USNORTHCOM and NORAD history. However, they also maintain a small historical archive of both commands' historical documents and records. This archive includes the following:

NORAD histories (declassified);
NORAD agreement;
NORAD historical reference papers;
Cheyenne Mountain.

Air Mobility Command, Office of History

Register of Berlin Airlift documents.
Box 1, folder 31, letters between Kuter and Tunner.

National Archives and Records Administration

Records of the US Army Air Forces (Record Group 18).
Record Group 263: Records of the Central Intelligence Agency, 1894–2002 Series: Articles from "Studies in Intelligence," 1955–1992 File Unit: Winter 1958: 12–5-2: "Concepts for a Philosophy of Air Intelligence," by Lewis R. Long.
Records of Joint Commands (Records Group 349).

National Security Archive, George Washington University

"Founded in 1985 by journalists and scholars to check rising government secrecy, the National Security Archive combines a unique range of functions: investigative journalism center, research institute on international affairs, library and archive of declassified U.S. documents ('the world's largest nongovernmental collection' according to the *Los Angeles Times*), leading non-profit user of the U.S. Freedom of Information Act, public interest law firm defending and expanding public access to government information, global advocate of open government, and indexer and publisher of former secrets" (http://nsarchive.gwu.edu/nsa/the_archive .html). The collection includes the following:

Chief of Staff of the United States Air Force, Commanders Conference, April 25–27, Notes;

Pueblo Committee Report to President, Sixth Draft, February 7, 1968. Top Secret;

Air Operations in the Taiwan Straits Crisis, 1958;

Cold War Air Defense Relied on Widespread Dispersal of Nuclear Weapons, Documents Show, National Security Archive Electronic Briefing Book no. 332, 16 November 2010.

Midway Village Museum, Rockford, Illinois

In 1981, Ethel Kuter donated her husband's medals to the Rockford History Center. "Midway Village Museum, the best institution for collecting, preserving and interpreting the history of the Rockford region, is committed to educating and enriching our community by providing state-of-the-art exhibits, programs and events" (http://www.midwayvillage.com/about-midway.html).

Secondary Sources

Arnold, Henry H. *Global Mission.* New York: Harper & Bros., 1949.

Benton, Jeffery C. *They Served Here: Thirty-Three Maxwell Men.* Maxwell Air Force Base, AL: Air University Press, 1999.

Biddle, Tami D. *Rhetoric and Reality in Air Warfare: The Evolution of British and American Ideas about Strategic Bombing, 1941–1945.* Princeton, NJ: Princeton University Press, 2002.

Bright, Charles D., ed. *Historical Dictionary of the U.S. Air Force.* New York: Greenwood, 1992.

Buell, Thomas B. *Master of Sea Power: A Biography of Fleet Admiral Ernest J. King.* Boston: Little, Brown, 1980.

Byrd, Martha. *Chennault: Giving Wings to the Tiger.* Tuscaloosa: University of Alabama Press, 1987.

———. *Kenneth N. Walker: Airpower's Untempered Crusader.* Maxwell Air Force Base, AL: Air University Press, 1997.

Cameron, Rebecca H. *Training to Fly: Military Flight Training, 1907–1945.* Washington, DC: Air Force History and Museums Program, 1999.

Chapman, Richard G., Jr. *Legacy of Peace: Mountain with a Mission, NORAD's Cheyenne Mountain Combat Operations Center.* Albuquerque: New Mexico Engineering Research Institute, University of New Mexico, 1996.

Cooke, James J. *Billy Mitchell.* Boulder, CO: Lynne Rienner, 2002.

Corum, James S. *The Luftwaffe: Creating the Operational Air War, 1918–1940.* Lawrence: University Press of Kansas, 1997.

———. *Wolfram Von Richthofen: Master of the German Air War.* Lawrence: University Press of Kansas, 2008.

Crane, Conrad C. *Bombs, Cities, and Civilians: American Airpower Strategy in World War II.* Lawrence: University Press of Kansas, 1993.

Craven, Wesley and James Lea Cate, eds. *The Army Air Forces in World War II.* 7 vols. Washington, DC: Office of Air Force History, 1983.

Daso, Dik A. *Architects of American Air Supremacy: General Hap Arnold and Dr. Theodore von Kàrmàn.* Maxwell Air Force Base, AL: Air University Press, 1997.

Davis, Richard G. *Carl A. Spaatz and the Air War in Europe.* Washington, DC: Center for Air Force History, 1993.

———. *Hap Arnold and the Evolution of American Airpower.* Washington, DC: Smithsonian Books, 2000.

———. *Bombing the European Axis Powers: A Historical Digest of the Combined Bomber Offensive, 1939–1945.* Maxwell Air Force Base, AL: Air University Press, 2006.

Doolittle, James H. *I Could Never Be So Lucky Again.* Atglen, PA: Schiffer, 1995.

Douhet, Giulio. *The Command of the Air.* Washington DC: Office for Air Force History, 1983.

Drea, Edward J., et al. *History of the Unified Command Plan.* Joint History Office. Washington, DC: Joint History Office, Office of the Chairman of the Joint Chiefs of Staff, 2013.

Dysart, Mary Dixie. *The Archives at the Air Force Historical Research Agency.* Maxwell Air Force Base, AL: Air Force Historical Research Agency, 2012.

Ehlers, Robert S., Jr. *The Mediterranean Air War: Airpower and Allied Victory in World War II.* Lawrence: University Press of Kansas, 2015.

Finney, Robert T. *History of the Air Corps Tactical School, 1920–1940.* 1955. Washington, DC: Air Force History and Museums Program, 1998.

Frisbee, John L. *Makers of the United States Air Force.* Washington, DC: Air Force History and Museums Program, 1987.

Futrell, Robert Frank. *Ideas, Concepts, Doctrine: Basic Thinking in the United States Air Force, 1907–1960.* 1971. Maxwell Air Force Base, AL: Air University Press, 1989.

———. *Ideas, Concepts, Doctrine: Basic Thinking in the United States Air Force, 1961–1984.* Maxwell Air Force Base, AL: Air University Press, 1989.

Gaston, James C. *Planning the American Air War: Four Men and Nine Days in 1941.* Washington, DC: National Defense University Press, 1982.

Griffith, Charles. *The Quest: Haywood Hansell and American Strategic*

Bombing in World War II. Maxwell Air Force Base, AL: Air University Press, 1999.

Griffith, Thomas E., Jr. *MacArthur's Airman: General George C. Kenney and the War in the Southwest Pacific.* Lawrence: University of Kansas Press, 1998.

Hall, R. Cargill, ed. *Case Studies in Strategic Bombardment.* Washington, DC: Air Force History and Museums Program, 1998.

Hansell, Haywood S., Jr. *The Air Plan That Defeated Hitler.* Atlanta: Higgins-McArthur/Longino & Porter, 1972.

———. "Gen. Laurence S. Kuter." *Air Force Magazine,* June 1980, 94–97.

———. "General Laurence S. Kuter, 1905–1979." *Aerospace Historian,* June 1980, 91–94.

———. *The Strategic Air War against Germany and Japan: A Memoir.* Washington, DC: Office of Air Force History, 1986.

Harrington, Daniel F. *Berlin on the Brink: The Blockade, the Airlift, and the Early Cold War.* Lexington: University Press of Kentucky, 2013.

Holley, I. B., Jr. "An Air Force General: Laurence Sherman Kuter." *Aerospace Historian,* June 1980, 88–90.

Hughes, Thomas A. *Over Lord: General Pete Quesada and the Triumph of Tactical Air Power in World War II.* New York: Free Press, 1995.

Hurley, Alfred H. *Billy Mitchell: Crusader for Air Power.* Bloomington: Indiana University Press, 1964.

Huston, John W., ed. *American Airpower Comes of Age: General Henry H. "Hap" Arnold's World War II Diaries.* Maxwell Air Force Base, AL: Air University Press, 2002.

Johnson, David E. *Fast Tanks and Heavy Bombers: Innovation in the U.S. Army, 1917–1945.* Ithaca, NY: Cornell University Press, 1998.

Kennedy, Paul. *Engineers of Victory: The Problem Solvers Who Turned the Tide in the Second World War.* New York: Random House, 2013.

Kenney, George C. *General Kenney Reports: A Personal History of the Pacific War.* Washington, DC: Air Force History and Museum Program, 1987.

King, Ernest J., and Walter Muir Whitehill. *Fleet Admiral King: A Naval Record.* New York: Da Capo, 1976.

Knaack, Marcelle Size. *Encyclopedia of US Air Force Aircraft and Missile Systems.* Vol. 1, *Post–World War II Fighters, 1945–1973.* Washington, DC: Office of Air Force History, 1978.

Kohn, Richard H., and Joseph P. Harahan, eds. *Air Superiority in World War II and Korea: An Interview with Gen. James Ferguson, Gen. Robert M. Lee, Gen. William Momyer and Lt. Gen. Elwood R. Quesada.* Washington, DC: Office of Air Force History, 1983.

———, eds. *Strategic Air Warfare: An Interview with Generals Curtis E.*

LeMay, Leon W. Johnson, David A. Burchinal, and Jack J. Catton. Washington, DC: Office of Air Force History, 1988.

Kuter, Laurence S. *Airman at Yalta.* New York: Duell, Sloan, & Pearce, 1955.

———. *The Great Gamble: The Boeing —747: The Boeing–Pan Am Project to Develop, Produce, and Introduce the 747.* Tuscaloosa: University of Alabama Press, 1973.

———. "How Hap Built the AAF." *Air Force Magazine,* September 1973, 88–93.

———. "The General vs. the Establishment: General H. H. Arnold and the Air Staff," *Aerospace Historian,* December 1974, 183–89.

———. "JFK and LBJ Consider Aerospace Defense." *Aerospace Historian,* March 1979, 1–4.

Libbey, James K. *Alexander P. de Seversky and the Quest for Air Power.* Washington, DC: Potomac, 2013.

Meilinger, Phillip S., ed. *The Paths of Heaven: The Evolution of Airpower Theory.* Maxwell Air Force Base, AL: Air University Press, 1997.

———. *Airmen and Air Theory: A Review of the Sources.* Maxwell Air Force Base, AL: Air University Press, 2001.

———. *Bomber: The Formation and Early Years of Strategic Air Command.* Maxwell Air Force Base, AL: Air University Press, 2012.

Mets, David, R. *Master of Airpower: General Carl A. Spaatz.* Novato, CA: Presidio, 1997.

Miller, Donald L. *Masters of the Air: America's Bomber Boys Who Fought the Air War against Nazi Germany.* New York: Simon & Schuster, 2006.

Miller, Roger G. *Billy Mitchell: "Stormy Petrel of the Air."* Washington, DC: Air Force History and Museum Program, 2004.

Mitchell, William. *Winged Defense: The Development and Possibilities of Air Power—Economic and Military.* New York: Dover, 1988.

Momyer, William W. *Airpower in Three Wars (World War II, Korea and Vietnam).* Maxwell Air Force Base, AL: Air University Press, 2003.

Mortensen, Daniel R. *Airpower and Ground Armies: Essays on the Evolution of Anglo-American Air Doctrine, 1940–43.* Maxwell Air Force Base, AL: Air University Press, 1998.

Nalty, Bernard C., John F. Shiner, and George M. Watson. *With Courage: The U.S. Army Air Force Is World War II.* Washington, DC: Air Force History and Museum Program, 1994.

Orange, Vincent. *Coningham: A Biography of Air Marshal Sir Arthur Coningham.* London: Methuen, 1990.

Overy, Richard J. *The Air War, 1939–1945.* Washington, DC: Potomac, 2005.

Parton, James. *"Air Force Spoken Here": General Ira Eaker and the*

Command of the Air. Maxwell Air Force Base, AL: Air University Press, 2000.

Pincus, Walter. "Eisenhower Advisers Discussed Using Nuclear Weapons in China." *Washington Post,* 30 April 2008.

Porch, Douglas. *The Path to Victory: The Mediterranean Theater in World War II.* New York: Farrar, Straus, Giroux, 2004.

Rast, Vicki J. *The Air University: Pantheon of Air, Space, and Cyberspace Power Thinkers.* Maxwell Air Force Base, AL: Air University Press, 2009.

Rein, Christopher M. *The North African Air Campaign: U.S. Army Forces from El Alamein to Salerno.* Lawrence: University Press of Kansas, 2012.

Rolf, David. *The Bloody Road to Tunis: Destruction of the Axis Forces in North Africa, November 1942–May 1943.* London: Greenhill, 2001.

Shaughnessy, Ryan. *No Sense Dwelling on the Past? The Fate of the U.S. Air Force's German Air Force Monograph Project, 1952–1969.* Maxwell Air Force Base, AL: Air University Press, 2011.

Sherry, Michael S. *The Rise of American Air Power: The Creation of Armageddon.* New Haven, CT: Yale University Press, 1987.

Spires, David N. *Air Power for Patton's Army: The XIX Tactical Air Command in the Second World War.* Washington, DC: Air Force History and Museums Program, 2002.

Tate, James P. *The Army and Its Air Corps: Army Policy toward Aviation , 1919–1941.* Maxwell Air Force Base, AL: Air University Press, 1998.

Tunner, William H. *Over the Hump.* 1969. Washington, DC: Air Force History and Museums Program, 1998.

Underwood, Jeffery S. *The Wings of Democracy: The Influence of Air Power on the Roosevelt Administration, 1933–1941.* College Station: Texas A&M University Press, 1991.

Unger, Debi, and Irwin Unger. *George Marshall: A Biography.* New York: HarperCollins, 2014.

Wells, Mark K. *Courage and Air Warfare: The Allied Aircrew Experience in the Second World War.* London: Frank Cass, 1995.

Werrell, Kenneth P. *Blankets of Fire: U.S. Bombers over Japan during World War II.* Washington, DC: Smithsonian Institution Press, 1996.

Wolk, Herman S. *Planning and Organizing the Postwar Air Force, 1943–1947.* Washington, DC: Air Force History and Museums Program, 1984.

———. *The Struggle for Air Force Independence, 1943–1947.* Washington, DC: Air Force History and Museums Program, 1997.

———. *Cataclysm: General Hap Arnold and the Defeat of Japan.* Denton: University of North Texas Press, 2010.

Index

American Airlines, 125
American English: made the official language of aviation, 127
American Museum of Natural History, 141
Amoy, 156
Anders, Bill, 170
Andrews, Frank, 45, 46
Andrews Air Force Base, 134–35
antiaircraft artillery, 41, 66
Army Regulation 95–5, 46
Arnim, Hans-Jürgen von, 80
Arnold, Bee, 125
Arnold, Henry H. "Hap": Air Force Advisory Council and, 57; Airmail Scandal and, 24, 26; "Air Operations in Western Europe in 1944," 103; Air War Plans Division–Plan 1 and, 47, 49, 187n13; arrival in Europe after D-Day, 109; assessment of Kuter in 1945, 123; Cairo Conference, 101–2; conflict with Alexander Seversky, 93, 94–95, 96–98, 99–100; control of US Army Air Forces, Pacific Ocean, 118; D-Day and, 106; death of Oliver S. Ferson and, 57; firing of Haywood Hansell, 119; head of US Army Air Corps, 46; George Kenney and, 89, 90; Earnest King and, 59; Kuter and, 3, 36, 41; Kuter as assistant chief of staff for, 87, 89, 92–93, 97–98, 99–117 (see also Air Staff—Kuter as assistant chief of staff for plans and combat operations); Kuter as deputy chief of staff for in 1942, 57, 58, 62; on Kuter at the Yalta conference, 112–13, 115; Kuter's critique of air–ground cooperation in North Africa, 84–85; Kuter's promotion to brigadier general and, 54, 55; Kuter's transfer back to Washington in 1943 and, 83–84; McNarney Plan and restructuring of the US Army Air Force, 56, 57–58; orders Kuter to Japan in August 1945, 122; overseas deployment of staff officers and, 63, 64; presents Kuter with the Distinguished Service Medal, 117; relationship with the Air Staff, 57, 58; retirement of, 125; return to the US from Europe in June 1944, 109; Gordon Saville incident and, 52; trip to Italy and North Africa following D-Day, 109–10

"A staff," 56
ATC. See Air Transport Command
atomic bombs: Taiwan Straits Crisis of 1958 and, 157–58
attack aviation: Kuter's clash with George Kenney over, 89–90
Australia, 105
AWPD-1. See Air War Plans Division–Plan 1
Azores, 104, 125

B-9 bombers, 22, 23
B-17 Flying Fortress bombers: bombing of German U-boat pens, 65–67, 68–69; effectiveness against U-boats, 67; first received by the 2nd Bombardment Wing, 21; Kuter's 1938 lecture on, 40; Kuter's command of the 1st Bombardment Wing, 64–72; LeMay's development of the combat box formation, 68–69; mission on D-Day, 108; Pacific theater and, 61
B-24 Liberator bombers, 61, 67
B-29 Superfortress bombers, 92, 101, 105, 121, 149
B-35 bombers, 92, 192n14

213